INDEX
TO
THE COLLECTED WORKS
OF
EUGENE HALLIDAY

INDEX

TO

THE COLLECTED WORKS

OF

EUGENE HALLIDAY

Melchisedec Press

Melchisedec Press

5 Taylor Road, Altrincham, Cheshire WA14 4LR
melchisedecpress.net
info@melchisedecpress.net

First edition published in the UK by Melchisedec Press in 2021

Edited by John Zaradin & Hephzibah Yohannan

ISBN 978-1-872240-45-9 (2021 paperback)
ISBN 978-1-872240-46-6 (2021 ebook)

A CIP catalogue record for this book is available from the British Library

The Melchisedec Press was founded by David Mahlowe
to publish the works of Eugene Halliday

Printed and bound by Ingram Spark
Set in Baskerville

In memoriam

Donald Sinclair Lord (1926–2012)

&

John Anthony Duckworth (1936–2016)

Contents

Editors' Notes

This Index to the fifteen books of Eugene Halliday's Collected Works is both a reference work and a guide to the range and understanding of the terms, expressions and symbols which he employed. It allows students of Halliday's work to follow his themes throughout his written works, rather than simply by reading his books one at a time.

In order to get a quick idea of the contents and value of a work before deciding whether or not to buy, both Eugene Halliday and Donald Lord recommended looking first at that book's index. We hope that both existing students and those new to Halliday's work will find this Index of interest and of use.

The idea of a comprehensive index of Halliday's books was initiated by Donald Lord, in the 1980s, but only the letters A-C have been found. His version was an index to Halliday's concepts, and, as such, they were paraphrased, not shown exactly as they appear on the page. Following Lord's death in 2012, the idea of the Index was taken up by Anthony Duckworth. He completed the letters A-Z, but again used many paraphrases. Subsequently Andrew Moore took up the task, this time making the entries consistent with the wording on the page. During this process, he noticed, with interest, the frequency of occurrence of certain words in Halliday's vocabulary, and a number of distinctive terms and combinations of terms, in his writing.

Andrew Moore's work has been compiled, typeset and prepared for publication by John Zaradin. The text has been edited by John Zaradin and Hephzibah Yohannan, checking and editing every entry against the books, and adding further entries. They have been assisted with the reference-checking by Sheila and Robert Taylor. The completion of the Index has been a labour of love and dedication to the work of Eugene Halliday, on the part of all involved.

****

Wherever practicable, the entries in the Index show the text exactly as it appears on the page. Hence, some entries are in capitals, some have initial capitals, some are in lower case, and some are in italics or brackets.

Where there are many occurrences of the same reference term, the first occurrence is preferred. Therefore, the style may not match every entry, exactly.

&	An ampersand (&) before an entry indicates an indirect connection to the Header; entries without an ampersand have a direct connection.
Self- / -consciousness	Where entry-words are hyphenated with the Header, the header-word is not included with the entry, unless it is needed for clarity; e.g. terms such as 'self-consciousness'.
see	means that there are several ideas relating to one term, on a page. In such cases, it would be better to simply read the page, rather than have several different headings / entries set up referring to a term.
[...]	Square brackets in italics indicate editorial comments; e.g. *[error: should read ...]*
(...)	A row of three dots indicates words omitted from a long passage.
Erratum:	"God is not dead" on the first line of text in Chapter One of *Essays on God*, should read "God is dead" (a quotation from Nietzsche).

1

KEY TO THE BOOKS

The books referenced here are the Hardback editions of The Collected Works of Eugene Halliday, published by David Mahlowe. All new editions of these books, including ebooks, incorporate the page numbers of the hardback editions. This Index, therefore, can be used to search all editions of these books.

Book	-	Book Title
DD	-	Defence of the Devil
RS	-	Reflexive Self-Consciousness
TC	-	The Tacit Conspiracy
C1	-	Contributions from a Potential Corpse 1
C2	-	Contributions from a Potential Corpse 2
C3	-	Contributions from a Potential Corpse 3
C4	-	Contributions from a Potential Corpse 4
CA	-	The Conquest of Anxiety
EG	-	Essays on God
B1	-	Through the Bible 1
B2	-	Through the Bible 2
B3	-	Through the Bible 3
B4	-	Through the Bible 4
P1	-	Christian Philosophy 1
P2	-	Christian Philosophy 2

A

A

& the Infinite, C3: 28-29
A E I O U, (*see* diagrams), C4: 30
a posteriori: man, C4: 38
a priori: the universe, C4: 38
A-theist, C4: 56
see English gematria, C3: 19-20, 84-88

Abba

& Infinite Power, B4: 47

Abel('s)

& Cain, B1: 77-78, 82, 127; B2: 8;
    B3: 89; CA: 88; DD: 64; P1: 63
& idea of the Scapegoat, B1: 78
& inter-relating of their diverse talents
    ceased, B1: 120
& sacrifice, CA: 89
& voice of murdered Faith, B3: 113
death was sacrificial, CA: 89
man of mere faith, B4: 173
suffered his death, CA: 91
ye shall become ..., when ye shall have slain
    Cain, DD: 64

Abraham('s)

& divine promise, B2: 137
& example, B2: 142
& faith in the Divine Power, B2: 104
& God's promise, DD: 59
& Isaac, B2: 140
& Jesus, B4: 68
& moral position of someone who is
    required to sacrifice, B2: 136
& Over-view, B2: 123
& sacrifice, B2: 136
& sacrificial situation, B2: 137
& Time and Matter, B2: 192
& vision, B2: 103, 105
"Abraham rejoiced to see my day" (Jesus),
    B2: 102
broke the idols, B2: 107
father of many nations, B2: 94
knew the ways of the eagle, B2: 123
man of persistence, B2: 105
rejoiced to see his day, B2: 140
seed, B2: 137

Abram

& addition of the "H" in the name ...
    changes its meaning, B2: 94
& Lot, B2: 91; P1: 114
& Melchizedek, B2: 92

& Sarai & Hagar, B2: 93
obeyed God's command, B2: 90

Absolute

& "Substance", C3: 60
& continuum, C1: 98; C3: 124
& created forms, C2: 46
& creative work, C2: 47
& creative act of man, C4: 63
& determinations, C1: 93-94
& Dracula Key, C2: 112
& Father, TC: 32
& individual consciousness, C1: 105
& individuality, C1: 105
& individuals, C1: 76
& Kosmic or Universal Master-tool, C2: 46
& non-dual awareness, C1: 106
& Nothing, C3: 14
& open Eye, C3: 29
& origin of all things, C1: 93
& otherness, C3: 67
& painful situations, C2: 112
& pains suffered by individuals, C1: 76
& prime matter, TC: 32
& sensorium, C1: 110
& solipsism, C3: 41
& souls, C1: 102
& the Origin of Sin, C4: 53
& Tower of Babel, B3: 179
& Truth, B3: 120; C1: 83
& Ultimate Reality, C3: 114
& wholeness, C1: 111
A polarises itself, C4: 30
an infinite ocean of light, C1: 86
as pointless, C3: 29
as complete synthesis (Schelling), C2: 96
awareness, C1: 112
Brahman, C1: 81; C3: 131
cause of all things, C1: 46
continuum, C1: 98; C3: 124
control (God), B3: 179
eternal continuum of motion, RS: 10
God, B2: 47
GOOD, C1: 94
"I am the Almighty God ...", B2: 94
Infinite Eternal, TC: 26
infinite ocean of light, C1: 86
is all value, C1: 112
is infinite sentient power, RS: 10
lacks nothing, C1: 111
man, RS: viii

motion, C1: 87, 110

motion of certain of the philosophers, RS: 7

non-dual awareness, C1: 106

not a thing, TC: 28

Origin of all things, C1: 93

otherness of, C3: 67

pains, C1: 76

philosophers call the, C3: 14

Power, TC: 32

power … fundamental to all things, B3 : 50

seen by Schelling, C2: 96

Self, C2: 46-47

Sentient Power, C2: 1, 46, 52, 66, 112;
     C3: 14, 25, 62, 72, 97, 98, 124; TC: 26

sentient power & 3D existential, individual,
     C3: 98

sentient power & forms, C3: 97

sentient power & impress, C3: 72

sentient power as Final Reason, C3: 25

sentient power as non-dual, C3: 25-26

sentient power, basis of all phenomena,
     C3: 2, 124, 125

sentient power, continuum of, C3: 2, 124

sentient power, grasping of itself, C3: 62

sentient power, ultimate reality, C3: 114

silence, C3: 57

SPIRIT NON-ROTATING IS, C1: 88

Subject, C3: 41, 112

Substance, C3: 60

supreme, infinite power, B2: 46-47

"that which remains when all
     determinations whatever are washed
     away", C1: 93

to love the, C2: 47

transcending all distinctions, C1: 82

transcends all souls, C1: 102

ULTIMATE REALITY, C3: 114

will of the, C4: 63

Absolute Sentient Power

& 3D existential, individual, C3: 98

& ectropy, C2: 47

& entropy, C2: 47

& evil, C4: 1

& forms, C3: 97

& impress, C3: 72

& the Origin of Sin, C4: 53

as Final Reason, C3: 25

as non-dual, C3: 25-26

continuum of, basis of all phenomena,
     C3: 124-125

God, C2: 7, 28, 46

Grasping of itself, C3: 62

Hinduism, C2: 102

his method is "Let", C4: 1

of the Infinite Eternal, TC: 26

phenomena, C3: 125

see C2: 1, 46, 52, 66, 112;
     C3: 25, 62, 72, 97, 124;

ULTIMATE REALITY, C3: 114

work is of two kinds, C2: 47

Absolutely

Free, C1: 107

Absoluteness

in act, C4: 92

see PHASES OF DEVELOPMENT OF
     MAN, C4: 91-92

Abstraction(s)

& reality, C1: 86

of the finite, C1: 86

abstractionist thought. RS: 10

appetites … not mere, B4: 6

As pure consciousness we deal with an,
     C1: 98

Eternal principles or concepts, B3: 78

Form without functional power would be a
     dead, C3: 92

'Infinity' without finity is an illegitimate,
     C1: 79

intellectual, RS: 7

is, C1: 86

Kant's "Ding an sich" … a final product of
     abstractionism, C3: 24

Logos [think of] … not as an, B3: 53

of male and female elements from each
     other, TC: 11

of the total visual possibility of the universe,
     C1: 36

of thought, C3: 28

Saturn and Jupiter are abstractions, if
     viewed apart from …, C4: 39

To think of less than this totality is to
     indulge in, B3: 107

two worlds … the dwelling places of living
     intelligences, not of, P1: 40

Abyss

& fear, B4: 84-85

& God the Father, B4: 84

Acceptable

picture of ourselves, CA: 65

Acceptance
  & adjustability, B3: 132
  of reality, CA: 36
  Total, B3: 132
Accident(s)
  & causation, C1: 50-51
  & fortuitous concourse of atoms, C2: 1-2
  & living body, C1: 50
  & non-accident, C2: 1-2
  & pre-set goals, B4: 150
  & the universe, B4: 149
  (contingency), C3: 46
  ("fortuitous concourse of atoms"), C2: 1-2
  (i.e. the way things *happen to fall* in the
     absence of intelligent guidance), C2: 82
  means, C1: 50
Accidental
  & Humanist, Rationalist, Materialistic
     Atheist, C2: 1
  & idea of causation, C1: 51
  Material particles, B4: 97
Accidentally
  formed organism, C2: 1
Accuser
  slanderer, devil, C1: 87
  Diabolos, DD: 7
  Satan, DD: 7
  self-, C2: 11
Ace
  & "Space", EG: 49
  high, is God transcendent, EG: 50
  is … letter H, EG: 50
  low, is God immanent, EG: 50
Acknowledge
  "Acknowledge Me and I will acknowledge
     you" (Jesus), B4: 98
Acquisition
  Cainan … means, B1: 92
Act(s)
  & Absolute (Schelling), C2: 96
  & choice, B2: 95
  & focussing, RS: 14
  & Hamlet, C1: 9
  & His (God) question, DD: 62
  & our own essence, P1: 12
  & sinning zone, C4: 54
  & spheres, C2: 70
  & TO ACT or NOT TO ACT (God's
     question), C1: 9; DD: 62
  & TO BE or NOT TO BE (not God's

  question), C1: 9, DD: 62
  "caught in the act", C2: 74
  Creative (nature of), B4: 92
  highest, C4: 103
  his last, C2: 74
  Man's highest act of will, C4: 103
  of Mercy, C2: 49
  of free will, C4: 21
  of Will, B4: 9
  "Pure Act" (God), B4: 24
Action(s)
  & applying a force, C1: 103
  & "Being", P1: 73
  & Egotism, CA: 79
  & feeling, B3: 69
  & laws of physical science, P1: 85
  & man of spirit, B3: 79
  & power, B3: 62
  & reactions, B3: 79
  & resistance, C1: 103
  & responsibility, B4: 153
  & soul's deepest centre, C4: 50
  & thinking, B3: 69
  conscious of an, CA: 65
  effects of … return, B3: 7
  fruits of our, B3: 7
  is interaction, B4: 12
  "law of action and reaction", B2: 124;
     CA: 79
  mould the form … of our … body … soul,
     B4: 63
  originates, C4: 50
  our physical body's, CA: 64
  see C2: 80
  splitting of our feeling, action and thinking,
     B3: 69
  unconscious of, CA: 65
Active
  feeling, C3: 92
  forms, a universe of, B1: 8
  Joy is, B2: 127
Activities
  exclusivist, C4: 54
Activity
  & Energy, B3: 58
  & Holy Ghost, EG: 18
  & metanoia, C2: 11
  creative, C2: 98
  key to everlasting life, C3: 93

Actor
  & mask, C2: 111
  "hypocrite", B2: 39
Actual(s)
  & potentials, C2: 13
  being, RS: 6
  things, B3: 58
  value, C4: 116
Actualisation
  & "being", B1: 115
Actuality(ies)
  & acts of will, B4: 9
  Jesus is all, P1: 73
Adam('s)
  & a fiery sword, TC: 37
  & birth, DD: 44
  & creature of God, B1:55
  & "Dispensation for Innocence",
    B3: 88
  & division of labour, B2: 15
  & division of reality, B1: 60
  & Edenic innocence, B1: 73
  & error, C3: 34; EG: 58, P2: 108-109
  & Eve, B1: 23, 52-55, 69, 79-81, 130;
    B2: 15; C4: 96; EG: 55-56
  & Eve, error of, EG: 58
  & Eve, stop the re-entry into Eden,
    TC: 37
  & evil, B2: 33-34, 36-37
  & expulsion from the garden of Eden,
    B1: 63
  & extrication of Eve, C4: 96
  & female principle, B2: 15
  & forbidden tree, DD: 47
  & forces contra life, B2: 33
  & help-mate, B1: 54
  & hinder-mate, B1: 55
  & his Creator, B1: 23
  & identification, fell into, B1: 72
  & image of God, B2: 14
  & Jesus Christ, P2: 109
  & nature of evil, B2: 37
  & Pain, DD: 44
  & self-alienation, B1: 53
  & self-imposed alienation, B2: 38
  & sin, B3: 89; DD: 58
  & Spirit of God, DD: 42, 47
  & spiritual death, B1: 53
  & split … conscious and unconscious mind,
    B1: 57

  & state of perfect harmony, B2: 36
  & tempter's suggestion, B1: 130
  & tree of knowledge, B1: 52; CA: 40; P2: 11
  & whole consciousness, B1: 72-73
  afraid, DD: 47
  ASKED FOR THE SPLIT, C3: 70
  bi-polar, C4: 96
  created in the image of God, male and
    female, B2: 14
  creature of God, B1: 55
  "Dispensation for Innocence", B3: 88
  divide the substance, DD: 42
  Fall, B4: 165; CA: 32
  first human ancestor, B1: 69
  first truly human being, B2: 165
  God had warned, B1: 23
  hiding, B2: 38
  Innocence, B3: 88
  "Old Adam", P2: 107-108
  prior to his fall, B2: 36
  Qadmon, C2: 1, 34; C3: 122
  Red One, DD: 10
  Sin, B1: 24; DD: 58
  type of all men, B1: 56
  type of innocent but disobedient figures,
    B1: 79
  weakness, DD: 47
Adamic Man
  first truly human being, B2: 165
Adjustability
  & total acceptance, B3: 132
Admiration
  & the child, B2: 56
Adult
  & child, B3: 155
Advaita
  Non-dualism (& paradox), C2: 68
Adversary
  Satan, DD: 7, 27
Aesthetic
  discrimination, C3: 36
  Mode & Original Appetite, C3: 36
Aether
  Soniferous (Akasha), C3: 51
Affect
  & cognition (balance of), C4: 74
  & Sushumna, C4: 74
Affection
  & values, B4: 8

Affirmation
of All Negations, DD: 71
Saves, B2: 170, 172
Yes/No, C4: 119

Afraid
"Be not afraid, only believe", (Jesus to
Jairus), P2: 1, 4, 9

Agape
-love, B1: 138-141

Agent
& modal complexes, C2: 52
"patient" & "agent", C2: 52

Aggression
& aggressor, P1: 95-96
& initiative, C3: 110
& other men, P1: 92
& self-defence, B2: 63
counter-, P1: 94

Aggressor
& free intelligence (man of), P1: 97
& self re-examination, P1: 96
plight of the, P1: 97

Ahasuerus
(see diagram), C3: 50

Ahriman(ic)
& Angra Mainyu & Ahura Mazda, C4: 8
& granularity, C3: 99; C4: 8
& The Devil, C3: 7
Angry mind, C4: 8

Ahura Mazda
& Angra Mainyu, C4: 8
& TWO MINDS, C4: 8
mind lit by the Absolute Light of   …,
C4: 8

Aidos kinesis
everlasting motion (Anaximander), RS: 4

Aim(s)
& *anxiety*, CA: 77
private (& *urgency*), B3: 148
private (& "sins"), B3: 19
unrealisable, CA: 77

Ain Soph Aur
see C4: 42

Air
& combustion, C1: 48
& Four Elements, C3: 122

Akarana Zarvan
Time-process, C3: 133

Akasha
Soniferous Aether, C3: 51

AKU-AKU
& awake, C4: 16

Alchemical
substances, C3: 80

Aleph
& Ayin, DD: 12
& Yod, C3: 28
& RELATION of the Infinite to the finite,
C3: 28
Accept whatever is, C4: 54
(see diagram), C3: 28, 51

Alienation
& "Salvation", B4: 127
of nation, P1: 116
of the self, C4: 52
"Sin", B4: 126

Alignment
with God's will, CA: 43

All
-Seeing Eye, B2: 76; B3: 136
-Seer, B3: 136
beings are *within* his consciousness, RS: viii
Totality, C1: 26, 28

All-Seeing Eye
Divine, B2: 76

Allah
& ASP, C3: 25
& community of Islam, C2: 124
the Absolute Sentient Power, C2: 124

Allegory
& the Bible, B3: 135

All-In-Oneness
Infinite simultaneity, CA: 44

All-One
Great Alone, B1: 132

Allopathy
& systems of healing, C2: 121

Alone
"take the flight of the alone to the alone"
(Plotinus), B1: 131

Alpha
-Alef, C3: 84
-light (Great), B3: 6
-Light-Omega-Body of God, B3: 6
& A-theist, C4: 56
& Omega, B3: 5; C3: 34-35, C4: 56; DD:
38; EG: 43; RS: ix
Idea held in God's mind, B1: 122

Alphabet
see English gematria, C3: 19-20, 84-88

Alphatheos
    & A-theist, C4: 56-57
    infinite creativity, C4: 57
    name of the God of the atheist, C4: 57
    Nothingness, C4: 57
ALTAR
    & TORAH, C4: 119
    of Cosmos, C4: 119
Amazon(s)
    & the Greeks, C4: 100
    women, TC: 11
Ambition(s)
    & a great name, B2:52
    & Babel-tower, B2: 56
    & externalisation of consciousness, P2: 78
America
    power via commodity production, C2: 37
American Indians
    teach dignity of the person, C2: 103
Amoeba
    & survival, TC: 3
AN
    & pleasure, C4: 1
    non-rational sensuous, C4: 1
Analysis
    & action, EG: 5
    & outer world, B1: 59
Analytical activities
    conscious mind's, B1: 61
Anamnesis
    & homoeopathy remedies, C4: 77
Ananda
    "bliss", C4: 12
Anaxagoras
    All qualities are eternal, C4: 31
Anaximander
    everlasting motion (*aidos kinesis*), RS: 4
    The flux of things is their punishment,
        C4: 31
Ancestors(')
    & bad conscience, B2: 180
    & companionship of failure, C4: 45
    & law of resonance, B2: 182
    & monsters, CA: 8
    & our unconscious mind, B2: 179
    & pain and fear, CA: 85
    & protoplasm, B2: 180; CA: 84
    disobedience, CA: 19
    errors of our, B2: 78
    male, C4: 70
    negative records, P2: 113
    our first, CA: 19, 85
    records, B2: 179
    self-pity, C4: 45
    tendencies to reactivity, CA: 84
Ancestral
    habit-patterns, B3: 25
    records, C4: 87
    records of ... experiences, P2: 112
Anchor
    -Man, CA: 34
    & body, C2: 111, CA: 28
    & self-image, B2: 113
    & soul, CA: 18, 21, 101
    & things of the outer world, B1: 44
    AN-CHOR, C3: 49
    Anchored Himself in Eternal Reality,
        CA: 44
    "Christ My ...", C2: 65;
        CA: 18, 21, 26, 28, 101
    gross material things, B1: 44
    Jesus Christ is our, CA: 34
    Serpent Hierarchy, C3: 49
Andocrats
    & gynocrats, C4: 99
Angel(s)
    & beings in Eternity, B1: 17
    & Lucifer, DD: 3
    & "their common source", DD: 2, 20, 37
    different "angles", B1: 17
    dissenting, DD: 3
    "messengers of God", B1: 17
    misoneist, DD: 4
    negativity of, DD: 4
Anger
    & behaviour patterns, P2: 99
    & Ego, C3: 54
    & impedence, B4: 115
    & physical body, P2: 99
    & pleasure pursuit, C4: 1
    see C4: 1
Angles
    see "angels", B1: 17
Angra Mainyu
    & Ahriman, C4: 8
    & Ahura Mazda, C4: 8
    & granularity, C3: 99; C4: 8
    & TWO MINDS, C4: 8
    angry finited mind, C4: 8

Anima
   & *Corpus* & *Spiritus*, C2: 89
   & God, Spiritus, C2: 126
   & Maya, C2: 89
   container or shell to house spirit, C2: 87
   empirical ego, C2: 87-89

Animal(s)
   & choice, P2: 21
   & choose only between pleasures   and
      pains, B2: 89
   & human beings & belief in freedom, B3: 74
   & human beings, B3: 122
   & Human beings (diverse tendencies),
      B2: 146
   & human work, C4: 84
   & locomotion, B4: 40
   & power of three-fold self-analysis, B3: 122
   & ram caught in a thicket, B2: 145
   & *Substitute Sacrifice*, B2: 145
   & survival, CA: 5; P2: 19
   & survival instincts, B3: 74
   & unconscious instincts, P1: 145
   & WANT, C3: 64
   & world of Spirit, P2: 20
   anxiety, CA: 2
   conditioned, CA: 5
   instinct(s), B3: 122; P1: 145, 147
   Male and female, B2: 7
   tendencies, B2: 146
   work, C4: 84

Annihilate
   we could … the human race, CA: 94

Annihilation
   & death, B4: 70
   & materialist, CA: 22-23
   & self-consistency, B3: 123
   & self-contradictory form of life, CA: 94
   fear of final, C1: 14

Anointed One
   see DD: 16

Answer(s)
   final, C3: 95
   to all problems, C4: 1
   ultimate, C3: 95

Anti-Beauty
   forces, P1: 42
   These anti-life forces in us are the forces of
      evil which are also anti-Truth, anti-
      Beauty, and anti-Goodness, P1: 42

Anti-Christ
   impulses in man, P1: 45

Anticipation
   free from formal definition, C4: 78
   of harm, CA: 2
   state of, C4: 64

Anti-life
   forces, P1: 42
   impulses, EG: 57
   These anti-life forces in us are the forces of
      evil which are also anti-Truth, anti-
      Beauty, and anti-Goodness, P1: 42

Anti-Truth
   forces of evil, P1: 42
   These anti-life forces in us are the forces of
      evil which are also anti-Truth, anti-
      Beauty, and anti-Goodness, P1: 42

Ants
   social systems, EG: 89

Anxiety
   & anticipation of loss, CA: 98
   & bad opinion / name, B1: 108
   & body, CA: 16-17, 100
   & civilised men, CA: 75
   & dream-condition, CA: 16
   & dreams, B1: 58
   & embodiment, CA: 17
   & failure, CA: 75
   & fear, CA: 1-2, 97
   & "fight the good fight", B2: 181
   & Fish symbol, CA: 34-35
   & guilt, B1: 73
   & harm, CA: 3, 97
   & memory, B1: 73
   & objective fear, CA: 2
   & record of this disobedience, P2: 112
   & tension, CA: 84
   & soul, CA: 16-17, 100-101
   & unconscious, B1: 58
   & *unrealisable aims*, CA: 77
   & unshakeable belief, C2: 64
   & whole human race, CA: 19
   & excessively vibrating energies, P2: 2
   animal, CA: 2
   decreases, CA: 77
   first step towards the conquest of, CA: 13
   generalised, P2: 7
   ocean of, CA: 34
   origin of, CA: 13
   pre-creational, CA: 25

primal, CA: 104
primary, CA: 16
sea of, CA: 13, 19
states, CA: 75
unconscious, P2: 115
undefined, CA: 2
vast sea of, CA: 19

Anxious Mind
& Time, CA: 50

Apeiron
source of the world, RS: 4

Aphrodite
non-hierarchical power-substance, C4: 75

A posteriori
& A PRIORI, C2: 125; C4; 38
"after the fact", C4: 38

Appearance(s)
& duality, TC: 37
Phenomena, B4: 60

Appetite(s)
& ethical ideas, C4: 93
& female, C4: 93
& "Food", C2: 92
& food's chemistry, C4: 63
& form, C4: 65
& formed restraints, ethical ideas
    of conduct, C4: 93
& hunting, P2: 47
& inner, P2: 49
& Man, C4: 93
& women, C2: 92
crucifies itself, C4: 63
infinite, C4: 63
magnetism, C4: 62
Object of, C1: 94
ORIGINAL, C3: 36
primal, C2: 63
primordial, C4: 45
real forces, B4: 6

Appetival power
self-manipulative (& the magician), C2: 92

Application
of terms, C1: 83

Appropriation(s)
& eternal proprium of energy, C4: 15
capable of, C4: 15
is …, C4: 18

A priori
& A POSTERIORI, C2: 125; C4: 38
IDEA, C4: 38

Aquarius
[*Zodiac sign*] *see* C3: 12, 114; C4: 30, 32-33
& pure logic, cosmic science, C3: 12
& memory, C3: 114
& Logos (The Divine Spirit), C4: 32
intellect, C4: 30

Arche
telos, C3: 35

Architect
Grand, C2: 46-47

Argument
& pursuing truth, C1:102
clash of wills, C1: 102

[*Aries*]
[Zodiac sign] Ram C3: 114

Aristotle
& God, EG: 7

Ark
& protective vessel, B1: 97
Noah's, B2: 48; B3: 134

Arkana Zarvan
Time-process, C3: 133

Armageddon
& super-biograms, C2: 131
meaning of, C2: 131

Art(s)
& centred consciousness, C2: 138
& colours, C4: 80-81
& divine science, P1: 83
& forms, C4: 80-81
& junction point (WHERE THREE
ROADS MEET), C4: 87
& Music … "the type of the…", B4: 108
& new possibilities, C4: 80
& supreme aesthetic sensitivity, C4: 40
efficient employment of means, C4: 84
IS NOT MERELY TO PLEASE, C4: 80
mankind, C4: 80
open the mind and heart, C4: 80
science, art and philosophy (WHERE
    THREE ROADS MEET), C4: 87
work of, C2: 38-39
see C4: 80-81

Articulate
speech, B4: 41

Artist(s)
& male and female characteristics, B2: 14
& pattern of local self intensification, EG: 11
& psychosomatic unity, C2: 38-39
& religion, C4: 115

& sacrifice & training, CA: 92
& significance of all forms of being, C4: 113
& work of art, C2: 38-39
articulator of forms, C4: 114
group, B2: 14
interrelatedness (conscious of), C4: 113
pattern of local self-intensification, EG: 11
see C4: 113-115
widest sense, C4: 113

Ashlar (Law of Spirit)
Law of the Hexon, C3: 101

Asklepios
& infinite sentient power continuum, C3: 48
(see diagram), C3: 48

A.S.P. (Absolute Sentient Power)
& A Sphere (self-precipitated zone), C2: 66
& Chaos, C4: 29
& Cosmos, C2: 1
& every so-called entity,   C2:3
& Infinite Creativity, C2: 27
& intensest compaction, C2: 138
& Law of Being-Encapsulation, C2: 106
& Mary, (personification of the substantial
   aspect), C2: 86
& realisation of, C2: 94
& SACRIFICE, C3: 91
& salvation, C2: 94
& science and faith, C4: 56
& sin, C2: 7
& so-called Entity, C2: 52
& test situations, C2: 64
& the Origin of Sin, C4: 53
& things, C2: 30
& Truth, C2: 102
& Voice of the field of, C2: 111
absolutely self-made, C2: 69
Allah, C2: 124
catalytic act (universe), C4: 38
indissoluble trinity, C2: 83
individuated concrete existence, C2: 138
infinite extent in every area, C2: 46
leads every entity into test situations, C2: 64
Logos Voice, C2: 111
non-dual substance, C3: 26
Non-dualism and Non-pluralism, C2: 101
Prior to encapsulation, C2: 60
sphere of the, C2: 66
ultimate source and origin, C4: 53
Wonder-Eye and God of gods, C2: 33

ASP (Absolute Sentient Power)
see A.S.P.

Assembled ones
& As young trees, DD: 39
& common source, DD: 20, 37
& God's promise to Abraham's seed,
   DD: 59
& Jesus, DD: 57-60
& mercy, DD: 29
& MERIT?, DD: 15
& sixth day, DD: 40
& the Spirit of God, DD: 39
& virgin .. daughter, … handmaid, DD: 22
& weak, DD: 29
& woman to wife, DD: 22
gaze (with mild eyes), DD: 31
said to themselves, DD: 28
turned their eyes upon me (Lucifer), DD: 28

Assimilation
& meditation, C2: 62

Association
& contents of the mind, CA: 73
& our interests, CA: 73
of ideas, C2: 59

Astral
light, C2: 63; C3: 40
travel, C4: 24

Astronauts
& sacrifice & training, CA: 92

Atheist
& Alphatheos, C4: 57
Humanist, Rationalist, Materialist …, C2: 1
theist of the Alpha, C4: 56

Athlete(s)
& sacrifice & training, CA: 92
Olympic, B2: 107

Atman
is Brahman, C3: 131
Sentient Power operative, C4: 52

Atmosphere
see B4: 179

Atom
-Mota, C4: 63
& Atomic research scientists, B1: 32
& naive materialism, C1: 50
& scientists, B1: 32, 59
insentient, non-sentient, C2: 4
uncuttable, B1: 59-60

Atomism
19ᵗʰ century, C2: 4

Democritus, C4: 31

Atomists
materialistic scientists, C1: 67

Atonement
At-one-ment, B4: 64

At-one-ment
& Jesus, P1: 82
God's own, C3: 94
is Atonement, B4: 64

Atrocities
history of human, EG: 85

Attack(s)
& physical bodies, CA: 88
chess-player's favourite maxim, B2: 64
counter-, B1: 127
real or imaginary, CA: 89

Attainment
& way to this (at-oneness), P1: 83
of state of at-oneness with the will of
God, P1: 83

Attention
& Eve's suggestion, B1: 55
& reflexion, C4: 117
& sentient spiritual field, C2: 62
& visual field, C1: 36
Adam externalised his, B1: 55
of the observer, C4: 117
shift of, C2: 62

Author
Bible, C4: 70

Authority
& creation of Man, B1: 21
& Jesus Christ, P1: 14-15
God conferred the, B1: 21

Autistic
children, C4: 72

Awakened
& "Sons of God", B3: 24
Ones, B3: 24

Awareness
& being on guard, RS: iv
& rate of per-ception, B2: 129
evolution of, C4: 12
feeling-intensity, B2: 118
field, C1: 70
Has many degrees, P2: 68
heightened, B2: 128
immediate and therefore unconditioned,
RS: 3

inner, C4: 25, 87
lost, B3: 12
non-dual, C1: 106
objectless, C4: 112
of awareness, RS: 3
of our existence, B2: 117
Old English "waer", RS: iii
on guard, RS: iv
Sentiency = field, C1: 70
sharpen our, B1: 49
spiritual, B1: 41

Axis
East-West & living *(see diagram),* C4: 66
North-South & dead *(see diagram),* C4: 66

Ayin
& Aleph DD: 1

B

B
see English gematria, C3: 19-20, 84-88

Babel
foundation of, DD: 14
judgement of, B2: 52
Tower, B2: 53, 56; B3: 179

Baby
& Christopher, a Christ bearer, C2: 69
& externality, C4: 86
Focussing on its outer visible activities,
C4: 24
loves pleasure, B1: 25
newborn, CA: 84
see EG: 76-77

Bad
& "good", B1: 59, 77
& conscious mind, B1: 59
Fight, B3: 157
give displeasure or pain, B1: 59
inefficient, B1: 75
logic of their obscurantist argument, DD: 3
marksmanship, B1: 77
motives, B1: 112
name, B1: 108, 110, 112
opinion, B1: 108, 110
will, B1: 75

Baihoom
system of the attainment of
supremacy, C3: 17

Bait
pleasure-giving ("hook" situations), CA: 9
Baker('s)
& pralaya, C3: 12
Daughter, C3: 12
God the Father, C3: 13
Balance
& energy, C2: 87
& Messiah, C4: 60
& reason, C2: 87
& spiritual ecology, B3: 81
& temper, B1: 148
& whole consciousness, C2: 87
actions, C2: 49
Beauty = (Qabalah's definition of
    Tiphareth), C4: 40
Heaven & balance of power, B3: 179;
    C4: 75, 103
inner, CA: 82
Justice and true, C2: 49; P1: 20
original perfect, C4: 78
perfect, C3: 50; C4: 60, 78, 119
place between blood and nerve, C4: 74
point, C3: 35
see B1: 40; C3: 50, 62; P2: 104
Sushumna, C3: 30; C4: 74
THREE PHASES: PUSH, PULL, C3: 30
re-establish our, P1: 20
Balancer
of total Reality, B3: 181
Banishment
& Socrates, CA: 81
Basic
motive of life, B1: 114
Battle
inner, B1: 38
inside us, B4: 6
Battlefield
man is a, B1: 26
Be
"BE" as a fit dwelling place for my crucified
    spirit, DD: 10
"Be it unto me as unto the handmaiden of
    the Lord", TC: 45
"LET" ..."THERE" ... "BE"
    ... "LIGHT", DD: 9-10
"to be or not to be", C1: 9; C2: 67; DD: 62
Beard
BLUEBEARD, C2: 67
goat, C4: 72

high priest, C4: 72
Beast
Great, C3: 45
number of the, C4: 69
Beau Geste
Great Accomplishment, C2: 140
Beautiful
& True & Good (see diagram), C4: 40
Beauty
& intelligent power, B3: 42
& Kali, C3: 79
& Truth & Goodness, C3: 23 *(see diagram)*,
    C4: 102; P1: 43-44
= Balance (Qabalah's definition of
    Tiphareth), C4: 40
anti-, P1: 42
Become
consciousness itself, RS: vi
reflexively self-conscious, RS: 40, 58
ye shall ... Abel, when ye shall have slain
    Cain, DD: 64
Beelzebub
Lucifer & Satan, DD: 7
Bees
& social systems, EG: 89
Beethoven
"Help thyself, O Man", C2: 34
Begets
He begets Himself wholly (God), B2: 158
Beginning
& End, B4: 102
& generation of *Time,* B1: 13
& the Word, B4: 41
head of a series of actions, B1: 15
opening of a possibility, B1: 2
Begotten Son
God's Onely, P1: 82
Behaviour(s)
Civilised, B2: 42
of beings, C1: 68
of energy, B1: 60; C4: 65
of the unredeemed "dead", B3: 21
Schizoid, B3: 37
Behaviourist(s)
mechanistic, P2: 36-37
theories of mechanistic, CA: 22
Being(s)
-zone, C2: 58
& act of Creation, B1: 4
& INFINITE Sphere, C3: 133

& *interest*, C2: 93
& Logos, C3: 94
& Love … development of the possibilities
 of, B1: 111
& machines, B1: 44
& "Non-being", B2: 67
& RITUAL, CEREMONY,
 PROCEDURE?, C3: 95
& "seeming", P1: 67
& "self", C2: 48
& SPIRIT, C3: 106
& the Absolute paradox, C2: 139
& verb "to be", P1: 72-73
Absolute, P1: 73
a portion of the Supreme Power,   B3: 50
absolute Ground of Being, C4: 20
action-pattern continuity, P1: 73
actualisation, B1: 115
are substantially one, C4: 116
"being-awareness", C4: 43
Beyond Being (Parontos), C2: 60
Christalised Being is the Supreme Beloved,
 C2: 139
created, B1: 32; B3: 98
embodied, B3: 98, B4: 72
encapsulated, C4: 60
form of activity, C4: 53
FOUR *PLANES* OF, C3: 99
higher, C3: 62
His Being (Jesus), P1: 74
human, B1: 8, 39
identification of Jesus with the totality of all,
 B4: 80
INFINITE Sphere, C3: 133
intelligent (the universe), B1: 8
is a doing, is a verb, C3: 24
Law of Being-Encapsulation, C2: 106
living, B1: 144
located sphere of energy, C3: 61
LOGOS IS THE WHEEL OF, C3: 40
Loss of, B4: 146
means *actualisation*, B1: 115
of God, B1: 21
of Perfection, C3: 16
"ordered realm of …", B1: 46
organic, C4: 65
our three-fold, B4: 72
our whole, CA: 63
planes of, C3: 82, 99
purposive intelligent, B4: 152

rotatory zone, C4: 13
Sacrifice is the Law of, C3: 83
see P1: 72
self-posited zone of sentient power, C4: 101
singleness of, B3: 44
solidarity of all, C4: 112
Spirit requires each, C3: 106
still centre of, B3: 107
substantially one, C4: 116
The is-ness of all, C2: 146
True, P2: 88
unity of, C3: 91
Universal, B3: 126
vibratory pattern of wave-clusters, C2: 77
Belial
Lucifer & Satan, DD: 7
Belief(s)
& faith, B2: 85
& judgment, C4: 19
& Nietzsche, CA: 11-12
& sanity, C2: 64
& soul, CA: 10
about God, P1: 53
act of our will, B3: 6
Christian, B3: 110
conditions of our receiving this Spirit,
 P2: 108
confess our, B4: 99
in freedom, B3: 74
highest, B2: 85
in Christ Jesus, P2: 90
is an act of our will, B3: 6
man's, C4: 19
not merely passive acceptance, P2: 88
of the gross materialist, B2: 85
our pretend-, B4: 99
periods of, P1: 67
real & pretend, B4: 99
see P2: 88, 90
that Jesus Christ, P2:108
unshakeable, CA: 99
will to believe, P1: 53
Believe
Be not afraid, only believe, P2: 1, 4, 9
Believer(s)
Abel was a, B4: 173
in free will, B4: 45
Belle dame
sans merci, TC: 15

Berkeley
& Dr Johnson, RS: 4
Beth
Zone of is-ness, C4: 54
Beware
"Beware of pity!" (Nietzsche), EG: 68
Beyondness
characteristics of total reality, B3: 130
the source of the humility, B3: 130
Bhagavad Gita
"What truly *is* can never cease to be …",
C1: 9
Bhakti Yoga
& Indian Sages, C3: 93
Bias
towards the acquisition of knowledge (Cain),
B1: 127
Bible
& Cosmic Law, C4: 70
& enlightenment, B1: 22
& FEAR … intelligent, C4: 70
& levels of interpretation, B1: 94; B3: 135
& mystery of this fall, B2: 35
& names of persons, B4: 189
& system of symbology, B3: 38
& true interpretation, B1: 2
66 books bound together, C4: 70
canon for man, C4: 70
continuous restatement that God, B1: 11
Divine Plan of World evolution, B1: 22
handbook, B1: 35
handbook of principles, B2: 44
history of the workings of God's Love,
B1: 132
mirror, B4: 195
names of persons, B4: 189
not … a single book, B1: 1
not merely a "religious" book, B2: 29
One Cosmic Book of the Logos, C4: 70
one-volume library of the wisdom of the
ancient world, B2: 29
"The Word", B1: 102
theme, continuity of, B1: 11
Biogeny
Recapitulates phylogeny (philogeny),
C2: 127; C4: 84
Biograms
& Armageddon, C2: 131
buried in the unconscious, C2: 131

Biological
Blood brothers, B3: 31
Bio-magnetic field(s)
measured (in America), C1: 54
record, C4: 47
recorder, C4: 47
Bio-plasma
& soul, C2: 110
Bi-polar
human being, C4: 93
name (Tetragrammaton), C4: 95
Bi-polarity
of God, C4: 100
Birth
a coming out of thyself, DD: 44
first, C4: 108
in Bethlehem, P2: 96
into time, CA: 27
new, P2: 108, 113
of water, CA: 32
physical, B4: 30
rebirth into the divine spirit, P2: 112
second, C4: 108
spiritual, B4: 37
What is birth? (Adam), DD: 44
Bishop
overseer, B2: 6
Bitty-ness
& bitterness, B4: 14
& suffering, B4: 15
Evil is, B4: 14
Blackness
Deep, C3: 57
Blake
& excess & "enough", B4: 27
& Lucifer, B4: 27
English mystic, B4: 27
"Opposition is true friendship", C4: 120;
DD: 1
"The world is a fiction made up of
contradiction", C4: 111
Blame
No longer can blame be laid at another's
door, C2: 11
Blind
Pharisees, P1: 60
Bliss
& impedances, C4: 2
& life energies, B4: 123
"ananda" of Hindu philosophy, C4: 12

inherent property of God, B4: 91
"let" motion, C4: 12
state in which, C4: 2
state of unalloyed, B4: 91

Blood
& balance place, C4: 74
& nerve, C4: 74
& Sushumna, C4: 74
brothers, B3: 31-35
one original human, B2: 176

Bluebeard's
last wife, C2: 67

Boat
on a rough sea, C4: 8

Body(ies)
-boat, B1: 97
-conservation tendency, TC: 17
-language, C3: 79
-object & sleep, C1: 60
-process awareness, B2: 12
& Absolute Truth, B3: 120
& anchor, C2: 111, CA: 28
& anxiety, CA: 15, 17
& BONES, C3: 42
& bounding skin or integument, CA: 14
& chemical elements, B2: 116
& Christ's incarnation, C2: 64
& danger, P1: 39
& death, C1: 17-18; C3: 31; CA: 26
& embodiment, CA: 17
& feeling-sensitivity, B2: 12
& haptic experience, C4: 76
& health of, CA: 99
& incarnation, CA: 15, 17
& inner battle, B1: 38
& intelligence and will, B4: 42-43
& life-force, C1: 48
& light-field, C3: 56
& love, C1: 66
& packets of energy, CA: 25
& periodicity of the energy spin, EG: 33
& psychic plasma, C2: 110
& Satanic dust, B1: 26
& self-comforting memories, B4: 78
& soul, C2: 110-111; CA: 14-18, 100-102
& space, B3: 78; CA: 24
& spirit, C3: 58; C4: 95; EG: 4
& stresses and strains, B1: 38
& Sufism, C2: 103-104
atoms and molecules of our, B3: 43

bondage, C1: 30
centre of reference, CA: 100, C1: 59;
    C2: 104; P2: 26
Christ's, B4: 142
condition our, CA: 53
Damage, CA: 15
discrete, C4: 76
disintegration of the, B3: 126
Each organ in the, B2: 3
earthy material, C1: 18
energies, B4: 78
finite (*at the existential level*), RS: 13
finite zone, RS: 13
"fire-body", CA: 29-30
fleshly, CA: 30
food, C4: 62
GOD'S, C1: 70; EG: 16-19
hara centre, C2: 110
human, C1: 30
immortal, B4: 139
is composed of, B2: 2
is spirit, C3: 58
Jerusalemic, CA: 102
Jesus Christ … entered into a …
    physical, CA: 31
key to gaining and stabilising of our highest
    part, our spirit, CA: 26
"leib", B1: 7
lives from inside out, C3: 56
love of, C1: 66
mass inertia of energy, TC: 16
of … memories, B4: 78
of Adam, B1: 24
of Christ, B4: 142
of energies, B4: 78
of ideas (energy-patterns), B4: 78
of ideas (self-consistent), B4: 139
of reactive matter, B4: 42
of Universal Truth, B4: 142
One's body is God modalising …, EG: 18
orientation or inertia, TC: 16
physical, B1: 6, 24, 26, 61; B2: 2; B3: 108;
    B4: 78; C3: 99; C4: 76; CA: 25, 26, 29,
    53, 99; P1: 38-39; P2: 28
processes, B2: 3; CA: 63
real, B4: 78; C4: 62
Satanic dust, B1: 26
spiritual; CA: 102; P2: 59
subtle (of ideas), C3: 31
survival motive … tied to our physical,

B3: 28
Temple of the Living God, P1: 38
three-dimensional system, C1: 30
vehicle of experience, C1: 5
"water-body", CA: 29-30
Weakness of, EG: 87
wholly living, P1: 76
zone of spin, EG: 33

Boehme
"The worst is as good as the best", C4: 120
"Where is the hammer that can strike my bell?", C3: 108

Bondage
& existentialist evolution, TC: 18
& Free Will, C4: 20
& freedom, B3: 7; P2: 120
& inclination, RS: 21
Christ … release all … from, DD: 55
degrees of, B3: 7
escaping from, C1: 30
implications, C1: 29
of matter, TC: 18
see RS: 21
state, C1: 29
willing is called "creation", C4: 20

Bone
& centre, C3: 42

Book(s)
& Sacred Law, C4: 80
& Teth, C4: 55
AGAINST ISOLATION, C2: 70-73
BEYOND SYMBOLISM, C2: 68
Bible, B1: 1, 11
Cosmic (of the Logos), C4: 70
FEAR A MAN who reads only one book, C4: 70
message of the, C4: 51
of Life (Logos), C4: 91
of the Logos, C4: 70
of Truth, C2: 72
PARADOX … philosophy of Non-dualism (Advaita), C2: 68-69
THE ETHICS OF THE CONTINUUM, C4: 75-76

Boredom
Absolute, P2: 57

Born
"Except you are born again … "(Jesus), EG: 76
"To the born, certain is death" (Buddha),

B2: 16
Twice-, C4: 108
two ways of being …, B4: 29

Boundaries
creation of, B3: 3

Boustrophedon
root "kra", TC: 26

Box
= Vox, C2: 16

Brahman
Atman (self of man), C3: 131
Cosmic Breather, C4: 52
Ground of Ishvara, C1: 81

Brain
-structures, RS: v
-cell aggregate …, RS: v
-washing, B3: 135
& intelligence, B2: 84
& THE FOOD-TUBE, C3: 77
inner battle, B1: 39
mechanical, CA: 10
recent evolute, C3: 77
TWO HALVES of the, C3: 82

Brain-washing
& free spiritual expression, B3: 135

Bread
& stones in the desert, B4: 16
& word of God, DD: 30
Bread of Heaven, C3: 13
external material, P2: 45
internal spiritual, P2: 45
"man does not live by bread alone", P2: 44
of this stone must I make (Lucifer), DD: 30

Breath
& spirit, C1: 48
of life, B1: 25

Brethren
love the, B2: 1, 4

Brightness
degrees of, B1: 19

Brilliance
highest limits of, B4: 27

Broad
& "narrow way", P2: 53-57
"broad way", P2: 53-57, 77

Brother(s)
& hunt & war, B2: 2
biological, B3: 31
blood, B3: 31, 33, 35
"brotherliness", B2: 2, 4

"brothers in arms", B2: 1
Lucifer … brother-in-arms, DD: 4
organs & cells, B2: 3
spiritual, B3: 31-35
we use the word, B2: 1

Buber (Martin)
& Kierkegaard, C2: 31

Buddha
& compassion, B4: 15
& Jesus, Mahavira, Jina, Lao Tse,
    Zarathustra, Socrates, RS: 52
Diamond Body of the Buddha, C2: 139
origin of all beings, RS: 52
The father of Gautama, B4: 15
"To the born certain is death",
    B2: 16; C1: 18

Buddhi
Active Intellection, C2: 10

Buddhism
analyses a way, C2: 102
Japanese, C4: 89
"jijimuge", C4: 89

Buddhist
doctrine of "No Mind", C1: 23

Burden
& self-responsibility, B3: 7

Bureaucrats
Six-legged, C4: 69

Business
& caste system, C3: 65
& survival, P2: 46
men, C3: 65
UNFINISHED, C3: 27

Butterfly
& caterpillar, B1: 135-136
& spiritual birth, B4: 38
"psyche", B1: 136
soul, B1: 136

C

C
see English gematria, C3: 19-20, 84-88

Cain('s)
& Abel, B1: 77-78, 82, 90-91, 120, 127, 129;
    B2: 8, 24, 64; B3: 89; B4: 173; CA: 88;
    C3: 34; P1: 63
& God, B1: 78, 83-84, 131; B4: 173
& knowledge, B1: 128-130

& nuclear power, B1:129
Cain-man, B4: 174
daughters of, B1: 92
delver in the ground, B1: 130
embodied (desire to know), B1: 130
first murderer, B1: 120
forgot The Great Law, CA: 87
murderous act, B2: 74
raising of, B1: 125-126; B3: 89, 113
tiller of the ground, B1:74
ye shall become Abel, when ye shall have
    slain, DD: 64

Cainan
Seth [*son of*], B1: 92

Camel
-state (Nietzsche), EG: 75
& ancestral heredity, EG: 74

Cancer
[*Zodiac sign*] *see* C3: 113; C4: 30, 32
& Logos, C4: 32
& rebel cells, B1: 118
& Spirit, C4: 30
uncommittedness of feeling, C3: 113
water-life, C4: 32

Capacity
Choice-, B4: 67
for *choice*, B4: 68; P1: 13
for choosing *wrong*, B1: 143
for suppression, B4: 32
of creation, P1: 12
of *discrimination*, B1: 142
to *choose freely*, B2: 62

Capricorn
[*Zodiac sign*] *see* C3: 114

Casket
of Muhammad, C2: 100

Caste
& India, B3: 26

Cat
symbolises "fixity of purpose", B2: 168

Catalyst
Consciousness is a, C2: 133; C4: 51; CA: 65

Catalytic
act of Absolute Sentient Power, C4: 38

Categories
mutually exclusive (e.g. sentience,
    insentience), C2: 83

Caterpillar
& apparent death, B1: 135
& butterfly, B1: 135-136

& spiritual, Birth, B4: 38

Causation
& "accidentally", C1: 51
idea of (in Europe & oriental philosophies),
    C1: 43

Cause(s)
& determinists, C2: 148
& effect, B1: 7; B3: 124; C1: 46; C3: 23
& generative power, B3: 140
& "power", C1: 42
applied force, C1: 94
Original, C4: 85
to strike (Latin), C1: 51; RS: 10
Ultimate, B2: 58

Cave
of the heart, C2: 6

Ceiling
(sealing) velocity, C2: 139

Cell(s)
-multiplication, C4: 81
& life-force, B1: 118
& memories of Injuries, EG: 15
& "self", B1: 117
& Suryayana and Pitryana, C4: 81
interfunction, B1: 118
rebel, B1: 118
see B1: 117-120

Celtic
Christianity, B2: 78

Centrality
loss of inner, B4: 161

Centre
& Adam, B1: 63
& "Eden", B1: 63
& empty, C1: 101
& power-sentience, C2: 138
& Reflexion, C4: 117
& state of rest, C3: 61
& vortex, C1: 101
complex of contradictions, C4: 110
is everywhere (real God), C4: 57
innermost, B1: 32
of the human soul, B1: 63
"off-centre person", P2: 128

Centred
consciousness, C2: 138

Ceremony
& RITUAL, C3: 95

Certainty
& will of the Creator, P1: 49

Eye of, C2: 104
In Sufism, C2: 103
Knowledge of, C2: 104
Truth of, C2: 104

Chains
of separativity ideas, B4: 80

Change(s)
& development, B1: 135
& Energy … eternal … cannot, B3: 58
law of, C4: 73
production of (Magic), C4: 65
things of time and matter, B3: 1

Changeless
eternity is, B3: 1

Chaos
& Order, C4: 29; EG: 24
& Satanic energy, B1: 22
& spirit, C4: 36
forces of, B3: 117-118
state of, B3: 117

Character
& choice(s), B2: 53; C2: 74; C3: 69;
    CA: 53, 58
& inclinations, P1: 106
& soul, C1: 88

Characteristic(s)
& genes, C4: 24
of the materialist, B3: 35

Charge
emotional, C1: 39

Chariot
vehicle of expression (God), EG: 18

Chasten
"Those I love I chasten" says God, B1: 123

Cheek
turn the other, P1: 35, 83

Chemical
electro-chemical … systems, B1: 30
elements, B1: 29-30; B2: 183
laws, B1: 30

Cherubim(s)
& full lesson of knowledge, EG: 92-93
Garden of Eden, B1: 63

Chess-player's
favourite maxim, B2: 64

Cheth
see & hierarchy, C4: 55

Child('s)
"child-man", EG: 75
-face, B2: 139

& idolatry, B2: 57

& man & woman, C4: 55

& music, B2: 56-57

& restoration of the mind, B4: 4

child-bearing process, B2: 12

deprived, B2: 9

errors, B1: 148

"Except you become as a little child
    …" (Jesus), EG: 74

new beginning, EG: 74-75

new born, & Christopher, a Christ bearer,
C2: 69

see B1: 148; B2: 57, 77; B3: 155-156; C3: 1;
    C4: 6, 55, 104

values, B2: 57

Children

& Fall & "Sin of Adam", B1: 23-24

& laws of heredity, B1: 23-24

& parents, B1: 23; B2: 57

& the Tacit Conspiracy, TC: 49

& work of world reclamation, TC: 49

aim to acquire qualities, B2: 56

autistic, C4: 72

copy … any "superior" type of behaviour,
    B2: 56

of Time, CA: 48

"The sins of the fathers are upon the
    children", B2: 77

Chladni (y)

Figures, C1: 27; C2: 99

Choice(s)

-capacity, B4: 67

-possibility, B3: 130

& Abraham, B4: 68

& Abram, B2: 90

& action, P2: 35

& Blind laws, B4: 43

& character, CA: 53, 58

& consequences, C2: 113

& effects, B4: 95

& faith, C2: 113

& free will, B1: 123; C4: 3

& freedom, CA: 6, 24, 98; C4: 3

& God's omniscience, C2: 73

& Karma, C2: 113

& orientation, B4: 35

& primal anxiety, CA: 104

& self-creators, CA: 57

& Spirit, CA: 98

& time-process, P2: 123

& Will, CA: 56

act of, B4: 61

capacity for, B4: 60, 68; C2: 73; CA: 55;
    P1: 13

first wrong, B1: 149

free, CA: 55, 86, 104; P1: 160; P2: 42, 116

infinity of, C4: 3

man has a … (Saturn / Jupiter), CA: 48

possibility of, P1: 8

power of free, CA: 66

power of, B2: 91

problem of, P2: 35

self-, CA: 103

single, B3: 131

unavoidable, B2: 96

Choose

& highest conceivable aim, C2: 35

chop away, C2: 21

power to, B2: 88

"Therefore choose Life", P2: 83

to select from all possibilities, B3: 129

Chosen

"Many are called but few are
    chosen" (Jesus), P1: 7

Chrism

Sacred, C2: 139

Christ('s)

-child, C2: 69, 128

-Logos, C2: 9

-love, CA: 96

& ancestral dictatorships, C1: 97

& Ascension, C2: 88

& Body of Truth, B4: 142

& Christopher, C2: 69

& continuum, C1: 9

& devil, C1: 106

& Gethsemane & Golgotha, CA: 95

& *grace*, B3: 81

& locks of heaven and hell, DD: 55

& money-changers, C3: 19

& peace, C2: 73

& Religion or Philosophy, C1: 96

& resurrecting power, CA: 96

& Temple, C3: 19

& the world, P1: 26, C4: 57; CA: 87

& Unity with the Creator, P1: 4

& Word of God, B4: 142

Anchor, C2: 65;
    CA: 18, 21, 26, 28, 34, 36, 101

Body of, C4: 63

"Body of Christ", B4: 142
Christ-child, C2: 69, 128
Christ-Logos, C2: 9
cross, CA: 91, 95
crucifixion, C3: 33; CA: 92
dialectic of … crucifixion, CA: 92
died, CA: 91
Fish, CA: 34
"fool for Christ's sake", B2: 80, 83
His Ascension, C2: 88
His symbol is Fire, CA: 28
"I have food you know not of", C4: 105
incarnate, B3: 52
Incarnation of, CA: 15
Key, CA: 43
"Kindly Light", C2: 9
"Mind of Christ", B3: 16; CA: 51
Mystical, Body, C4: 63
"Our Father which art in Heaven …",
    CA: 13
our helper, CA: 36
path, B2: 163
pleroma, C4: 63
power in us, CA: 30
pray, CA: 13
sacrifice, CA: 36
seamless garment, B1: 32; B3: 165; B4: 10;
    C1: 9; C2: 15, 41; C4: 57; CA: 87; P2: 4
seamless garment & Reality, B4: 11-12
seamless garment … that we shall wear
    eternally, B4: 10
see DD: 55
see quotations (words of Christ), B3: 112, 134;
    C2: 41; C4: 35, 64, 86, 105;
    CA: 13, 92; P1: 15
show us how to die, CA: 92
show us how to live, CA: 92
source of our *initiation*, CA: 30
symbol, CA: 28, 34
total self-knowledge, B3: 81
Truth, C1: 96
value of … for us, CA: 31
victory over the devil, P1: 38
"water of Life", P1: 143
way, B2: 81, 163
words, P1: 2, 5, 15

"Christ my Anchor"
Jesus Christ is our Anchor, CA: 34
see C2: 65, CA: 18, 21, 26, 28, 101

Christal
Sphere, C2: 139
Christalisation
conceptual structure, C2: 139
Christalised
Being is the Supreme Beloved, C2: 139
Christian(s)
& the Messiah, B3: 118
& true Divine Way, B2: 163
belief, B3: 110
Philosophy, P1: 1, 2, 47
Christianity
& Incarnation, C4: 10
& Judaism & Islam, C2: 12
& Neighbourly Love, C2: 12
& Nietzsche, CA: 12
& sacrifice, P1: 121
Celtic, B2: 78
Mystery of, C2: 111
Christification
& Diamond Body, C2: 139
Christopher
& Christ-child, C2: 69, 128
Church
& Mary, C2: 85
& Roman Catholic Teaching, C2: 85
coordinated assembly, B2: 6
Ekklesia Para Hexon, C3: 32
leaders of the, B3: 110
Of God, C3: 32
Circle(s)
& binding conture, C1: 28
& figure of eight, B1: 42
& greatest conceivable being, C1: 32
& sentient power, C1: 33
& space, C1: 29
Cross in the, C3: 122
KIRK EL, C3: 32
limited being, B1: 44
of being, C1: 28
perfect, B2: 17
represents the whole of Nature, C1: 32
sacred space, C2: 143
two, B1: 42
zone of rotating motion, RS: 8
Circular
& energy patterns, B3: 21
Circulation
band, C1: 33
easy, B4: 123

Circumcision
  external symbol, B2: 95
  of the chosen, TC: 28
  spiritual act, B2: 95
  symbolic act, B2: 94
Circumscription
  & Creation, C1: 77
  & motion, C1: 68
  & finite existence, C1: 68
  & "finity", C1: 78
  zone of, C1: 78
Civilised
  behaviour, B2: 42
Civilisation(s)
  & controls, B4: 115
  began, B2: 42
  Human, P1: 6
  Materialistically Based, P1: 5
Clarity
  & "distinction", C2: 97
  & intellect, B1: 50
  & "perfect knowledge", C2: 97
  & Reality, P1: 151
  FEAR GENERATES, C3: 72
Classification
  & Adam, B2: 26
  system of, B2: 26
Clay
  & woman, DD: 45
Cloak
  & spiritual poverty, C2:100
  form-totality of creation, C2: 100
  (inside) a casket of white pearls
    (Muhammad), C2: 100
Cocoon
  & caterpillar weaving, B1: 135
  shroud, B1: 135
Cogniser
  & interest, C1: 91
  & shell seen as silver, C1: 91
Cognition
  & Sushumna, C4: 74
Cold
  & hot, CA: 54
  & lukewarm & indifferent, CA: 54
Collective
  spark, EG: 47
  unconscious mind, B2: 175
Colours
  & ART, C4: 80-81

& forms, C4: 80-81
see C4: 113-114
tone-values, C4: 113-114
Comforter
  & God-Man within, P2: 92
  His actual presence, P2: 92
Commandment
  "A new commandment I give unto you, that
    you love one another ..." (Jesus), P1: 6
Commit
  ONESELF TO SPIRIT, C3: 106
  ourselves, CA: 54
Common
  origin, P1: 119
  source, DD: 2, 4, 14-15, 20-23, 31-32, 37,
    40-41, 43
Communicate
  to live we must, CA: 92
Communication(s)
  & autistic children, C4: 72
  & Christ, CA: 91-92
  & language, B3: 116
  essentiality of human life, CA: 88
  inter-, CA: 90
  non-, CA: 91
  Self-, CA: 90
Communal
  unity of the ... group, CA: 82
Community
  human, CA: 82
  In the ancient world, CA: 81
  of the Holy Ghost, B3: 88
Compact
  [between God and Lucifer], DD: 48
Compaction
  centre of, C2: 63
  self-, C2: 138
Compassion
  & Fiat, C2: 17
  & self-pity, EG: 68
  & suffering, B4: 14-15
  infinite, P2: 56
  infinity of all His mercies, C2: 17
Complexity
  High ... of our mental life, CA: 73
Composer
  & cacophony, C4: 113-114
  musician-, C4: 113-114
Compounds
  & corruption, C1: 35

Comprehension
pattern, C4: 91
Compression
(Saturn), C4: 68
Compromise
& Truth ... Falsity, P1: 40
Compulsion
& dualistic thinking, C1: 77
external, P1: 101
without ... from the outer stimulus?, P2: 35
Computer
acts as programmed, C4: 51
cannot disobey, CA: 66, 71
has *no free will*, CA: 66
man is *not* a, CA: 71
not built to be arbitrary, CA: 71
properly designed, CA: 66
Conation,
& separation, C4: 67
see C2: 2; C3: 15, 83, 121; C4: 67
Concealment
& Noah & covering, B2: 28, 32
& veil, B2: 28, 32
Concentration
& continuum, C2: 93
centring process, C3: 53
energy, B2: 108
symbol of, C2: 142
Concept(s)
& "logos", C4: 84
& "mythos", C4: 84
& percept(S), C2: 114; RS: 44
"Finites" are but, C4: 9
governing, CA: 77: P1: 22
highest possible, C4: 94
hypostasised, C4: 17
master, C4: 27
of God, C4: 94
OF THE God-Man, C4: 94
tuning device, C3: 74
Conceptual
essence(s), C2: 121, 124, 138; C3: 56;
C4: 31, 77
Concrete
"grown together", C1: 86
Concretion
& power, B1: 134
of energy-units, B1: 134
Condensation
& highest poetry, C2: 6

Condition
object-slavery, B4: 174
our mind, CA: 53
Conditioned
conditioned-reflex, RS: 25
Confidence
TRUE SELF-CONFIDENCE, C3: 122
Conflict
between the exclusive and inclusive will,
B2: 178
cure of ... restoration of true interfunction,
B2: 9
of polarised beings, TC: 39
Confound
language ("Babel"), B2: 54
Confucianism
& communal living, C2: 102
& social rituals, C2: 37
Confusion
& elements of truth, P2: 32
"Babel", B2: 54
fusing together of forms, C1: 69
of purposes, B2: 54
Conquest
of anxiety, CA: 13
of Anxiety, *see* the Book *Conquest of Anxiety*
(CA)
Conscience
& Abraham, B2: 136-137
& ancestors, B2: 180
& knowledge, C4: 19
& theatre, B2: 39
bad, B2: 180
becomes clear, B2: 181
clear, B2: 181
good, B2: 182
records in ourselves, B1: 90
see B2: 179-182
source true, C1: 101
totality of one's knowledge of oneself, B1: 89
Conscious
& realities (inner world / outer world),
B1: 41
& "unconscious" ... mind(s), B1: 57, 60-61;
B2: 176-178; B4: 121
& unconscious suffering, B4: 121
battle, B1: 61
creator, C1: 81
gap in one's Being, C2: 79
hidden, B4: 153

individuals, B4: 191
knowledge, B2: 81
mind, B1: 57-62
of an action, CA: 65
of his freedom, P2: 21
self-sacrifice, CA: 95
suffering, B4: 121
struggle, B2: 178

Consciousness
& ability to ignore, B4: 172
& act of reflexion, RS: 41
& Absolute awareness, C1: 105
& body-object, C1: 62
& bone, C3: 42
& dim, EG: 46-47
& divide / division, B1: 35, 40
& divine dissatisfaction, RS: 50
& dot or point, C2: 142
& field of awareness, B3: 173
& freedom, P2: 21
& God-in-him, B4: 175
& higher self, C4: 24
& "I", C1: 67
& Identity, C2: 54
& infinite self-sentient power, C1: 8
& inner / inside & outer / outside,
   B1: 35, 40-41
& involutionary process, RS: 50
& Light *(see diagram)*, C4: 28
& "light", B2: 97
& limit of mind, C3: 119
& "living death", B3: 22
& Materialistic science, C4: 48
& materialistic scientist, B4: 170
& matter, C1: 81
& mental disorders, RS: 41
& "Mind", C2: 46
& "Mistakes", C4: 24
& MONOCELLS, C3: 109
& motion-complex, RS: 49
& object-identification, RS: 21, 49
& outer world's realities, B1: 41
& physical body, CA: 26
& Power, B3: 67; EG: 48
& reflexive act, RS: 39
& sentience, C1: 2
& sleep, C1: 60
& Space, EG: 48
& STING of intensest compaction, C2: 138
& symbol, C2: 142

& the Absolute, C2: 97; RS: 32
& the resec act, RS: 15
& the Self, RS: 2
& understanding, B4: 191
& WHOLE ORGANISM AWARE, C3: 29
& will, RS: 32
& word, C1: 22
back-flow of, RS: 46
catalyst, C1: 56-57; C2: 123, 133;
   C4: 51; CA: 65
cause of, C1: 52
centred personal, C2: 138
civilised, B2: 175
clear, P2: 114
concentrated or diffused, EG: 48
content(s) of, C1: 53; C3: 61; EG: 46;
   RS: vii
defines analytically, RS: iii
degrees of, B2: 119
evolutionary process of our, RS: 50
external modes of, C4: 86
extroversion of, B1: 30
focal point for, C2: 71
God the Son, EG: 49
higher, B3: 16
highest activity of our Bodies, EG: 44
Human, P1: 147
"I", C1: 67
infinite ocean of sentiency, C1: 84
Infinite, C1: 24
is a catalyst, C2: 133; CA: 65
key to ... freedom, RS: 46
lack of, P2: 68
"Light" (symbol), B4: 191; P2: 69
light of, C4: 120
loss of, B4: 74; RS: 30
mysterious, B1: 42
nature of, B4: 171
observing, B4: 169
of consciousness is immediate, RS: i
peripheralisation, C4: 108
personal, EG: 46
pre-condition of all freedom, B3: 162
Pure, B3: 81, 106; B 4: 175; C1: 91, 97
quickness of, C1: 104
reference point, C2: 71
Reflexive, B3: 65
return of health to that, RS: 41
sentient power, RS: 50
shift of, C3: 61; C4: 24-25

stable reference of, CA: 26
symbol of, P2: 69
turns back upon itself, RS: 39
two parts, B1: 40
whole, C2: 87; EG: 46

Conservation
& Mother, C4: 109
of power, C4: 106
principle, C4: 109

Consideration
& fear, C4: 41
deep, serious, P1: 11

Consistency
& humanness, B3: 123
of things in the material world, C2: 95
perfect mental, P1: 64
self-, B4: 146; C2: 108
"*Sin* is within itself a *consistency*, and in this
    consistency of evil within itself it possesses
    a certain power" (Kierkegaard), C2: 107

Consort
& Man … necessary for the development of,
    TC: 43

Conspiracy
& Tacit, *see* the Book, TC

Consummation
(of days or enlightenments), EG: 17

Contact
& existence of finite things, C1: 111

Contemplation
& inspired writers … of the Bible, B1: 16
& sages, B1: 16-17
highest stages, B1: 16
in a single comprehensive moment, B3: 102
pure, B1: 16

Continence
& conservation of power, C4: 106
& incontinence, C4: 106

Contingent
& Real Self, C4: 107
self, C3: 46
stimulation, C4: 90, 107
stimuli, C4: 90, 107

Continuance
physical, B1: 41

Continuity
of action, P1: 73
see P1: 72-73
of theme (Bible), B1: 11

Continuum
& Absolute Sentient Power (ASP), C2: 30
& Christ, C1: 9
& energy, C4: 105, 112, 116
& Fear, C2: 145
& motion, C1: 99; C2: 62
& no "empty" places, C2: 145
& "Fear of the Lord is the beginning of
    wisdom", C2: 145
& partless ocean of sentient power, C2: 93
& PHENOMENA, C3: 2; C4: 106
& shift of attention C2: 62
& "sin" or separation from the Source,
    C4: 107
& Supreme Power, B1: 32
& the "Fall", C4: 107
& the substance of the Absolute, C1: 98
& ULTIMATE REALITY, C3: 114;
    C4: 21
& vibratory action, C3: 2
field of sentient power, C3: 30
infinite, C1: 41; C2: 62; C4: 53, 120
is no-fear, C2: 145
modalisings" of the, C4: 76
modalities of a, C2: 93
NON-DUAL, C4: 57
non-mechanical, C2: 12
not subject to disintegration, C1: 9
partless ("seamless garment"), B1: 32, 60
PARTLESS, is not restricted, C4: 78
power-, CA: 87
Reason of the, C2: 82
seamless garment of Christ, B1: 32, C1: 9,
    C4: 57
seamless indestructible whole, C1: 9
Self, C4: 106-108
Self, the only real, C4: 56
sentient power, C1: 8; C2: 137; C4: 57, 105
space-time-energy, B1: 133
The Ethics of the Continuum, C4: 75
transcends, C3: 48
Universe, C4: 112
Wisdom intuits the, C2: 145

Contours
binding, C1: 31

Contraction
stressed feeling, C1: 39

Contradiction(s)
& self-consciousness, C4: 110
& The Real, C4: 95

hidden, B4: 33
see C4: 110-112
self-, B3: 40, 123

Contradictory
elements, B3: 40

Contrariness
source of, B4: 112

Control(s)
& civilised people, B4: 115
& impulsive behaviour, B1: 107
& language, B3: 116
& words of truth, B1: 107
dialectic, P2: 120
formal, C3: 95
immediate, C1: 89
inner (yogi), C4: 87
limits, P2: 120
matter of self-knowledge, C4: 17
of impulsive energy, B1: 104
of irrational impulses, B2: 29
of pleasure-pain reaction tendencies,
    B1: 114
of "shift of attention", C2: 63 of the name
    (Shem), B2: 28
possibility of total, B3: 68

Convergence
of energy ... mind ... will, P2: 80
Exercises in consciousness, C2: 63

Co-operation
& non-free Beings, C3: 106
& well-being, B2: 10
"brotherliness", B2: 2, 4
Creation implies, B4: 156, 158
harmonious working together, B4: 158
intelligent, B2: 10
"working together", P2: 1

Co-operative
interfunction, B2: 4

Co-ordination
function, B2: 6
lack of, B3: 50
original state of, B3: 60

Corinthian
& architectural orders, C3: 30

Corner
-stone, B3: 83, 109

Corpus
& Subjectivity, C2: 89
Anima, Spiritus, C2: 89, 126
principle of substantialisation, C2: 126

Corruption
& first error of Adam and Eve, B1: 93
tends to accelerate, B1: 93

Cosmic
Book of the Logos, C4: 70
intelligence, B4: 167; P1: 84
Logos, C2: 147
Man, C2: 1
Mother, C4: 109
Observer, B4: 167
ocean (*Mare*), C2: 86

Cosmopolis
non-accident, C2: 2
perfect, C2: 2

Cosmos (Kosmos)
& Altar of, C4: 119
& last judgement, C2: 74
& the soul, C4: 64
& Time, C3: 133
is maintained in being, C2: 117
SCRYING BALL of God, C3: 24
supreme intelligent organism, C2: 1

Council
of perfection, P1: 23

Count
count all, OR COUNT NOT AT ALL,
    DD: 63

Counters
& the assembled ones, DD: 14
& players, DD: 65
count the cost, DD: 51
men, DD: 14, 63
worshippers of Mammon, DD: 64

Counting
& pregnancy, C4: 55
Coins, DD: 63
end of, DD: 51
evaluating, C1: 24
evil which ... makes, DD: 65
false, DD: 64-65
lovers of, DD: 63
thinking process, C1: 24

Cou-rage
see C2: 70; C4: 6-7

Cour-age
Logos-God, C4: 7
see C2: 70; C4: 6-7

Courage
& cowardice, C4: 6-7
opposing forces, C2: 70

see C2: 70; C4: 6-7
Coward
  & slavery, EG: 87
  man who guards his Q, C4: 5
Cowardice
  & cure of, C4: 6
  is female, C4: 7
  see C4: 5-8
Create
  "ark" / "arc", TC: 26
  encapsulate, B4: 92
  root "kra", TC: 26
  see C1: 11
  signifies, DD: 8
  "to circumscribe", C1: 28
  Why does God ...?, C1: 76
Created
  being, B3: 98
Creating
  & forms of His (God's) omniscience, EG: 3
Creation
  & anxiety, CA: 25
  & biological forms, TC: 7
  & divine purpose, B3: 33
  & energy, B2: 149
  & infinite power, B1: 2
  & Infinite Spirit, C4: 23
  & infinity, C1: 72
  & intelligence and will, P1: 123
  & The Greatest Sin, C2: 19
  & Ultimate Reality, C4: 21
  act of, B4: 92; P1: 123
  act (willed), C1: 77
  activity of the Power of God, B1: 6
  before, B1: 3, 23; B2: 155; C4: 89; CA: 25
  beginning of the control of this force,
      B2: 149
  capacity of, P1: 12
  circumscription, C4: 89
  Divine Will's, P1: 160
  encapsulation, C4: 89
  formation, C4: 89
  God's, DD: 3
  implies co-operation, B4: 156, 158
  Infinite Creative Power, B4: 92
  INTELLECT IS A, C3: 71
  mechanical, C1: 77
  of a finite encapsulated zone, C4: 107
  process, P1: 12; C1: 77
  purpose of, B1: 6

releases the beings of Eternity, B1: 4
special act, B1: 4
source of, P2: 5
view of, C1: 77
work of, P1: 13, 16
Creative
  act (nature of), B4: 92
  activity, C1: 79; C2: 98
  capacities, B4: 151
  imagination, C4: 73
  intelligent living, B1: 37
  Love (His Law of), CA: 79
Creativity
  & INTELLECT, C3: 71
  & man's soul, P2: 41
  & psychoanalysis, C4: 80
  pure, C2: 12
  "spiritual ...", DD: 70
Creator('s)
  & each soul, C4: 64
  & relationships, P1: 51
  God (7): THE ORIGINAL, C3: 90
  of the Universe, B1: 147; C4: 100
  see B1: 46
  self-encapsulated, C4: 86
  Shall we co-operate with our, P1: 162
  Will-power, B4: 101
Creature(s)
  being of limitation, B1: 18
  finite, C1: 14
  God is not a, B1: 19
  limited in our physical bodies, P1: 138
  limited in power and knowledge, CA: 86
  Man as a, B1: 130
  must become God, B1: 130
  of free will, B1: 146-147
  self-created (therefore God), C4: 86
  spheres of enclosed energies, B4: 92
  UTTER IMPOTENCE of the, C3: 70
Cricket-players
  & causation-doctrine, DD: 8
Criticism
  & an exercise in self-control under injustice,
      TC: 43
  of others, B4: 28
Cross
  & embodied love of God, CA: 95
  & Jesus, CA: 39, 91; DD: 60
  & significances of vertical and horizontal,
      C2: 144

antwort of the, C2: 112
Cosmic, C4: 119
George, C3: 84
in the Circle, C3: 122
meaning of the, B3: 137
of Golgotha, C4:35
of our own individual existence, CA: 95
symbol of, B3: 137

Crucified
God-Man, the Omega and Telos, C3: 31
King, C3: 15, 16

Crucifixion
& our own, B4: 110
of Christ, C3: 64
of Jesus, P2: 56
ST (SELF-CRUCIFIXION), C3: 47

Crux
Ansata, C3: 17, 101 (*diagram*); C4: 92
  Crystal
    precipitating itself in a solution, C4: 59
    see C2: 51-52
    Seed, C2: 51

Cube
(*see diagram*) C3: 100, 121

Culture
& *work* (Marxism), C4: 58
tora-ruled, C4: 14

Cup
functions like the soul, C2: 79

Cure
& fears, B2: 189
& expectancy, C4: 79

Curiosity
& Cat, B2: 168
& forgetfulness, B2: 168
& fringes, B2: 168
& "subjective" processes, P2: 38
Kyriosity, EG: 17

Cycle(s)
of birth and death (ancient view), CA: 47
of egg-embryo-child ..., C1: 80
of mental events, P2: 41

Cyclic
& Non-cyclic motions, RS: 14
actions, B1: 46
Time, B1: 14
wheel of the physical world, P1: 67

D

D
see English gematria, C3: 19-20, 84-88

Daat
between eternity and time, C3: 15

Dakini
the Red Goddess, C3: 79

Daleth
Divide the consolidated zone, C4: 54
Door of Life, C3: 26

Damage
& anxiety and fear, CA: 15
& inconsistency, B4: 33
& state of anxiety, CA: 1

DAN
(judgment). D-AN, C4: 22

Danger
& freedom, CA: 87
being talented, B3: 55

Darkness
" ... upon the face of the deep", B1: 21;
  DD: 8
deep blackness, C3: 55
Deep, C3: 57
"from excess of light came darkness", B1: 20
"great interjection", C1: 87
"Men love darkness rather than light ...",
  P1: 54
mental, B2: 98
No-saying to light, DD: 18
privation of light, C1: 106
substantiated content of consciousness,
  C3: 40
symbolises unconsciousness, B2: 97

Darwinian
evolutionists, C1: 49

Data
& the computer, CA: 71

David
Star of, C3: 80

Day
dawn, DD: 9
star, DD: 18

Dead
& Divine Will, P1: 24
& inner creativity of Emanuel, B3: 9
& machines, B1: 144
& "quick", B1: 144; B3: 10-11, 22-24;
  CA: 92; P1: 24; TC: 7
asleep, B1: 144

"dead in their sins", B3: 19
"dead to something", P2: 14
Father raiseth the, P1: 17, 23
"God is dead" (Nietzsche), C2: 128, EG: 62
God Is Not Dead (EH), EG: 62-97
person, C2: 77
routine behaviour patterns, B3: 11
routine-ruled people, B1: 144
unredeemed, B3: 21

Death
& body, C4: 62
& caterpillar, B1: 135
& change our form, B2: 110
& different levels of being, B2: 33
& dishonour, C4: 15
& Eve, EG: 55
& expulsion from the Garden of Eden,
    B1: 67
& "Hell", RS: 40
& instinct, C1: 15
& "last judgement", CA: 58
& *mode* of dying, C1: 16
& North-South axis, *(see diagram)*, C4: 66
& ritual burials, C3: 76
& sleep, B1: 68
Abel's, CA: 88
approach to, B2: 71
AT ONE'S SIDE C3: 31
Beyond, B4: 2
disconnection from life, P2: 14
disintegration, B3: 126: C1: 17; P2: 58
enemy of life, C4: 49
escape from ... ceaseless mechanicality,
    B1: 70
Every man's, B1: 121
fall into identification, RS: 35
forshadowing ... of Jesus Christ, CA: 89
"GREAT LEVELLER", C3: 38
"I have this day set before you Life and
    Death", P2: 83
Jesus has overcome, B4: 70
life between birth and, C1: 2
loss of the self-determination of the soul,
    B4: 70
moment of, B4: 137
near-, B1: 135
physical, B2: 71; B3: 30; B4: 142
re-entry into God, B3: 177
second, B4: 142, C3: 32; CA: 26; P1: 79
source of, B1: 48

spiritual, B1: 53
survival of, CA: 23
there is no ..., DD: 46
"To the born certain is death" (Buddha),
    B2: 16
wrong kind of, C4: 18

Decision
& own ... to correct oneself, C2: 11
free, CA: 98

Declaration
formal, TC: 20

Dedication
attainment of reflexive self-consciousness,
    C3: 90

Deed(s)
& deliberate evil, CA: 58
& *quality* & *quantity*, CA: 37
"In the beginning was the *Deed*", B3: 167

Deep
Blackness / Darkness, C3: 57
"darkness upon the face of the ...", B1: 21

Defence(s)
means of, C2: 135
system of, B4: 118

Defensive
mind, CA: 89

Deficiency(ies)
& Diseases, C4: 77
& talents ... may appear, P1: 113

Definition(s)
& division, B1: 39
& form and function, B1: 50
act of, C1: 83
define what we mean by, C1: 21
of the anxiety cause, CA: 2
Transcendence of all, C4: 71

Degrees
of feeling awareness, B2: 118

Deification
"making like God" of man, B3: 51

Delegate
educate potential workers to take over,
    C3: 52

Delight
in the misfortunes of other persons, CA: 41

Delilah
& Samson, TC: 45

Delphic
Oracle, B3: 37, 133

Deluge
see B1: 96-97
Democritus
(Atomism), C4: 31
Demon
alienated portion of one's being, B3: 59
Depression
& loss of power, RS: 50
& suicide, C1: 6
Description
refers only to finites, C1: 95
Desert
Then the man went forth into …, DD: 53
Design
see B3: 43
Designer
of total Reality, C2: 47
Desire(s)
& Fame, B2: 56
& fear, DD: 49
& human anxiety, CA: 79
& "Love", B2: 125
& charm or assumed merit, B1: 140
energy driving living beings, B3: 47
own, B2: 98
see B3: 47
to harm another human being, P1: 65
Despair
& disparity, CA: 17
& soul, CA: 17
devil's, C2: 106
Destiny
goal which one freely chooses, C2: 127
Destruction
& preservation, P1: 123
our possible, P2: 5-6
The Broad Way, P2: 81
un-structuring, CA: 25
Detensification
& intensification, EG: 10
Determinism
Free Will or DETERMINISM?, C2: 134
Determinists
SEE the present situation, C2: 148
Deuce
& the Devil, EG: 49
Developing
life-forms, B1: 122
Development
& artists, B2: 23

& caterpillar to butterfly, B1: 135
& child prodigy, B2: 23
& choice, B4: 35
& extra-ordinary changes, B1: 135
& Love, B1: 111; P1: 159
& resistance, B2: 23
great law of talent …, B1: 120
of all beings, B3: 99
of his gifts, B2: 23
of the chastened, B1: 123
PHASES OF … OF MAN, C4: 91
true self-, B1: 85
Devil
-Lucifer, DD: 5
& English gematria, C3: 20
& Messiah, C4: 111
& principles of Mammon-diabolism, P1: 27
& Saturn, Mercury, Jupiter, C4: 111
Accuser C1: 87; DD: 7
and God, C4: 111
Anti-Christ, P2: 81
Deuce, EG: 49
"devil-player", C2: 7
disintegrating forces of identification, C1: 87
grip of the, B4: 194
is sheer spirit (Kierkegaard), C2: 106
Murderer and liar from the beginning,
     P1: 61
one with the Christ (Logos), C1: 106
Prince of Evil, P1: 28
Prince of Lies, P1: 32
"principle", P2: 30-31
resistance needed for God, C2: 56
slanderer, C1: 87
Devious
man, B1: 86-87
Diagonal
through GOnaD to GOD, C3: 51
Dialectic
& Christ, P2: 56
& Controls, P2: 120
& freedom & bondage, P2: 120
& Logos, C4: 35
& "paradox", P2: 56
& Truth, C4: 35
equal value of opposites, C4: 9
Eternity, C3: 69
of sacrifice, CA: 92
of the narrow way, P2: 57
Time, C3: 69

true, C4: 9

Dialectical
Master of all ... Oppositions (Messiah), C3: 8
Necessity, P2: 120

Differences
diversity of ideas, B3: 128

Differentiation
of modes of activity, C4: 53
of powers, B4: 148

Direction(s)
six, C3: 100
two, B1: 55

Disciples
tread the same path, B2: 81

Disbelief
is an insulator, B2: 132

Discovery
self-, B1: 6

Discrimination
capacity of, B1: 142
free, B1: 143

Discussion
real aim of, P1: 41

Disease(s)
& "agent", C2: 52
& allopathy and homeopathy, C2: 121-122
& deficiency, C4: 77
& excess, C4: 77
& expectancy, C4: 79
& healing of, C2: 121-123
& homoeopathy, C2: 121-122; C4: 77
& "patient", C2: 52
& Tension in the organism, B4: 117
modal complexes, C2: 52
of mankind, C4: 10

Discontinuum
cannot be ultimate, C4: 106

Disharmony
we act in ways that ... produce, B3: 69

Dishonour
& Death, C4: 15

Disintegration
& death, C1: 18
& evil, B4: 195
& fear, P2: 6
& illusion, C1: 40
soul, B3: 127; B4: 64
& unifying purpose (lack of), B2: 108
scattering energy-units, B1: 134
soul, B3: 127; B4: 64

Dislike(s)
& our likes, CA: 69
the word "God", B2: 74

Dismemberment
& Will-to-be, B4: 64

Disobedience
first act of, P2: 103
first ancestors', CA: 19
result of, CA: 21

Disorder(s)
& order, B1: 38
disintegrates us, B1: 38
stress, B3: 61, 152

Disparity
& non-despair, C2: 140

Dispensation
"Dispensation for Innocence", B3: 88

Disquiet
& untruth, P1: 65
(experienced, P2: 3

Disregard
wilful, B4: 172

Disruption
& Luciferan precipitation, B1: 21

Dissolution
Saturn/Jupiter/Mercury & Unbalance,
    C4: 38

Distraction
pre-condition of destruction, P2: 78

Distrust
suppose we ... our reason, B1: 109

Dis-unity
& divine Unity, B4: 161

Diversity
& pure unity, C4: 116

Divine
& new birth, P2: 113
& ultimate results of actions, C3: 83
dissatisfaction, RS: 49
grace, B4: 38, 128; C2: 44; C3: 16; P1: 98
Hermaphrodite, C4: 74-75
Human, B2: 170
intelligent power, B4: 22
joy, B1: 147
Life, EG: 7
Light, B3: 5
love, B1: 150; CA: 39
names, C2: 99
Order, C2: 98
Origin, B4: 47

Plan, B1: 22; CA: 70
Purpose, B3: 33
Self-revelation, P2: 87
Son, B2: 158, 161
Spirit, B4: 111-112; C2: 86; CA: 16;
    P2: 28, 40, 87, 113
Will, P1: 18

Divinity
can confer, B4: 54
hidden, B4: 128
Inner, B4: 21
power that divines, B4: 39

Divinisation
rules of our, B4: 127

Division
& consciousness, B1: 35
& Principle of Order, B1: 39
a necessity, B1: 37
of labour, B2: 6, 15
of reality, B1: 60
original … of peoples, B2: 54
primary, B1: 45

Doctrine
Law of Being-Encapsulation, C2: 106
of the Tacit Conspiracy, TC: 16
True, C2: 105

Do
"to be or not to be" … "to *do* or not to *do*",
    C2: 67

Dog
-brained (The coward), C4: 5
Cooperation of pack, C3: 91

Do-gooder
position of the, DD: 1

Domed
& the Free, C1: 107

Donna
La donna e mobile, TC: 10

Door
"I am the Door; no man comes to the
    Father but by me", P1: 129
Son Jesus, P1: 18
of understanding, CA: 39

Doorways
of Eternity, CA: 49

Doric
architectural orders, C3: 30

Doubt
& Thomas, P1: 52
doubleness, P1: 49, 50

no true unity, CA: 12

Dove(s)
& peace, B3: 134
"as harmless as doves", P2: 48
harmless … as a dove, yet … wily as
    serpents, DD: 56
"I send you as sheep among wolves.
    Therefore, be as wily as serpents and as
    harmless as doves", B3: 134; P2: 46
in man, B3: 134
Jesus accepted the … in man, B3: 134
seem harmless …but, B3: 137
symbology of the, P2: 51

Dream(s)
-condition, CA: 16
& sleep, B1: 68
& the sleepers, DD: 9
& unresolved problems, B1: 58
awareness, B2: 118
state, B1, 69; C3: 120
World, C4: 83

Drifting
not willing, B2: 106

Drop
penny to, C4: 42

Drunkenness
Noah, B2: 28

Dual
nature, B3: 67

Dualism
& LOGIC, C3: 25
absolute, TC: 36
avoid falling into, RS: 11
is impossible, B3: 141
ultimate, B3: 141

Dust
physical body of Adam, B1: 24
Satanic, B1: 26
we are not merely "dust of the ground",
    B3: 39

Duty
& Beethoven, B3: 147

Dynokinetic
process, B2: 156

E

E
A E I O U, *(see diagrams)*, C4: 30

life relation-making, C4: 67
life-field of sentience, C4: 30
see English gematria, C3: 19-20, 84-88

E=Mc2
see B4: 87

Eagle
double-headed, B2: 122
symbol of the "over-view", B2: 122-123
"The snake will one day coil affectionately
   around the eagle's neck" (Nietzsche),
   C3: 117

Ear(s)
& sound, C1: 109
for God, B3: 176

Earth
-Mother rites, C4: 71
& Cain, B1: 74
& Four Elements, C3: 122
& furtherance of life-forms, B4: 152
& Lucifer's fall, B1: 24
& Mammon-mind, B4: 153
& our duty, B4: 152
deforest the, B4: 153
DENSE ATMOSPHERE, C3: 67
Divinisation, C4: 119
God, C4: 37
new, B2: 148
paradisical garden [or] totally unfit, B4: 153
R discontinuity *(see diagram)*, C4: 95
(Tauros), C4: 30
we can make or mar our, B4: 153
Without proper care, B4: 152
woman is as, DD: 45

Earthy
material body, C1: 18-19

Eater
& Jupiter, C4: 63

Ecclesia (Ekklesia)
Para Hexon, C3: 32, 45

Ecological
balance (little sense of), B3: 69

Ecology
of spirit, B3: 71; P2: 71
spiritual, B3: 73, 75, 80, 82

Ecologists
observers for God, B3: 178

Economic(s)
& intelligence, B4: 28
& pollution, B1: 100

ECT
see C2: 50

Ectropy
"entropy", B1: 134; C2: 47, 77

Eden
& Cherubims, B1: 63
& guarded place, B1: 47
& state of innocence, B1: 63
& the subtle serpent, DD: 10
centre of human soul, B1: 63
paradisical harmony, B1: 23
re-entry into, TC: 37
zone of non-judgment, C4: 74

Education
& impedances to ... knowledge, B2: 98
& "scientistic" & critical mind, C4: 26
educational systems, government-controlled,
   B2: 98
Way of Play, C4: 80

Effect(s)
& cause, C1: 42-43, 46; C3: 23
& infinite sentient power, C1: 42
& the Father, B3: 140
law of "cause and effect", B1: 7
of power, B2: 58

Efficiency
& marksmanship, B1: 77
& words "good" and "bad", B1: 77
inefficiency, B1: 75
least energy expenditure, B4: 28
means, B4: 28
reduction of, B1: 110

Efficient
& nature of "good" and "evil", B1: 74

Effort
grossest level of existence, C2: 44

Egg
ovum, CA: 29; TC: 6
wisdom, DD: 19

Ego(s)
-anger, C3: 54
-basis, C4: 37
-bound mind, B3: 7
-centred power, P1: 27
-Eye, C3: 89
-in-the-world, C3: 73
-man(men), B3: 59
-pattern, B3: 83
-self, B3: 83-86
& Bad choices, C3: 69

& "devil principle", P2: 30
& outer, C3: 50
& self-defence process, B3: 85
& TIM-ID (Time-Form), C3: 50
exclusivist, B2: 188
finite (intent), C3: 39
heart, C3: 56
isolated and nescient, C3: 76
mistakes, C4: 24
non-ego, C3: 54
our individual, B3: 57
petty, B2: 62, 64
phenomena-complexes, C4: 107-108
pursuit of power, C3: 39
squirm, C3: 69-70

Egotism
& creative spiritual life, B3: 25
& law of action-and-reaction, CA: 79
actual, B3: 63
self-defensiveness, B4: 126
"selfishness", B1: 115

Egotist
& The Jesus prayer, C3: 96
total, B1: 115

Eight
figure of … (8), B1: 42

Elect
& right motive, B4: 63
& phenomena produced by … science,
    B4: 62
& supreme question, B4: 62
ask, P4: 62
avoid being deceived, B4: 57
deceive the, B4: 56
deceive(d) (avoid being / cannot be / not
    possible to be), B4: 56-57, 61
life is simple, B4: 63
oneself, C2: 23-24
say, P4: 62
special test, B4: 56
supreme question, B4: 62
themselves to live a life of sacrifice, CA: 92
those … turn the other cheek, P1:108

Electrical
impulses, B4 76
processes, CA 63
properties, CA 62

Electro-
-chemical … systems, B1: 30
-magnetic systems, B1: 30

Electron
electron-field & haptic experience, C4: 76
Electronic
action, B1: 39
Elements
contradictory, B3: 40
Four, C3: 122; TC: 3
male and female, TC: 1
of the human being, TC: 3
pattern comprehension, C4: 91
Eleusinian
octave, DD: 35
Eleven
to do his will (Jesus), DD: 57
Elixir of Life
& Philosopher's Stone, C4: 38
& Saturn/Mercury/Jupiter, C4: 38
of Life, C4: 38
Else
& God's, C4: 71
WHAT, WHERE, WHEN, WHY, WHO,
    How and If / Else, C2: 89-91; C4: 71
Em(m)anuel
& first ancestor, B2: 62
Divine Origin is, B4: 47
"God with us", B2: 62; B3: 5; P2: 92
God-within-us, B3: 15
innermost centre of our being, B3: 5
Embodied
& "turning the other cheek", B2: 47
created being, B3: 98
force, a force incarnate, P1: 35
life-force, P1: 31
love of God, CA: 95
love-seed, B3: 34
secret of sacrifice, CA: 92
"the Word made Flesh", B1: 102
truth(s), B3: 112; B4: 72
worthiness, B3: 112
Embodiment
& anxiety, CA: 17
& body, CA: 17
& incarnation, B3: 109; P1: 34
& instinct, C1: 15
& Jesus, P1: 74
& dialectical significance, B3: 109
& Messiah, B3: 109
& rejected stone, B3: 109
& soul, CA: 17
& spirit, B2: 169; B3: 109; B4: 112

material … veiling process, TC: 39
of an experience, C1: 15
of God, B2: 169; B4: 112
of … spiritual powers, B3: 109
of the principle of Truth, P1: 35

Embody
God, B2: 189, B3: 52
Man, B3: 52
Souls, B3: 128
Truth, B4: 74

Emergents
intelligent evolutionary, C4: 70

Emerson
"Every man is God playing the fool",
    C1: 105

Emotion(s)
& Feeling, C4: 76
& our complex organism, B4: 6
feeling mobilised, C1: 37, 39

Emotional
charge, C1: 39
conditions, P2: 60
potentials, B2: 10
responses, P2: 63
starvation, B2: 10

Emotive
charges, C4: 5
states, C3: 78

Empedocles
(Will as Magia), C4: 31

Empirical
ego, C2: 35, 87, 88, 102, 114; C3: 54
science, C2: 37; EG: 20
scientist, B3: 76

Encapsulation
& absolute infinite sentient power, C2: 60
& identification, C2: 148
& parontic field, C2: 61
beginning of a world, C4: 96
creation, C4: 89
monism, C2: 101
zones, C4: 107

Enclosure
megalo-cosmic primary condensation,
    C4: 37

End(s)
& the Beginning, B4: 102
& MEANS, C4: 85
no loose, C4: 14, 33
of time, DD: 59

Enemies
of freedom, CA: 7
Our greatest, B3: 172

Enemy
inertia, B4: 193
Last, C4: 18
Self-imagery, B4: 194

Energism
& materialism, B3: 36

Energy(ies)
-behaviour system, B4: 89
-field, C3: 55
-form(s), C2: 62
-mass C1: 19
-patterns, B1: 104
-system, C3: 27
-units, B1: 134
& *all* phenomena, C3: 61
& anxiety states, CA: 75
& bodies, B3: 43
& body movements, P2: 2
& design, B3: 43
& form, B2: 110
& God, P1: 125
& Greeks, B4: 162
& idea, C2: 123
& ideas, P2: 59
& intelligence, B2: 86
& interplanetary space, B2: 131
& Man, C4: 92
& matter, B1: 72; B2: 104; B3: 17; B4: 139;
    C3: 10; C4: 17; P1: 84, 122
& memory, B4: 105
& private thinker, C4: 67
& rational mind, C3: 27
& reality, B4: 72
& Space, EG: 43
& thinking, B3: 168
& unfulfilled purposes, CA: 76
& Universe, B2: 85, 130
ability to do work, B4: 105-106
can feel, B4: 88
constitutes all things, B3: 58
continuum, C4: 112, 116
creation, CA: 25
eternal, B3: 58
FIELD MOTION, C3: 97
God … supreme concentrator of, B2: 108
God's first act, CA: 21
impersonal, B1: 7, 11

levels, B1: 63
life, C4: 15
limited amounts of, B1: 56
nervous, B4: 116
non-reason, C2: 87
nowhere where ... is not, B2: 131
One Universal, B4: 80
ordered, B3: 169
original raw, B2: 149
originating, P1: 123
PAIN EXPERIENCED BY GOD, C3: 89
Ram, B2: 149-150
rationalising, C4: 92
"Reason-Word", B3: 54
Satanic, B1: 25
self-devouring, C2: 147
source-energy, CA: 23
spherically rotating, B1: 46
spinning, EG: 33
Spiritual world's, B2: 133
Spiritual, C3: 28
Supreme Source, B2: 58
Sushumna, C4: 74
types, B4: 87
universal requirement, C4: 105
vibrant B4: 179
wastage, B2: 107
wave-forms, B4: 88
working force or power, B3: 58
zone, C4: 65

Enerhy
causation motion, C3: 97

Enlightenment(s)
& The Bible, B1: 22
awareness of Eternity, B1: 16
(consummation of days, or enlightenments),
    EG: 17
final freedom, B3: 77

Enmity
act of, C2: 49

Enoch
= field intelligence, C4: 4
(Cain) built a city ... and called it after his
    son, Enoch, B1: 91

Enos Son of Seth
ancestor of Jesus Christ, B1: 92
"Man in his frailty", B1: 92

Enslavement
Ingrained habits, B4: 75

Entity
modality of the ASP, C2: 52

Entropy
& "ectropy", B1: 134; C2: 47, 77
pralaya, C2: 47, 77; C3: 64; C4: 100
two tendencies, B1: 134

Environments
two, P2: 44

Envy
giant, DD: 29

Epiphenomenon
Materialistic science, C4: 48

Epoché
& Skepticism, C3: 36-37
Sushumna, C4: 74

Equilibrium
& *conscious self-opposition*, C2: 80
& organism's total energy-system, C3: 27
Perfect, C2: 80

Eros
-love, B1: 138-139
& Plato, B1: 136
Greek God of love, B1: 136
realm of human desires, B1: 137

Error(s)
& extroversion of consciousness, B1: 30
& human race, CA: 21
& lustration of, C4: 80
& mankind, P2: 11
& self-pity, B3: 98
& Time Process, TC: 18
Adam's and Eve's EG: 58
ancestors, B2: 78
consequences of, B3: 92
"Law of Persistence of Error", C4: 69
our own, B2: 78
possibility of, CA: 86
unavoidability of, B3: 96

Espionage
among very small groups, B3: 153
international, B3: 153

Essence(s)
Conceptual, C3: 56; C4: 31
Divine Spirit, P1: 11-12
of darkness, C3: 55

Essentiality
of human life, CA: 88

Eternal
-looking, B2: 121

-Way, B2: 121-123
& Eternity-aware man, B2: 19
& work, B4: 107
Anaxagoras, C4: 31
City, C2: 33
Context, B4: 13
energy-play, B4: 108
Feminine, C3: 26
Forms, B2: 18
"Here", CA: 47
immediacy, C4: 92
is spirit ... intelligent power, B3: 2
Jesus saw Himself as, B4: 68
"Life-Three-fold", B4: 68
mind, C2: 76
"Narrow Way that leads to Eternal Life",
    B4: 133
noumena / noumenal, EG: 11-12
Now, B2: 192; CA: 47
Now-Being, B2: 193
Pattern, C2: 33
principles or concepts, B3: 78
Reality, B2: 193; CA: 36, 44
Recurrence, C2: 128; C3: 114; C4: 78
Soul of the Universe (Jesus), B4: 15
Spirit, B2: 192; C4: 16
Time-moments, C2: 74
Triangle, C3: 30
work, B4: 107
World, B2: 18

Eternality
Anaxagoras, C4: 31

Eternity
-aware man, B2: 19
& Creation, B1: 23
& "Enlightenment", B1: 16
& fall of Lucifer, B1: 20
& first birth, C4: 108
& God, B2: 191
& harmony, B4: 103
& Life-Trinity, B4: 133
& music, B4: 107-108
& The Will, C4: 87
& Time-events, B4: 96
& Time-moments, B4: 13
& Time, B1: 14; B2: 16; B3: 1; B4: 96, 107
= He-Trinity, C3: 50
believer's entry into, C4: 91
DIALECTIC OF, C3: 69
dweller in, CA: 4

great Now, B1: 125
infinite concrete whole, (purna), C2: 75
infinite Power of God, B1: 3
is changeless, B3: 1
is not ... unending time, B2: 191
is spiritual ... power, B2: 191
"mind of ...", CA: 51
perfect map, B4: 96
"Time is the moving image of Eternity"
    (Plato), B2: 18; B3: 2

Ethics
& focussed consciousness, P2: 71
& Man, C4: 93
Ethics of the Continuum, C4: 75

Euclidean
point, C2: 142

Evaluation
& centred consciousness, C2: 138
& consciousness, C1: 24
of experience, centred consciousness,
    C2: 138

Eve
& Adam, B1: 23, 52-55, 69, 79-81, 130;
    B2: 15; C4: 96; EG: 55-60
& bi-polar, C4: 96
& serpent, EG: 55-56
basis of developmental possibility,
    C3: 12
embodied (desire to know), B1: 130
furious, C3: 70
help-meet, TC: 41
image of God, C4: 96
means "to develop life's potential", TC: 41
original mother, P2: 11
Prime Matter, TC: 32
her son Cain, B1: 130
state of innocence, B1: 79
voice of, B1: 56

Events
generation of *Time*, B1: 13

Evidence
& Jesus, P2: 122
external sign, P2: 119

Evil(s)
& Adam and Eve, B1: 81
& choice, C3: 69
& death, DD: 11
& good natured people, P1: 55
& Good, B2: 32, 36, 174
& *good* fight, B2: 174

& living beings, B2: 34
& Love, C2: 131
& tree of knowledge, B1: 48;B3: 69; B4: 14;
    C2: 66; CA: 19; DD: 42
Adam's sin, B1: 24
"against life", B1: 82
anti-life forces, P1: 42
bittyness, B4: 14
Cain did, B1: 82
deed, B1: 82
definition ... of, B1: 82
deliberate, CA: 58
disintegration ... death, B4: 14
experience, B2: 37
fall of Lucifer, B1: 26
inefficient, B1: 74
is a force acting against life, B2: 32
man, P1: 54
meaning of, B2: 34
men, C4: 1
origin of, P1: 28
our body, P1: 38
painful, DD: 47
path of knowledge of good and, B4: 195
problems of, C2: 101
"Resist not evil", C2: 135
source, B4: 82
"Sufficient unto the day is the evil thereof",
    CA: 37
will, B1: 83

Evolution
accelerate, TC: 22
Creative, B3: 14
man's, TC: 41
of Awareness, C4: 12
painful situations, C2: 112
spiritual, B3: 4
towards the goal, B3: 8
universal, B1: 122

Evolutionary
intelligent ... emergents, C4: 70
movement of the universe, B1: 16
plan, B3: 4
process, B3: 5, 17

Evolutionists
materialist, B1: 13

Excess
& diseases, C4: 77
Lucifer, B4: 27
William Blake, B4: 27

Exchange
-process, B2: 117
Excitement
sperm's, TC: 5
Exclusive
way, B2: 178
Exclusivist
egos, B2: 188
Execution
self-, C2: 11
Executioner
God ... He is His own, C4: 85
Exhortation
"Two thousand years of Christian
    exhortation has produced little
    result", B3: 40
Ex-ile
see diagram, C3: 50
Existence
& non-existence of a personal God, C4: 115
& Saturn-moments, C4: 68
awareness of our, B2: 117
creation of zone of rotation, TC: 29
human & centred consciousness, C2: 138
individual (sense of), C4: 101
Existentialist(s)
& Truth, C4: 101
philosophy, P1: 5
Expectancy
& disease, C4: 79
negative ... or positive, C4: 79
see C4: 78-79
state of sentient power, C4: 78
Experience(s)
& protoplasm, CA: 85
& Psychic Release, C4: 46
& spermiforms, C4: 82
Conscience, B1: 90
emotional, EG: 85
evaluation of & centred consciousness,
    C2: 138
haptic, C4: 76
painful, B4: 121
path of, B1: 85
record(s), B4: 114, 116
repeated, B1: 7
vehicle of, C1: 5
Explorers
& sacrifice & training, CA: 92

External
(collision) stimuli, C4: 13
material things, B1: 55
modes of consciousness, C4: 86
response-abilities, C4: 25
response-abilities (*cf.* outer responsibilities),
    C4: 25
sources, C4: 13
subjection, B4: 92
work, B4: 106
world, B1: 57, 64
Externalised
conscious mind, B1: 58
materialism, B1: 64
Externality
MAN ... is captured into, C4: 86
Extrojection
& introjection, C3: 83
Extroversion
& Adam, B1: 64
& introversion, B1: 42
of consciousness (Materialism), B1: 30
Eye(s)
-blink, B2: 120
& Art, C4: 80
& brother Lucifer, DD: 12
& certainty in Sufism, C2: 103
& focus for consciousness, C3: 29
& fringes ... attract, B2: 168
& problem of life, B2: 168
& serial consciousness, C1: 72
& sharp definitions, P2: 69
All-seeing, B3: 136
and ears for God, B3: 176
deception, C1: 109
directional organ, C1: 36
Eye-ness (I -ness), C3: 43
forms or shapes, C1: 26
"God shall wipe away all tears from their
    eye", B4: 118
"If thine eye be single, thy whole body is full of
    light" (Jesus), B3: 44, 50, 60
Light & Reft, C3: 107
observing Ego-, C3: 89
observing I, C3: 105
of God, EG: 17
of Horus, EG: 19
of pure consciousness, B4: 175
organ of superficiality, P1: 144
single ... "full of light" (Jesus), B3: 60

sub-entities, C1: 92

F

F
see English gematria, C3: 19-20, 84-88
Fabricator
Master, C2: 46-47
Fact
physical, C2: 68
spiritual, C2: 68
Failure
& anxiety, CA: 75
Faith
& Abraham, B2: 104; P2: 117
& God-believers, B4: 86
& guiding power, B2: 129
& science (HOW TO RELATE), C4: 56
& the Cain-man, B4: 174
& True Reason, C2: 114
& Will, B2: 106
an act of Will, C2: 3, 113; P2: 95, 126
an attitude, P2: 131
and good works, P2: 127
beneficial, B2: 85
Eye of Faith, P2: 125
"faith may move mountains", B3: 143
gives us our greatest positivity, B3: 144
in our ability to survive, B3: 144
in our free will, B3: 80
in our own freedom, B3: 80
is power, B3: 143
is the power, B4: 7
is present when, C2: 40
lack of, B2: 132
lost, CA: 22
makes the leap, P2: 95
man of faith-in-spirit, B2: 84
of Jesus Christ, P2: 130
prayer at work, B3: 143
substance of things hoped for, B2: 104, 106;
    B3: 143; B4: 6
that God has a purpose, CA: 20
that power in us ..., B2: 81
true, P2: 134
"Without faith it is impossible to please God",
    B2: 81
work of God, P2: 130

Falcon
   & resec priest-kings, RS: 37
Fall
   & alienation from God, B3: 62
   & condition of forgetfulness, B4: 23-24
   & CURE & reversal, C2: 117
   & excessive interest in *parts*, B3: 60
   & "Golden Age", B3: 12
   & great religions and philosophies, B3: 68
   & Luciferan, Pride, B4: 26
   & our troubles, B3: 69
   & reversal of the, C2: 117
   & separativity, B3: 61; B4: 83
   & story of Lucifer, B4: 184
   & subjection, C4: 108
   act of God, B3: 15
   Before the, B3: 12-14
   CURE OF THE RESULTS of, C2: 117
   dissociation of the inner and outer being,
      C4: 13
   doctrine, B3: 75
   enslaved to outer stimuli, B4: 93
   external subjection, B4: 92
   "Fall from Grace", B4: 91, 161
   from the eternal. C2: 14
   into *identification*, CA: 32
   into sin, C2: 15; CA: 67
   into the temporal, C2: 14
   is reversible, C4: 12
   loss of inner centrality of the free will,
      B4: 161
   loss of internal awareness, B4: 90
   mystery of, B2: 35
   of Adam, B4: 165; TC: 22
   of Lucifer, B1: 17; TC: 22
   of Man, B2: 164
   of Satan and Mankind, B2: 22
   separation from the Source (the
      Continuum), C4: 107
   state of religious systems, C4: 90
Fallen
   ego-self, B3: 86
   man, B2: 32
   men (reclamation of), B3: 33
False
   ego, B3: 86
   relationships, B3: 165
Falseness
   in our self-image, B4: 127

Falsity
   statements … check them for truth or,
      B4: 193
   Truth & war / battle against, B3: 165;
      P1: 40
Fame
   is the spur, B2: 56
   mere opinion, B2:82
Fantastic
   behaviour (of M2), TC: 45-46
Farthing
   "paid the uttermost farthing", P2: 51
Fate
   & Destiny, C2: 127
Father(s)
   & Absolute, TC: 32
   & Christ, P1: 15
   & fructifying power, TC: 35
   & haemophilia, C4: 6
   & Mother, TC: 35-36
   & polarity, TC: 3
   & Prince of Lies, P1: 32
   & Prodigal, C4: 90, 103
   & The Logos, C2: 27
   "Abba", B4: 47
   All-Father, B3: 141
   and the Son, C4: 109
   Da and Ma, C4: 96
   divine, B1: 148
   earthly, B1: 148
   Eternal, C3: 70; C4: 35
   Generative Power, B3: 41; C4: 67;
      CA: 13-14, 23-24
   God as the, B2: 157
   God the, C4: 34: CA: 48; P1: 18
   Heavenly, C3: 58; C4: 35, 103; CA: 23;
      TC: 35
   Holy Trinity, C4: 108
   human, B1: 148
   "I and my Father are One" *(Jesus)*, C4: 86;
      P1: 15
   Infinite Eternal Initiative, TC: 36
   intellect, C3: 5
   "Jupiter" means, CA: 48
   of All, C3: 47
   of Gautama Buddha, B4: 15
   One Supreme Source, B4: 111
   "Our Father", B3: 41, 140
   Power, B3: 113
   Principle, TC: 36

"The Son can do nothing of Himself but what He seeth the Father do; ...", P1: 17

"the sins of the fathers have their effects in the children", B1: 91

"The sins of the fathers are upon the children", B2: 77

Undying, C2: 132

"What the Father does in secret, that I do openly" (Jesus), B4: 111

"Who seen me has seen the Father", (Jesus), B4: 111; EG: 18

(WILL) POSITS the Son, C3: 111

Fatherhood
of God, B1: 142

Fathomless
meer, DD: 16

Fear(s)
& anxiety, CA: 97
& discontinuity, C2: 145
& *freedom*, CA: 58
& life energies, P2: 1
& monsters, CA: 8
& Prejudice, B3: 171
& unpleasant ideas, P1: 66
A MAN who reads only one book, C4: 70
ancestral, B3: 172
anticipates possible destruction,   P2: 6
anticipation of damage, B3: 171
basis of, P2: 9
carries our mind away, P2: 7
closes the mind, B3: 171
conflict of inhibiting forces, RS: 55
cure, B2: 189
deep, B4: 34
disintegrates ... unity, P2: 7
excessive vibration, P2: 7
"Fear of the Lord is the beginning of wisdom", C2: 145
FR is PR. Fear is Reason, C2: 133
free from, B4: 143
GENERATES CLARITY, C3: 72
love triumphed over, CA: 95
objective, CA: 2
OF ALONENESS, C3: 76
of nothingness, B4: 69
of nuclear war, B2: 34; B3: 144
of physical pain, B2: 71
of ... reprisal(s), B3: 152; C4: 64
origin, P1: 97
"Perfect Love casts out fear", B4: 117, 143;

C2: 35; C4: 7; CA: 58, 84, 86; P1: 97
physical, B2: 71
problem, of CA: 1
real danger situations, C2: 136
root of, B2: 70
two kinds of, B2: 70
zone, P2: 8

Feel
field-state, RS: ii
"sentire", B4: 178; B2: 117

Feeling
-awareness, B2: 119
-emotion(s), B3: 78; C4: 74
-intensity, B2: 118
-sensitivity, B2: 12-13; B4: 180
& consciousness, C1: 55
& "indifference", B4: 88
& intellect, C4: 74
& Materialism, B1: 30
& Quality, C2: 55
& separate functions of the human soul, B2: 8
& special zones in the brain, B1: 97
& thinking, B4: 77, 192; C4: 77; P2: 60
and Fielding, C1: 35
assessing condition, P2: 63
assessment, P2: 64
assuages, C4: 76
basic, RS: ii
belongs to love, C4: 77
contradiction or opposition, C4: 110
degrees of, B4: 180
experience, B4: 89
fine, P1: 148-149
general, RS: ii
love, C4: 77
may be vague or well defined, B2: 117
one of the factors in a human situation, B2: 165
Rejected, C4: 77
self-feeling, B4: 89
soul is ... being, CA: 54
splitting of our feeling, action and thinking, B3: 69
state, a sentient condition, B4: 154

Feign
"Triple-F' response, B3: 29

Fellowship
& idea of human community, P1: 114

Female(s)
  & EQUALITY, C3: 17
  & Hysteria, TC: 13
  & oviforms, C4: 82
  & Qabilistic, Tree of Life, C3: 30
  and male, C4: 100
  differences between male and, B2: 9
  elements, TC: 3
  inertia, C3: 33
  Intolerance … mark of the female female,
    C4: 72
  mascprot semi-females, C3: 18
  Merriment, C2: 108
  non-rational, C4: 92-93
  principle MO, C4: 99
  sentience, C3: 128
  sentience and substantiality, TC: 3
  sun, C3: 110
  symbolism of male and, C4: 96-97
  The Severity Pillar of the Tree of Life,
    C4: 71
  vulnerability, C4: 5
Feminist
  movement, C4: 100
Fence
  -sitters, P1: 15
Few
  "Many are called, but few are chosen",
    P1: 7
Fiat!
  Creative, C2: 17
  Fiat Lux, C3: 56
  FOHAT! Let there be, C3: 3
  God says, C2: 17
  mountain-moving, C2: 9
Fibonacci
  APPLICATION of the widdershins cycle,
    C3: 112
Fiction
  "The world is fiction made up of
    contradictions" (Blake), C4: 111
Field
  -state, RS: ii
  & ENERGY, C3: 97
  electron-, C4: 76
  electron-field, C4: 76
  'field-forces" & "resistance", C4: 76
  FILED, C3: 97
  hexonic, C3: 97
  in electronic theory, RS: ii

  of Absolute Sentient Power (A.S.P.), C3: 97
  of activity, C1: 41
  of awareness, C4: 9
  of sentience, RS: iii
  of sentient power, C4: 27, 44-45
  OF THE LIVING ORGANISM, C3: 41
  sentient, C3: 28
  visual, C1: 36
  volitional, C3: 45
  zone of feeling, RS: ii
Fiery
  "fiery sword", EG: 58; TC: 37
Fight(s)
  Bad, B1: 34
  Good, B1: 34; B2: 174, 176;
    B3: 153, 157, 160, 174
  "Triple-F" response, B3: 29
  "Two fight three, and three fight two in one
    house" (Jesus), B3: 78
Figure
  of eight (8), B1: 42
Fikr
  and zikr, C2: 8
  (meditation), C2: 8
Finger
  of God, B4: 176
Finite(s)
  & Continuum, C4: 78
  & Infinity, C1: 77
  are but concepts, C4: 9
  being, B1: 130
  beings, C4: 56
  creatures, C1: 14
  "eye", C1: 72
  individual, C1: 76
  knowledge, B1: 131
  negation of the, C1: 95
  not-, C1: 31
  SPIRIT, C1: 101
  subject, C1: 73-74
  zone of sentient power, C4: 46
Fire
  & first men, C2: 135
  & Four Elements, C3: 122
  fire-body, CA: 29-30
  Fire-Fighting Rules, C4: 71
  "fires of life", CA: 28
  Heracleitus, EG: 77
  representative of Spirit, EG: 77
  symbol is … (Christ), CA: 28

symbol of spiritual life, CA: 28
symbol of Truth, C2: 104
Firmament
binding circle of our skin, B1: 45
Genesis, B1: 39
Heaven (Balance of Power), C4: 75
First
birth, C4: 108; EG: 77
Cause, C4: 85; EG: 79
"first death", CA: 26
immediacy, C2: 58
Inclination, C4: 41
Fish
Jesus Christ is a, CA: 34
NOW as N - VVV, C4: 16
"Reality is an ocean full of fish; if there were
    no shark there would no fast swimmers",
    C4: 120
sign of a, B4: 81
symbol of Jesus Christ, CA: 34-35
"to swim one must be a fish", B4: 83
Five
days, C3: 80
modalities, B3: 78
sense organs. RS: vii
Flaming
sword, DD: 66
Flesh
Old Adam, P2: 107-108
pain, B4: 78
protoplasm, P2: 110
"sins of the flesh", B4: 74
"the flesh lusts against the spirit, and the
    spirit lusts against the flesh", P2: 98
"the law in the flesh", P2: 111
Fleshly
body, CA: 30
life, CA: 30
Flight
"Triple-F" response, B3: 29
Flood
& Ark of Noah, B1: 97
psychological meaning, B2: 46
Flooding
submergence … emotion, B2: 45
Flower
"flower in the crannied wall", EG: 17
Flux
Anaximander, Heraclitus, Parmeniges,
    C4: 31

dream, C4: 83
Focus
attention, B1: 55; B2: 120; B4: 83
focus-enslaved mind, B4: 84
forgetting, C2: 74
of consciousness, C2: 75
FOHAT!
Let there be, C3: 3
Followers
& forerunners, DD: 24
Folly
birth of wisdom, DD: 19
Food
-TUBE, C3: 77
& body, C4: 61
& energy system, C4: 61
Food-Tract, C2: 57
"I have food you know not of", (Christ),
    C4: 105
materials (Gross), C4: 64
solar energy, P2: 52
substantial appetite, C4: 63
without salt, EG: 61
Fool(s)
& Goose, B2: 79
"Fool for Christ's sake", B2: 79, 80, 83
laughter of, B2: 138
Force(s)
& field, C1: 41
& matter, B3: 76
alien, C2: 3
continuous causal field, EG: 32
interfunction of, CA: 78
motions of the absolute sentient power,
    C1: 8
of Chaos, B3: 118
of good, B1: 26
of Order, B3: 118
opposing, B1: 12
ordering, EG: 25
patterned play of, B2: 156
Satanic, B1: 33
Forgetfulness
condition of, B4: 23-24
Forgetting
& "Time consciousness," CA: 46
absolute & relative, C2: 74-75
letting focus lapse, C2: 74-75
of our real properties, B4: 52

Forgive
  and *remember*, B3: 97
  erase, B3: 91
  "Father forgive them, for they l know not
    what they do", CA: 95
  forgive others' trespasses, B4: 27
Forgiveness
  & evil actions of others, B4: 27
  & self-pity, B3: 98
  all in need of, B3: 99
Forked-Tongues
  Ye philosophers, DD: 62
Form(s)
  -discrimination, C3: 36
  -principle (Sound), C3: 51
  & ART, C4: 80-81
  & ASP, C3: 115
  & Astral Light, C3: 39-40
  & colours, C4: 80-81
  & Consciousness, C1: 105
  & Cosmic Mother, C4: 109
  & Divine Order, C2: 98
  & energy, B2: 110; CA: 23
  & function, B1: 49
  & Hermes, C4: 75
  & hexonic field, C3: 97
  & I & P, C4: 98
  & "Identification", C1: 75
  & Identity, C2: 54, 58
  & knowledge, B1: 50
  & MAGICAL PROCEDURE, C3: 126
  & meditation, C2: 62
  & phenomenon, B4: 57
  & point & line & plane, C4: 98
  & principles of Reality, B3: 113
  & re-cognition, C4: 68
  & real God C4: 56
  & Sensuality, C3: 117
  & Sophia, Cosmic Wisdom, C4: 110
  & substance, P1: 132
  & Supreme Spirit, EG: 5
  & Sushumna, C4: 74
  & the artist, C4: 114
  & 3-D tangible, C4: 98
  & TIM-ID (Time-Form), C3: 50
  & Trinity Law, C3: 92
  & Truth, B4: 31; C3: 21; C4: 101
  & Truth, Beauty and Goodness,   P1: 43
  & vision, C2: 53
  activation of SP, C2: 82

  active, B1: 8
  at death we change our, B2: 110
  beginning of all, C4: 98
  behaviour of energy, C4: 65
  "character", C1: 73
  circumscription, C1: 106
  clarity of, B1: 53
  contour, C1: 27
  During our life we change our, B2: 110
  form-differences, B3: 128
  function creates, C4: 65
  "idea", B2: 17
  individual thing, C2: 3
  inertia, C4: 109
  male, C3: 128
  Namarupa (name-form), C2: 43, 53
  origin, C1: 24
  Nama-rupa, C2: 16
  power-form, C4: 75
  rationalised appetite, C4: 65
  Rotation, C3: 75
  sound-phenomenon, C3: 2
  visible, tangible aspect of reality, C2: 16
  visual, C1: 35
  will of the Will, C2: 147
Formal
  clarity, B1: 53
  content, C1: 74-75
  differences, B3: 128
Formation
  creation, C4: 89
Formless
  & void, DD: 8
  "void" (Genesis), B1: 21
Free
  -will, B2; 15; B3: 7
  Absolutely, B3: 98; C1: 107
  act of will, P2: 113
  action, B1: 146
  Adam, P2: 104
  being(s), B2: 160; C2: 25; CA: 67
  Choice, CA: 66, 86; P1: 160; P2: 42, 116
  condition of grace, P2: 99
  decision, CA : 98
  discrimination, B1: 143
  Eternity, C4: 16
  Free-dome, C1: 107
  from all restraints, B3: 98
  human being, P2: 27
  "know the truth and the truth will make you

free", B2: 128

man, B3: 77

our belief that we are, B3: 75

our mind from misinterpretations, B4: 193

real Self, P2: 28

relationship, B1: 115

response, P2: 117

soul, P2: 112

spirit, C4: 10, 112

Total SELF-Determination, DD: 70

will, B1: 5, 123, 146-147; B2: 15; B3: 45,
    76, 79, 80, 105; C2: 44, 134;
    CA: 24, 27, 66, 67; P1: 161;
    P2: 117

Freedom

& balance of forces, P2: 104

& believing C4: 34

& bondage, B3: 7

& *discrimination*, B1: 142

& divine creative act, B1: 6

& free man, B3: 77

& Greek citizens, EG: 69

& *responsibility*, CA: 87

& self-responsibility, B3: 7

& separation CA: 14

& the soul C4: 50

& void, DD: 8

= the condition for new creations, C3: 71

absolute, B3: 7

attaining, C3: 5

belief in, B3: 74

beloved, C3: 123

capacity for choosing *wrong* as well as right,
    B1: 143

conferred upon Man, B1: 142

Do Not Attribute, C4: 4

each creature has *in the presence of other
    creatures*, B1: 6

enemies of, CA: 7

essential spiritual CA: 98; P2: 29

external, P2: 120

gift of CA: 6

gift of God's spirit, P2: 134

Grace, B4: 82; C4: 35; P2: 115

"His worship is perfect freedom",
    C4: 34-35; P2: 117

Human CA: 6

implies self-responsibility, B3: 7, 79

in our innermost soul, P2: 97

innermost, CA: 67

lost, P2: 13, 110, 112

man's greatest gift, CA: 86

of action, P2: 24

of choice, B1: 123; CA: 6, 7, 24

of will, B2: 160

perfect, B3: 75, 99, 101; C4: 34-35; P2: 117

permitted, B4: 25

relative, B3: 75

responsibility, CA: 87

see CA: 86-87

spirit of, P1: 139

Spirit of God … is our, CA: 86

spiritual, CA: 26, 98; P2: 21, 23-24

the essential eternal, P2: 33

total, CA: 20

true centre, CA: 33

Free-willed

act, RS: 26

Freud

& Uncontrolled forces, B2: 46

Friend

Lucifer, DD: 55

Friendship

"Opposition is true friendship" (Blake),
    C4: 120

Frightened

psyche, C4: 46

Frightening

thoughts, B3: 79

Fringes

& curiosity, B2: 168

& problem of life, B2: 168

attract the eye, B2: 168

Fruits

& actions, B3: 7

Frustration

& soul's will, C1: 88

feelings of, CA: 75

Fulfil

aim is to "fulfil all righteousnes"
    (Jesus to John the Baptist), B4: 14

Function(s)

& form, B1: 50; B3: 114

& identity, C2: 58

& intellect, B1: 50

& Mary (Roman Catholic Teaching),
    C2: 85

& origin of sin, C4: 53

& Spiritual ecology, B3: 82

& THE LIVING ORGANISM, C3: 41

& Trinity Law (Form-function-power),
      C3: 92
& Truth, Beauty and Goodness, P1: 43
co-operative, B2: 4
creates form, C4: 65
function-pattern, C4: 53
God the Holy Spirit, B3: 114
inner, C4: 11
interfunction, B2: 7, 74; B4: 12; C2: 78
inter-function, B2: 3, P1: 154, 156; B4: 12
levels of, B2: 7
of energy (matter), P1: 122
of religion, B3: 113
of science, B3: 113
perfect, P1: 43, 134
self-separating, C4: 53
"Shem function", B2: 42
two kinds of, B4: 44; C4: 11
use, P1: 132

Future
cause, C2: 148
present is the cause of the, C2: 148
God *creates* His, B1: 148

G

G
see English gematria, C3: 19-20, 84-88
Gain
& evolutionary advance, B2: 150
Gamma
Darkness, C3: 32, 40
Garden
& God's universe, B1: 87
& Spirit of God, DD: 39
Eden, B1: 23, 47, 68
guarded place, B1: 46
Garment
& concealment, B2: 28, 32
& fringes, B2: 168
& Noah & covering ... nakedness,
      B2: 28, 32
& veil, B2: 28, 32
& waking Self, B1: 68
& will, B4: 9
of absolute power, C1: 50
of cosmic creative form, C2: 100
of pure truth, B4: 10
of wool, B4: 141

of words, B4: 141
outer waking Self as a kind of, B1: 68
seamless ... of Christ, B1: 32; B3: 165;
      B4: 10-12; C2: 15, 41; P2: 4;
      C4: 57; CA: 87
special kind, B4: 9
that we shall wear eternally, B4: 10
well knitted, B4: 140
Gathering
& scattering, B4: 49, 162-163
opposite movement of, B4: 163
Geb
& Goddess Nut, C4: 37
earth God, C4: 37
gematria
English, C3: 19-20, 84-88
Gemini
[Zodiac sign] see C3: 113
endless ratiocination, C3: 113
Generate
we ... *Time,* CA: 46
Generative Power
& cause, B3: 140
"Father", B3: 41; C4: 67; CA: 13-14, 23-24
God, CA: 14, 24, 99
see B3: 41, 140; C4: 67; CA: 14, 23-24, 99
Genes
& inheritance, C4: 23-24
Genesis
book of, B1: 2, 13, 36, 39, 47, 53; CA: 19
Genius(es)
& source of intelligent power, B3: 42
marks of P1: 113
& protoplasmic evolution, RS: 24
Genuineness
& imaginary society, EG: 90
George
CROSS, C3: 84
Gethsemane
& Jesus, P1: 36: P2: 130
personal, B4: 117
Giant
envy, DD: 29
Gift
of the divine spirit (Each special talent is a),
      B1: 119
Gimel
Consolidate, C4: 54
Glory
& love, P1: 117

Gnits
out-response of the compacted A.S.P. field, C2: 138

Gnosis
& "Gnits", C2: 138

Goad
& fear, C2: 131

Goal
& evolution, B3: 8
lack a defined, B3: 38
value, C4: 58, 85

Goat(s)
& BEARD … high priest, C4: 72
& sheep, DD: 55
Scapegoat, B1: 78-79, B4: 27
stand alone on their mountains, DD: 55

God('s)
-as-Man, EG: 13
-believers live by faith, B4: 86
-contemplation, C2: 28
-disbelievers, B4: 86
-head, EG: 13
-Man, B2: 160: C1: 34;C2: 128, 140; C3: 31; C4: 94;EG: 13
-worship, B1: 53
& Ace, EG: 50
& God-given power to choose, B2: 88
& Godless, B3: 63
& Abel, B1: 78
& Abraham, B2: 94
& Abram, B2: 90-96, 99
& Ace high (God transcendent), EG: 50
& action-reaction law, B1: 147
& Adam, B1: 63; B2: 37, 74
& Agape-love, B1: 138-140
& Anti-God, C4: 111-112
& Cain, B1: 78, 82; B2: 74
& casket made of white pearls, C2: 100
& Christianity, EG: 8
& Cosmic Plan, P1: 99
& creating for Himself a sacred place, C4: 106
& destiny of all creatures, CA: 24
& DIA-GON-AL = Through GOnaD, C3: 51
& divine will, C2: 148
& Divine Will's creation, P1: 160
& Empirical science, EG: 20
& encapsulation, C4: 89
& Eros, B1: 137-139

& Essential Christianity, C4: 10
& Eternity, B1: 23; C2: 75
& Eternity is an infinite actuality, CA: 46
& Eve, B1: 130
& Eye of Horus, EG: 19
& *form*, C4: 56
& formless, void earth, DD: 8
& free will … gift of, B1: 123
& generation of *light*, B1: 21
& Good, EG: 35
& great plan of Universal evolution, the Alpha idea, B1: 122
& He-Al-TH (Life is God), C2: 56
& His absolute nakedness, C2: 100
& His own image, B2: 62
& His own indestructibility, C1: 9
& His own joy, B1: 147
& His own way of response, B1: 91
& His self-appreciation, EG: 11
& Holy Trinity, B3: 113-114; P2: 82
& human being, CA: 4
& human race, P2: 100
& human soul as co-creator, B4: 156
& human will, C2: 148
& images of, B2: 156
& justification of the works of God, C2: 100
& Kyriosity, EG: 17
& Laodiceans … lukewarm, CA: 54
& Large Self, the Soul given by, B2: 68
& law of Love, P2: 95
& Logos, P2: 46
& Lucifer, B1: 19; DD: 36
& man, B1: 130, 149
& man's Highest Act of Will, C4: 103
& man's motive, C4: 3
& material particles, C1: 70
& Muhammad, C2: 100
& mystics, EG: 8
& Nature, C1: 31
& Nietzsche C2: 128 CA: 10; EG: 62-70, 68, 81, 89
& Non-dualism & Monism, C2: 68
& Only begotten Son, B2: 158; P1: 82
& our own Self, B3: 44
& our physical body, CA: 26
& PAIN, C3: 89
& pantheism, C1: 25; C2: 25
& pantheist, C1: 31
& persona, the "through-sounder", C2: 112
& philosophers of Spirit, B4: 81

& Power, Form and Function (triad),
    B3: 113-114
& prayers said in Jesus Christ's name,
    C4: 34
& Pure intention ... key to right relation
    with God, C4: 61
& purpose for us, CA: 20
& real, true self, C2: 35
& realm of absolutely true love, B1: 114
& salvation, C2: 92
& Science, EG: 20-21
& self-consistency ... ground of Love,
    CA: 56
& self-contradiction, C4: 88
& self-examination, EG: 11
& self-glorification, EG: 11
& Silence, B1: 35
& sin, C2: 7
& Space, EG: 42-43, 49
& specially chosen people, EG: 84
& Spinoza, P1: 136
& spiritual freedom, EG: 94
& soul-capacities, B2: 55
& ST (SELF-CRUCIFIXION), C3: 47
& state of unalloyed bliss, B4: 91
& the devil, B4: 194
& the sceptic, B1: 13
& The soul, B3: 127; C4: 63
& Time, DD: 35
& Truth, DD: 35
& universal energy, P1: 125-126
& void, DD: 8
& Will, P1: 48; P2: 67
& woman, C4: 55, 92
& Word, P2: 46
"a devouring fire", C4: 92
a suitable Mother from Himself, B2: 160
A-theist, C4: 56
Absolute, B2: 47; RS: 25; TC: 42
absolute infinite power,, B1: 2
absolute power ... fundamental to all things,
    B3: 50
Absolute power fundamental to all things,
    B3: 50
Absolute Sentient Power, C2: 7, 28, 46
All-in-all, B2: 15
All-power, EG: 2
All-Power, Supreme Intelligence and
    Infinite Compassion, B3: 51
All-presence, EG: 2

All-seeing, EG: 2
All-Seeing-Eye, B2: 75
Alpha-theos, C4: 56
approach to, B4: 143
Being of, B1: 21
Body, B3: 6; C1: 70; EG: 16-19
can focus ... on any particular thing, CA: 45
cannot cease to be, EG: 1
CIRCLE: KIRK EL, CHURCH OF
    GOD, C3: 32
"common source", DD: 2, 31
consort, C4: 55
conversation which God holds with himself,
    RS: 10
Covenant, B2: 21
creates ... His own self-experience, B1: 146
Creative Intelligence, P1: 159
Creator of human beings, B1: 144
Creator of the Universe, B1: 147
deepest depth of Being, B1: 115
Door of realisation, C2: 100
Door that only God could open, C2: 120
double sacrifice, B2: 159
embodied love of, CA: 95
embody, B2: 169, B2: 189; B3: 52
Emanuel, B4: 47, 175
equals Good, EG: 35
eternal life, B1: 22
Eternal Light of God, CA: 48
eternal motion of God's will, RS: 7
ever-loved presence, B3: 54
"Every man is God playing the fool"
    (Emerson), C1: 105
Father, B2: 157; C2: 28; C3: 6, 47
Fatherhood of, B1: 142
first act of creation, CA: 21
first Being mentioned (in Genesis), B1: 13
First Cause, C4: 85
First Mover, EG: 7
Form is the Logos, the Son of God, C4: 34
Generative Power, CA: 14, 24, 99
Glory of, B3: 147
"God is dead!" (Nietzsche), EG: 68, 81, 89
God Is Not Dead, EG: 62-97
"God is perfect in His unity", P2: 82
"God loves us", P1: 159
"God needs me as much as I need Him",
    EG: 8
"God shall wipe away all tears from their
    eye", B4: 118

God so loved the world, C4: 88

Good of goods, B4: 46

Great Accomplishment of the Beau Geste, C2: 140

great drama (Abraham and Isaac), B2: 161

Great Leveller, P1: 117

had to play Abraham and Isaac and the sacrificed ram, B2: 161

"Hast thou an arm like Mine?" (to Job), B4: 101

hidden mystery, B2: 155

His Eternal immediacy, CA: 47

His Eternal "Presentness", CA: 47

His Man-form, B2: 159

His own … Saviour, C4: 85

His own Executioner, C4: 85

His own Logos-Self, C4: 106

His Reason is the Reason of Love, CA: 86

His self-actualisation, B4: 24

His Son-form, B2: 159

His will-to-Oneness, B2: 108

"I am that is, was and shall be" (Jehovah), B2: 19

immanent, EG: 50

"In the image of God made He them male and female" , C4: 96

incarnation of the Living God, C4: 10

Infinite, B3: 61

Infinite All-in-all, C2: 67

Infinite Eagle, EG: 18

infinite intelligent energy, B2: 86

Infinite intelligent power, B2: 70, 156

infinite Knower, C3: 118

infinite patience, B3: 46

Infinite Sentient Motion (for EH), EG: 8

Infinite Sentient Power, C1: 10;   EG: 13

infinite source-power, B4: 55

Infinity of, C1: 32

IO name of God (read Hebraica), C3: 104

is, C2: 67

is dead (Nietzsche), C2: 128; EG: 62

Is Not Dead (EH), EG: 62-97

is joyful, B1: 146

IS SPIRIT, C3: 58; C4: 35; DD: 66; EG: 37

is spirit, to be worshipped in Spirit and in Truth: B3: 112; C4: 35

Jupiter Deo-Pater, CA: 48

knows everything, CA: 44

life of God and of Man, C2: 57

light-power of, B1: 21

little gods, EG: 34, 36

Living God, C4: 10

local actualisations of God's power, P1: 137

Logos God, EG: 34-36

Love-seed, sown by, B3: 34

Love, B1: 86, 132; B3: 174;C4: 35; CA: 56, 86; P1: 117, 153

love of (embodied), CA: 95

mammon, DD: 65

mind of, P2: 46

Mind of God, B3: 181; B4: 143

"Mind of Christ", B3: 16

modalities of, C3: 75

Most High, B3: 120

motive, P1: 142

"My meat is to do the will of Him who sent me, and to finish His work", C4: 94

mysterious somewhat ("God"), B3: 141

mystery, P1: 125

mystery of mysteries, B3: 54

nature, B2: 156, 169

"Noah was a man who walked with God", B2: 25

Non-dual infinite continuum, C4: 57

not possible for Him to cease to be, B3 : 50

Observers-for-God, B3: 177

of the philosophers, EG: 7

Omega and Telos, C3: 31

omnipotent, omniscient and omnipresent, C2: 101

Omniscience, C2: 73

omniscient, CA: 44

One (thought of in three ways), B3: 114

One True, B4: 18

ORIGINAL CREATOR, C3: 90

OTHERNESS OF THE ABSOLUTE, C3: 67

PaMa God in the Hebrew Tetragrammaton, C4: 95

Perfection, CA: 55

personal, B1: 11; C4: 115

plan, B2: 27; B4: 97

pre-fection is our, *per*-fection, C4: 51

presence of, B1: 1; C3: 70

presenting himself, C2: 111

promise to Abraham's seed, DD: 59

problem of, C4: 96

problem, P1: 160

proper subject for worship, B3: 125

"Pure Act," B4: 24

sacrifice of God Himself, B2: 160

SCRYING BALL of, C3: 24
Self making its contribution (Else), C4: 71
self-activating power, B1: 2
Single One (Kirkegaard), C2: 31
Solid God, EG: 9
some people dislike the little word "God", B2: 70
"Sons of God", B3: 24
speaks to the ..., CA: 54
spirit, B1: 21-22
SPIRITUS, ANIMA, CORPUS, devil, C2: 126
still small voice, B1: 35
stretched Himself on the Cosmic Cross, C4: 119
suitable Mother, B2: 160
Supreme Author, P2: 96
supreme concentrator of energy, B2: 108
Supreme Creator, P1: 76; P2: 96
Supreme Source, B1: 28
Supremely worshippable Being, B3: 48
Temple of the Living God, B4: 145
Tetragrammaton, C4: 95
"the" God and "a" god, EG: 22-27
THEOSIS, C3: 96
(Thinker, thought, object of-thought), EG: 51
This mysterious somewhat, B3: 141
transcendent, EG: 50
Trinity, EG: 51
triplicity of powers, B2: 87
Ultimate Cause, B2: 58
Unity is the essence of His divinity, B4: 160
Unity of God, P1: 4
Universal Being, B3: 126; P1: 12
Universal Creative Intelligence, B4: 98
Universal Supreme Being, B3: 138
unlimited "all-in-oneness", CA: 44
"Vengeance is mine", CA: 43
visible ... & Satan, B4: 18
voice, B1: 56
What is God?, EG: 37-50
Will, B3: 51, 53
Wisdom, B1: 52, 124-125
Word, P1: 10, 68; B3: 53
word (short, convenient), P1: 125
work, C4: 34
worshipped "in Spirit and in Truth", P1: 39
Ye are Gods, DD: 57

God-Man
& Comforter, P2: 92
& Emmanuel, P2: 92
& Malkuth & Melekh-Tau, C3: 31
CONCEPT OF, C4: 94
conscious self-sacrifice, CA: 95
crucify(ied), C3: 31; CA: 95
Divine, B2: 162
Man-God, EG: 13-15
Goethe
& truth, C1: 6
WE SEE ONLY WHAT WE KNOW, C3: 74
Gold
signifies the Will, C4: 90
Golden Age
& Fall, B3: 12; B4: 90
& man, B3: 12
pre-encapsulationary, pre-creational play of the Will, C4: 90
Golgotha
& Jesus, B2: 82; CA: 95
& crucifixion, C3: 33
& His self-sacrifice in (Jesus Christ), CA: 44
"Father forgive them, for they know not what they do", CA: 95
personal, CA: 95
Lucifer prefigures the Golgotha sacrifice, DD: 4
GOnaD
& Naga-Snake, C3: 51
Good
& Adam, B2: 36-37
& conscious mind, B1: 59
& evil, B1: 48, 81; B2: 32, 36-37; B4: 195; C2: 66; C3: 69
& Garden of Eden, B1: 24
& soldier, B1: 77
& Supreme Source, B4: 81
& Tree of Knowledge, B1: 48; B3: 69; CA: 19; DD: 42
& True & Beautiful, C4: 40
definition ... of, B1: 82
efficient, B1: 74-75
equals God, EG: 35
Fight, B1: 34; B2: 174; B3: 157, 160, 174
force of, B1: 26
give pleasure, B1: 59
"God" as the supreme, B4: 46
"Good name ... is the immediate jewel of their souls / the soul" (Shakespeare),

B1: 107, 110; B2: 100
marksmanship, B1: 77
natured people, P1: 54
(see diagram), C4: 40
will, B1: 75

Goodness
& Truth, C3: 23
& Trinity of Truth, Beauty and, P1: 43-44
see C4: 102, P1: 43-44
anti-, P1: 42

Goose
& the Fool, B2: 79
symbolised the intention to share, B2: 79

Gospel
of John, EG: 22, 77

Grace
special act of, B3: 15
"the *grace* of our Lord Jesus Christ", B3: 81
& Spiritual Heart, B4: 82
& body-darkness, C3: 55
Divine, P1: 52
Jesus Christ is full of, P1: 98
Freedom, P2: 115

Gradient
of power in the universe, B1: 32

Grail
Holy, C3: 80

Grand
Architect, C2: 47
Master Tool, C2: 46
Puppeteer, P1: 139

Granular
Time, the product of granular interactions, C2: 82

Great
Leveller, P1: 113
NEGATION, DD: 11, 13
Pi-function of the original circulating force, EG: 26
Rota, DD: 11; EG: 25
Universe, C3: 16
Work (Kosmos), C3: 14

Greater
"Greater works than these shall you do, if you go to my Father", EG: 36

Greek(s)
& Amazons, C4: 100
& Eros, B1: 136
& law of polarisation, TC: 13
of the classical period, B2: 14

philosophers, C4: 31
saw the divine life as emotionless and self-sufficient, EG: 7
saw the world as eternal, EG: 7

Griffon
world of, C4: 17

Grip
& Saviour, P2: 15
& spirit-matter problem, C4: 17
Begriff & Griffon, C4: 17
his own ... upon himself, B3: 86
of Maya, C2: 89
of others, P2: 15
of the devil, B4: 194; C1: 104
saturnine, B3: 86

Ground
of Being, C4: 20

Group
& "Morality", B3: 94

Growth
& material world, C1: 80

Grudge
inner tension state, B3: 97

Guarded
place, an enclosure (Garden of Eden), B1: 47

Guardedness
impedes the free flow of life energy, B2: 9

Guilt
& anxiety, P2: 114
& delayed shock, C4: 81
& guilty people, B2: 39
& reprisals, B3: 152
& self-refutation, C2: 19
collectively guilty (world war), B4: 152
inner, CA: 82

Gynocrats
& andocrats, C4: 99
& mother-god, C4: 99

H

H
& Ace, EG: 50
addition of the "H" in the name "Abram", B2: 94
see English gematria, C3: 19-20, 84-88

H2O
  see C4: 32
HA!
  see DD: 10, 18
Habit(s)
  -patterns, B3: 25; B4: 77
  & inertia of energies, B1: 4
  A well-established, B3: 22
  energy patterns, B3: 21
  fixed routine, B1: 143
  Ingrained, B4: 75
Haemophilia
  & fearful children, C4: 6
Hagar
  & Abram, B2: 93
  & mis-interpretation, B2: 100
  conceived, B2: 99
Hagician
  & basic life-principle, C2: 92
  & women, magicians and hagicians, even of
    nagicians, C2: 92
Halliday
  Edgar, C2: 119
  Margaret, C2: 78
  "Only the Infinite Continuum of Sentient
    Power is" (Yadillah), C4: 120
  Peg, C2: 78
Ham
  & his father's nakedness, B1: 103
  & Noah, B2: 28
  descendants of, B2: 54
  impulsive, B1: 98; B2: 28, 42
Hamlet
  (his) problem, C1: 9
  "to be or not to be", C1: 9 C2: 67
Hand
  MANUAL OF POWER (*diagram*), C3: 123
  left & right, C3: 9
  Hierarchical Query (*diagram*), C3: 49
[Hand symbols]
  [*interpretations*], *see diagrams*, C3: 49, 123
Handmaid
  see DD: 22
Happiness
  precondition of true, B1: 83
Haptic
  & electron-field resisting, C4: 76
  experience, C4:76
Hara
  centre, C2: 110

Hardware
  outer world of, B2: 109
Harm
  & bad motive, B1: 112
  anticipation of, CA: 2
  desire to, P1: 65
  different kinds of, CA: 97
  see B1: 112-113
Harmless
  "Be ye therefore as wise as serpents and as
    harmless as doves" (Jesus), B3: 134
  harmless ... as a dove, yet ... wily as
    serpents, DD: 56
Harmonious
  Interaction, P1: 156
Harmony
  & Golden Age, B3: 70
  & human community, CA: 82
  & intercommunication, B3: 43
  & the soul, B4:64
  perfect, B4: 64, 103
H.A.R.P.S.
  *Hermeneutics, Art, Religion, Philosophy and
    Science*, C2: 120
Harpocrates
  thumb-sucking gesture, C3: 95
Hate
  arises, B1: 113
  destroy, CA: 25
  love, B2: 115; C2: 131; CA: 38
Hate-seed
  sown, B3: 34
Hating
  Heart, CA: 37
Hatred
  Effect, B4: 28
Haves
  "Have-nots", P1: 44
Hawk
  & falcon & eagle, RS: 37
He
  He-Trinity, C3: 50
  Live in accord with ..., C4: 54
  (see diagram), C3: 51
Healing
  disbelief, EG: 14
Health
  & act of reflexion, RS: 41
  & mental disorders RS: 41
  breakdown of, B2: 8

return of, RS: 41

triple self-crucifixion, C2: 56

wholeness, B2: 8; B3: 38

Hearing

& subtle body, C4: 24

sense, P2: 69

sight, hearing, taste, smell and touch, C1: 26

Heart

hating, CA: 37

innermost, CA: 37

loving, CA: 37

purity, B1: 137; C4: 14, 33, 45

secret, CA: 38

Spiritual, B4: 82

Heaven

& motion-complexes, RS: 55

& power, DD: 64, 67; RS: 21; TC: 50

always *Now*, C4; 103

balance of power, B3: 179; B4: 183; C4: 75

continuity (Tibetan Lha) *(see diagram)*, C4: 95

equilibration of power, TC: 50

harmonious interplay, B2: 36

is *within*, B2: 103

kingdom of, B1: 3, 40; B2: 103; C3: 58; C4: 108; P1: 110

new, B2: 148

Quick Way, C4: 103

see B2: 36, 103

Heavenly

Father, CA: 23; TC: 35

Hedonistic

view of the universe, RS: 16

Hell

& Jesus, B2: 175; B3: 21; B4: 65; DD: 60

"collective unconscious mind", B2: 175

encapsulated fears, B4: 119

greatest frustration, B4: 183

individual, RS: 57

Lake of Fire, C3: 39

personal, B4: 120

self-contradiction, B4: 65

total identification, RS: 40

Help

-mate (Eve), B1 54

-meet, TC: 41

& ONE'S DUTY, C3: 130

Heraclitus

A law governs the flux ... of things, C4: 31

"No man bathes twice in the same river"

(Heracleitus), EG: 77

philosopher of "fire", EG: 77

Herd

mob mentality, EG: 72

Here

Eternal Presence of God to Himself, CA: 47

spatial distribution, C4: 16

Heredity

laws of, B1: 23

Here-Now

Eternity is an infinite, CA: 44

INFINITE Sphere of Being, C3: 133

only time of action, C3: 52

Time-moments, C2: 74

HERM (HRM)

Hierarchy, Rulership and Anti-Hierarchy, C2: 126

Magazine, C2: 126

Hermaphrodite

& Perfect love, C4: 7

bi-polar name, C4: 95

Divine, C4: 74-75

Hermeneut

true interpreter, B4: 192

Hermeneutic(s)

& centred consciousness, C2: 138

action, C2: 138

interpretation of temporal things, C2: 2

of Eternity; of Time, C2: 2

Hermeneutic action

& centred consciousness, C2: 138

Hermes

& double nature (female ... male), B2: 14

& Messiah: Mercury ... Tehuti, C4: 39

messenger of the gods, B2: 14

"Waters below", C4: 75

Hermetic

axiom, C3: 75

Hero

& myth, C3: 94

Heroic

acts, EG: 87

He-She

& Hermaphrodite, C4: 75

& Tetragrammaton, C4: 95-96

hermaphroditic or bi-polar name, 95-96

He-Trinity

Eternity =, C3: 50

Hexagram

I Ching (*diagram*), C3: 101

Hexon
Law, C3: 101
Hexonic consciousness
body (energy-mass), C3: 25-26
Hexonic field
& archetypal forms, C2: 20
Filed Field, C3: 97
pattern, C3: 10
six-petalled flower, C3: 101
Hexonic level
& sense of effort, C2: 44
Hidden
divinity, B4: 128
Hiding process
"unconscious mind", B4: 116
Hierarchical(ly)
& Aphrodite, C4: 75
& Hermes, C4: 75
& non-, C475
H.Q. = Hierarchical Query: the law of
polarisation, C3: 49
religion, C4: 87
systems, C4: 75
"Waters above", C4 75
"Waters below", C4 75
Hierarchy
differences of power, B4: 159
of Being, C3: 4
of powers expressed in space (*see diagram*),
C4: 16
see HERM, C2: 126
sphere is the self-precipitated, C2: 70
High
& low, C1: 112
frequency radio waves, B2: 133
vibratory energies of the Spiritual world,
B2: 133
HIHU
Infinite Intelligent Power, C2: 115
Hillel
& Jesus, C3: 93
Hinder-mate
& Adam, B1: 54-55
Hinduism
& Absolute Sentient Power, C2: 102
declares the truth "Tat tvam asi", "Aham
Brahman", C2: 102
identity of the creature with the creator ...,
C2: 102
non-temporal world of spirit, C2: 37

Hiranyagarbha
Egg of Time, C4: 38
History
& Abram's descendants, B2: 91
& *conflict*, B2: 178
God who acts in, B1: 11
Hoi polloi
& state control, C3: 49
Holiness
whole-ness, B3: 82
Holy
& three-foldness, B4: 69
Ghost, B3: 88; C2: 18; C3: 111; EG: 49
Sin against the Holy Ghost, C2: 18
Spirit, B2: 184; B4: 111; C2: 85; C4:
108-109
Trinity, B2: 185; B3: 113; C4: 108-109
Whole Threefold Being, B2: 185
Homily
& allegory, B3: 135
Homoeopathy
& conceptual essences, C2: 121
Homoeopathic remedies
& conceptual essence, C3: 57
"potentised" materials, C4: 77
Honour
& Bluebeard, C2: 67
"Honour and shame are the same"
(Lao-Tse), B2: 82
is initiative, C4: 7
is male, C4: 7
Hook
situations, CA: 9
Hope
& Pandora's box, C2: 16
Horizontal
& GEORGE CROSS, C3: 84
Hot
& hot, CA: 54
& lukewarm & indifferent, CA: 54
How
WHAT, WHERE, WHEN, WHY, WHO,
How and If / Else, C2: 89-91; C4: 71
HRM
significance of, C2: 126
Hubris
& the Jewish people, EG: 84
Human(s)
& animals, B2: 7
& centred consciousness, C2: 138

& communication, CA: 88
& freedom, B3: 74; CA: 6
& humility, B3: 130
& power, B2: 147
& Self-determination, B2: 62
behaviour, CA: 2
being ... double nature ... male and female,
     B2: 14
capacities, B2: 11, 14
community, CA: 82
consciousness, P1: 147
counts, C3: 83
creativity, B4: 152
dignity, CA: 37
Divine, B2: 170
evolution, EG: 67
existence, C2: 138
fully developed ... being, B2: 14
higher form of life, B2: 146
intellect, EG: 12
life (essentiality of), CA: 88
middle position on ... ladder of life, B4: 39
race, B4: 51; CA: 19; P1: 115
responsibilty, CA: 6, 87
self, C4: 43
society, C3: 65
soul, B3: 121; B4: 50; CA: 19, 87
specially designed capsules, C2: 72
truly, B2: 165-168
work, C4: 84

Human Being(s)
& *a priori* thinking, C3: 64
& belief in freedom, B3: 74
& humility, B3: 130
& Jesus, B4: 19
& King of Kings, P1: 83
& matter, B3: 76
& purpose beyond, B2: 7
& responsibility, B4: 153
& self-knowledge, CA: 21
& technical know-how, B4: 153
& total self-contradiction, C4: 88
& two Trinities, P1: 43
& world-court of all humanity, B4: 153
are composites of Spirit and Matter, B3: 38
are intelligent, B1: 12
centres of responsibility, B4: 153
divinely appointed, B4: 55
elements (four basic), TC: 3
first, CA: 66

individual, B4: 153; C2: 1
male and female elements, TC: 1
personalised expressions of the originating
     power, B3: 175
physical body, CA: 28
polarised being, TC: 2
power ... to turn ... earth into a ...
     paradisical garden ... [*or*] pollute it,
     B4: 153
right polar relation, TC: 16
see B1: 8, 141, 145; B2: 146, 170;
     B3: 122-123; B4: 53, 153, 183;
     C1: 45, 79; C2: 95-96; CA: 3-4,
     36; P2: 21, 27, 41-43, 49;
     TC: 16-17
special kind of being, B4: 39; CA: 5
spiritually minded, CA: 5
stand trial (world-court), B4: 153
unavoidably bi-polar, C4: 93
variously gifted, P1: 113

Human existence
& centred consciousness, C2: 138

Human race
& Cosmic Man, C2: 1
& language, P1: 115
& RITUAL, C3: 95
& sea of anxiety, CA: 19
has disobeyed, CA: 21
properties, B4: 51

Humanism
& theism / theanthropism, B4: 25

Humanist
Humanist, Rationalist, Materialistic Atheist,
     C2: 1

Humanity('s)
& RITUAL, CEREMONY,
     PROCEDURE?, C3: 95
Divine, B4: 110
essential, B4: 60
origin of ... troubles, B1: 60

Humanness
& capacity for choice, B4: 60,
Choice-capacity, B4: 67

Humility
& Beyondness, B3: 130
education of the soul, C1: 89
essential, B4: 54
feeling we experience when, B3: 171
reminds us, B3: 5

Humpty Dumpty
  see B1: 61
Hunt
  & war, B2: 2, 4, 12
Husband
  prima materia's, TC: 36
Hutzpah
  Jewish people, EG: 84
Hyakujo
  enlightened man, C3: 94
Hyle
  universal mother-substance, TC: 31
Hylozoistic
  continuum, C3: 30
Hypertension
  States, B3: 87
Hypocrite
  actor, B2: 39
Hysteria
  & men, TC: 13

I

I
  & every judgement, C1: 74
  & Indian myth, TC: 36
  & original void, C3: 103
  & P, C4: 98
  & pain, C3: 105
  & relation of the Infinite to finite, C3: 28
  & stage fright, C1: 67,
  & the Absolute, C4: 30; RS: viii
  & The Cross in the Circle, C3: 122
  A E I O U, (see diagrams), C4: 30
  each one thought "I", DD: 13
  group of ideas, C1: 39
  I AM, the Alpha and Omega, DD: 38
  I-ness Eye-ness, C3: 43
  objectively conscious, C3: 112
  see English gematria, C3: 19-20, 84-88
  that sensitive power basic to all things,
      B4: 182
Ida
  & THREE PHASES: PUSH, PULL,
      BALANCE, C3: 30
Idea(s)
  & a posteriori, C4: 38
  & a priori, C4: 38
  & egotism, B3: 63

  & every great work, B3: 57
  & language, C3: 104
  & mentation, B2: 13
  & our deep essential self, P1: 12
  & our intellect, B2: 61
  & purpose, C2: 59
  & series, B1: 16
  & simultaneity, B1: 16
  & thinking, C1: 20
  body of, B4: 139-140
  conceptual essence, C2: 123
  contradiction or opposition, C4: 110
  energy, P2: 59
  eternal form (Pure), C2: 83
  "form", B2: 17
  form in consciousness, C1: 22
  form of energy, C2: 62, 123
  forms of *power*, B3: 64
  granule or granular accretion (temporal
      form), C2: 83
  idea-differences, B3: 128
  images of things seen, P2: 62
  inner world of, B2: 17
  liking or disliking, CA: 68
  mental forms, B1: 131
  not *nothing*, B2: 18
  of being a visible God, B4: 18
  of being, C2: 138
  of motion, RS: 12
  one, C3: 38
  pass in *sequence* through our mind, CA: 72
  Pure (eternal form), C2: 83
  quantity of energy, B2: 18
  self-consistent, B4: 136
  separativity, B4: 80
  shape or form in the consciousness, B4: 133
  shapes or forms in our mind, B3: 64
  spermiforms, C4: 82
  structure of governing principles
      (Noah's Ark), B2: 48
  structures, B3: 127
  system(s) of, C1: 35; CA: 25-26
  true, B4: 142; CA: 26
  unfamiliar, B1: 104
Ideation
  & elements of human being, TC: 3
  & initiative, TC: 3
  & male, TC: 3
  & male-stressed consciousness, TC: 19
  & Will, C3: 11

power to formulate, TC: 2
SEPARATIVE, C3: 60

Identification
& confused state of mind, P2: 33
& external objects, C4: 108
& Fall, C4: 10-11; CA: 32
& loss of self, P2: 28
& mental disorders, RS: 41
& physical body, P2: 28
& state of forgetfulness, P2: 29
& THEOSIS, C3: 96
belongs in the objective aspect of being,
     C1: 73
cause of consciousness suffering, RS: 18
emotional charge, C1: 60
emotionally-charged contents of
     consciousness, RS: 41
fall into, RS: 16
falls easily into (a soul), B1: 96
form-function, C2: 58
formal similarity, C1: 105
of consciousness with an object, C1: 97
process of progressive, C2: 98
States of, C1: 55
wherever form occurs, C1: 75
with conceptual forms, RS: 45
with fallenness commits the fallen one,
     C2: 16

Identity
form-function, C2: 58
is form, C2: 58
of Opposites (Taoism), C2: 103
of the human battle, B2: 178
pre-condition for making real decisions,
     P2: 75
reference for consciousness, C2: 54

Idiot
"layman", C1: 105

Idle
& idol worship, B2: 59, 107
image, B2: 111

Idol(s)
& Abraham, B2: 107
idol-smashers, B2: 114
man's, B2: 113
of the theatre, B2: 56
worship, B2: 59, 107, 112

Idolatry
error of, B2: 57
worship is, B2: 58

If
WHAT, WHERE, WHEN, WHY, WHO,
     How and If / Else, C2: 89-91; C4: 71

Ignorance
of the law, B4: 172
self-imposed, RS: vi

Ignorant
lack humility, RS: vi

IHSV
In Hoc Signo Vinc, C3: 65

Illusion
& Parmenides, C4: 31

Ill-will
& stupidity, C1: 68

Image(s)
& mental life, CA: 73
& The Dream World, C4: 83
& the mask, C2: 111
at death occurs the flash, C2: 107
divine, B2: 114
of God, B2: 156
of ourselves, CA: 65
self-, B2: 101, 111, 114; B3: 182; B4: 1
Time as "the moving image of eternity"
     (Plato), B2: 120

Imagination
& Twilight, C4: 73-74
creative, C4: 73 economic way of creating,
     B1: 44
power in our mind, B1: 43

Immanent
Infinite Sentient Power is God ... immanent
     in Nature, C1: 33

Immanentism
Restrictive, EG: 5

Immediate
adequate response, TC: 24
"Good name in man and woman is the
     immediate jewel of the soul"
     (Shakespeare), B2: 100

Immortal
Soul, B3: 127

Immortality
& Eternal Truth, B4: 143
& "mortal", B3: 126
alone rescues all from vanity, TC: 25
eternal survival, B1: 121
gaining of, RS: 41
power to resist disintegration, P2: 58;
     TC: 25

problem of, B3: 126
Immortals
Band of, B4: 196
Impeccability
of Will, C4: 14, 33
Impedance(s)
& government-controlled educational
    systems, B2: 98
& motion, C4: 12
& pleasures, B4: 115
deliberately set up, B2: 98
source of, B2: 99
to … our knowledge and understanding,
    B2: 98
Impenitence
& Penitence (Jupiter/Saturn), C2: 34
Imperfection
& perfection, B2: 101
Importance
energy, C4: 28
stress of the will, EG: 2
Impression
of the infinite field of sentient power, C3: 72
Impulse(s)
afferent nerve, RS: 22
Inside our body, B1: 25
irrational, B2: 29
oppose … rational attempt to control, B4: 6
Impulsive
man, B1: 25
nature, B1: 104
son (Ham), B1: 98; B2: 28, 42
Incarnate
God-man, C1: 34
in a human body (Absolute Truth), B3: 120
Infinite, the true self-realiser, C4: 52
Logos, or Word, P1: 19
Incarnation
& a soul, CA: 15
& Essential Christianity, C4: 10
Christ's, C2: 64
Doctrine of, B2: 169
God's, C3: 28
of divine Spirit, B4: 111
Inclination(s)
"As the twig inclines, so grows the tree",
    P1: 104-105
first, C4: 41
little, P1: 105
of feeling, P1: 104

our organism is full of, P1: 106
tendency to fall into action, RS: 22
Inclusive
exclusive way, B2: 178
Incomprehensible
originating power, P1: 126
Inconsistency
& damage, B4: 33
& our soul, P1: 65
state of, B4: 99
Incontinence
& continence, C4: 106
painful results of, C4: 106
Indebtedness
to other men, B3: 56
Indestructible
soul is, CA: 16
Indifference
& lukewarm, CA: 54
& Laodiceans, CA: 54
failure to *commit* ourselves, CA: 54
So speaks God to the indifferent, the,
    CA: 54
Individual(s)
& self-awareness, CA: 21
& "the chain of the prophets", B1: 121
& truth, C3: 37
3-D existential, C3: 98
birth, B4: 153
consciousness, C1: 105; P2: 70
death, B4: 153
Destinies, P1: 113
developed, B4: 153
effort, B4: 153
existence, C4: 101
form and function, B1: 117
life, B4: 153
personal cross, B4: 110
reflexive self-consciousness of, C2: 64
responsibility, B4: 152-153
self, B1: 115; C1: 98
suffering of a finite, C1: 76
undeveloped, B4: 153-154
unique nature of each, C4: 114
uniqueness of character and talent, DD: 3
uniqueness of, B1: 122
we exist as, C1: 62
Individuality
& Faith & Will, C2: 3
& "law of increasing freedom", C1: 74-75

& unique nature of each spirit, C1: 93

depends on differentiation of forms and
 functions, B1: 117

depends upon the diverse experiences we
 undergo, B3: 128

differences of, C2: 58

empirical, C1: 75

human, C2: 120

Individuated

will (Leo), C4: 31

Individuation

& the vocal cords, C3: 103-104

formal separation of zones of sentience,
 C3: 116

road to freedom, C3: 43

Inefficiency

& words "good" and "bad", B1: 77

Inefficient

& nature of "good" and "evil", B1: 74

& mind of Cain, B1: 74

Inertia(s)

& an eternal spiritual being, CA: 28

& body, C4: 95

& disbelief, EG: 14

& female, C3: 33

& free will C2: 5; C4: 20

& habits, B3: 184

& identification, RS: 30

& Immediate Presence of Spirit, B1: 4

& initiative, B4: 36

& inner enemies, CA: 7

& The Absolute, TC: 31

after-motion of free will, C4: 20

after-motion of once-originating will, C2: 80

enemy, B4: 193

Finite Records of experience patterns,
 C4: 105

mass-, TC: 17

mental, B4: 77-78

of energies, B1: 4

of one's own past actions, C2: 25

past, C2: 74

patterns of motions once established in
 self-aware will, C4: 11

principle of, C4: 109

real force, B1: 104

resister of change, C3: 58

system (the material world), C2: 129

Inertic

resistance, RS: 30

Universal matter is, TC: 33

I-ness

Observer standpoint, C3: 43

Infinite

& finite, C4: 34

& the real God, C4: 56

awareness, C1: 101

beyond all being, C1: 31

BIG SECRET, C3: 28

Comprehension, C4: 89

continuum of Sentient Power, C4: 120

continuum, C4: 53

Divine Gestalt, C2: 17

excluded, RS: 9

"eye", C1: 72

feeling is, C1: 38

Field, B1: 133; C1: 74

God, B1: 132; B2: 169; C4: 103

Incarnate, C4: 52

intelligence & power ... not separated,
 B4: 21-22

light, B1: 19

negation of the finite, C1: 95

ocean of light, C1: 86

Power, B1: 8, 15, 130-133; B4: 47; C4: 67;
 CA: 13; P1: 24, 73, 81, 136-137, 141,
 153; P2: 1

power and infinite intelligence are not
 separated, B4: 21-22

Sentient Power, C1: 32-33, 60; DD: 70;
 C3: 14; C4: 102, 108, 120

Spirit, C1: 76-77

wisdom, B2: 169

Infiniteness

of sentience, RS: i

Infinity

& creation, C1: 72

Man cannot know, B2: 169

nothingness, C2: 40

of choices, C4: 3

supreme positive, beyond all
 circumscription, C1: 95

Information

inner and outer, B2: 131

Inheritors

"Woe to you who are inheritors", B1: 84

Inhibition

creation is, C1: 77

Initiating

Will is soul self-initiating, C4: 50

Initiation
  Source of our (Christ's power in us),
    CA: 30
Initiative
  & ideation, TC: 3
  & inertia, C4: 105
  & intellect, B2: 12
  & male behaviour, C3: 110
  & man of spirit, B3: 78
  & phenomena, C4: 106
  & Spirit, B4: 36; C4: 95
  & the now-moment, B3: 79
  & the "quick" in every situation,   B3: 11
  & will, B2: 12
  Grace, divine power within us, Emanuel,
    B4: 175
  introduction of change, TC: 17
  male, C3: 33
  nature of, B3: 159
  releases us, B3: 184
Injury
  "cellular neurosis", EG: 15
Inner
  & outer world, B1: 72; B2: 116, 131
  & two men, C4: 11
  awareness, C4: 25, 87
  balance, CA: 82
  chemical, CA: 63
  control, C4: 87
  divinity, B4: 21
  functions, C4: 11
  guilt, CA: 82
  invisible parts of its organism, C4: 11
  invisible processes C4: 11
  processes, CA: 63
  violence, B1: 62
  vision, B2: 105
  Voice, B2: 105
  world, B1: 72; B2: 116, 131
  world of our own true self, B4: 8
Innermost
  being, B1: 63
  centre, B1: 32, 94
  essence of things, B1: 32
  motivation, C4: 61
  soul, B1: 63
  spirit, B1: 94
  spiritual essence, B1: 73
Innocence
  "Dispensation for Innocence"

  (command to Adam), B3: 88
  Edenic, B1: 73
Instinct(s)
  animal, P1: 147
  basis of, B2: 81
  embodiment of an experience, C1: 15
  involved rational response, C1: 15
Instinctive
  love of life, EG: 66
  tendencies, EG: 6
Insulation
  absolute, B3: 137
  apparent, B4: 80
Integrate
  means that ..., B4: 130
Integration
  belief implies, P2: 6
  Jesus ... wills our, P2: 55
  of mind, soul and spirit, B4: 34
Integrity
  man of, P2: 79
Intellect
  & clarity, B1: 50, 53
  & feeling, C4: 74
  & initiative, B2: 12
  & Logos, C3: 111
  & need for an ordered world, C1: 85
  & pairs of opposite ideas, B2: 61
  & Truth, C4: 101-102
  knowledge; control; freedom; new
    creations,   C3: 71
  fully comprehensive, C4: 30
  "great interjection", the appearance of,
    C1: 87
  of man in his spiritually unenlightened
    state,   P1: 61
  quantity is in the, C2: 55
  rational facility, C3: 124
  see B1: 50-51, 53
  Will: initiator of the action of the, C2: 141
Intelligence
  & co-ordination, B3: 50
  & divine source, B1: 94
  & "efficiency", B4: 28
  & energy, B2: 86
  & God, B1: 13
  & purpose, B4: 22
  & realisation of a purpose, B1: 12; EG: 56
  & reductionists, C2: 84-85
  & sense of what is economic, B4: 28

& unity of our being, B3: 60
& will, B4: 42-43, 45-46, 73; P1: 124
a *Mystery*, B3: 124
creative, B4: 55
divine, B4: 22
enlightened, B1; 94; B2: 41
evolution as, B1: 10
free, B1: 94
human, B2: 84; P1: 125
Infinite, B4: 22
infinite, & infinite power … are not
    separated, B4: 21-22
instrument of survival, B1: 95
intoxicated, B1: 103
Man's, B2: 26
Noah's name, B1: 95
Noah-principle, B1: 105
Noah, B1: 99; B2: 30
Noetic principle, B1: 97
Nous, B1: 99
organising (body of sentient energy), C4: 61
power-intelligence & glory & danger, B4: 25
pure, C2: 88
quickness of consciousness, C1: 104
spiritual, B2: 39
Universal, B3: 125; P1: 84
Universal Creative …"God", B4: 98

Intelligent
& God, B1: 13
Awareness of true nature of reality, B3: 29
creative … living, B1: 37
divine intelligent power, B4: 22
evolutionary emergents C4: 70
Infinite intelligent power (the Eternal), B3: 3
Power, B1: 8; B3: 2, 42, 54; B4: 35; C4: 62

Intensification
& detensification, EG: 10
& phenomena, EG: 10

Intensity
(degrees of) inholdingness, C4: 68
stimulus energy, (of) RS: 17

Intension
of primal will, C3: 61

Intention
of the original infinite sentient power field,
    C3: 61
purity of our, C4: 61
willed, B4: 42; C4: 50

Intentional act
(in-tension-al) act, C4: 89-90

Interact
energy and intelligence, B2: 86

Interaction
& energy stimulus acting on a sense organ,
    B4: 58
& non-dual view, B3: 58
all action, is, B4: 12
intent, P1: 157
of inner and outer, B3: 57-58

Interactionist
view (non-dual), C3: 58

Interactivity
intimate, B2: 190
Life is *relational*, B2: 73
of our ideas, B3: 64

Interchange
mechanical, B4: 78
of feelings and emotions, B2: 10

Intercommunication
& harmony, B3: 43

Interest
& contents of the mind, CA: 73
& the continuum, C2: 93
& the eye, C1: 36
& The Infinite Power is interested, EG: 16
emotional charge, C1: 37
form of love, B1: 135
our unconscious, CA: 74
raises our temperature, CA: 28

Interference
& cause of undesirableness, C1: 76
& darkness, C1: 84
mutual, B3: 137

Interfunction
& Human beings, B2: 7
& interrelatedness, P1: 76
& a universe, CA: 78
all function is, B2: 3, 7, 74; B4: 12
evidence of, B2: 171
failure of, P1: 156
perfect harmonious, P1: 139
true, B2: 9

Interjection
"great interjection"
    (appearance of Intellect), C1: 87

Internal
work, B4: 106

Interpenetration
& first act of Creation, B1: 5

Interplay
Real life requires reciprocal, B1: 115
Interpretation
& an orderly life, B4: 58
Bible, B1: 2
level(s), B2: 137, 146
scriptural texts, B4: 1
Intolerance
& the female female, C4: 72
Introjection
& OUTER WORLD, C3: 83
Introspection
process of searching within ourselves, B3: 39
Introversion
& extroversion, B1: 42
Invention
has a mother, C2: 135
Investigation
FULL, C3: 41
our psychic capabilities, B1: 44
Invisible
no defining lines, B2: 168
power, B3: 168, B3: 62
source of all visibles, B3: 61
The One True God, B4: 18
Invocare
VOCARE EST INVOCARE,
C3: 1, 76; C4: 4
Invoke
"To voice is to invoke", B3: 141
Involution
& GOD (VII): THE ORIGINAL
CREATOR, C3: 90
IO
"enlargement of power", C3: 104
name of God, C3: 104
Ionic
architectural order, C3: 30
Irrefragable
Jesus, P1: 78
Is
verb "to be", C1: 25
I.S. (Inner sentience)
(see diagram), C3: 73
TENSION GENERATED BY, C3: 73
Isaac
& Abraham, B2: 139
& laughter, B2: 138-140, 147, 153
Ishmael('s)
& destiny, B2: 100

Hagar's child, B2: 93
Ishvara
& Brahman, C1: 81
Islam
& affirmation, C2: 37
& pursuit of the knowledge, C2: 102
stresses, C2: 10
taught, C2: 12
IS-NESS
of all beings, C2: 146
Is-now
against the Shall-be, DD: 51
Isolation
& death, CA: 88
& process of human evolution, CA: 90
& *relationship*, CA: 92
absolute, C4: 112
against, C2: 70
effects of Time, B4: 16
few men can long endure, CA: 82
self-isolation, CA: 89
total self-, B1: 5
Israel
& Abram, B2: 90

J

J
see English gematria, C3: 19-20, 84-88
Jacob's
ladder of being, B2: 176; C4: 4
ladder to all high designs, C4: 4
Jairus's
Daughter, P2: 1
Japan
Makoto, C2: 37
Japanese
sun-goddess, C3: 110
Buddhism, C4: 89
Japhet
& father's nakedness, B1: 103
& Shem, B1: 103; B2: 28, 39, 43, 54
descendants, B2: 54
signifies ..., B2: 25-26
he that persuades, B1: 98
Jehovah
Gee Whoa!, C2: 63
Jesus ... means, B1: 99
name of God, B2: 19

Jerusalem(s)
& Jesus Christ, C4: 35
Heavenly, C4: 15
New, C2: 139
two, P2: 133

Jerusalemic
Body, CA: 102

Jesus
& A rich young man, B4: 1
& Abraham, B4: 68
& abundant life, B1: 145
& Agape-love, B1: 139
& Being-action-pattern, P1: 74
& corner-stone, B3: 83
& covenant B2: 21-22
& divine Grace. P1: 98
& Divine Way, B2: 163
& error, B1: 51
& God's will, B1: 99; P1: 82
& good shepherds, RS: 52
& hell, B2: 175; B3: 21; B4: 65; DD: 60
& Herod, CA: 6
& insignia, DD: 56
& intelligent creative power, B4: 98
& Lucifer, DD: 55
& opponents, P1: 28
& power of God, B1: 134
& Ram-energy, B2: 153
& Reality, B4: 106
& "rejected stone", B3: 82-83
& rock of offense, B3: 83
& "Stone", B3: 83
& stumbling block, B3: 83
& the "dead", B1: 144
& the divine image, B2: 114
& the money-changers, P1: 100
& the "quick", B1: 144
& The Scapegoat, B1: 78
& "the Word made Flesh", B1: 102
& threefold temptation, P1: 27
& *total self-sacrifice*, B2: 164
& Truth, B1: 87; B4: 72; P1: 60
& Virgin Sophia-Mary, C3: 13
& Victory, P1: 78
& Wilderness, B4: 16
& "Worship", B3: 112
accepted the sheep, wolves, serpents and
    doves in man, B3: 134
"Acknowledge Me and I will acknowledge
    you", B4: 98

"Affirmation Saves", B2: 170
aim is to "fulfil all righteousnes" (Jesus to
    John the Baptist), B4: 14
all actuality, P1: 73
"all things to all men", B3: 81, 133
"As you sow, so shall you reap", B3: 79
battle, B1: 93
"Be not afraid" (Christ), P2: 5
"Be ye therefore as wise as serpents and as
    harmless as doves", B3: 134
"Before Abraham was, I am", B4: 68
beyond the Time-process, B4: 68
Buddha, Mahavira, Jina, Lao Tse,
    Zarathustra, Socrates, RS: 52
called twelve, DD: 57
"conscious intelligent self response", B3: 29
Demonstration on the cross, C3: 93
embodied, B1: 102; B2: 47, 82; B4: 111
embodies (the Word of Truth), B4: 143
embodiment of His Will, P1: 74
Eternal Soul of the Universe, B4: 15
eye (single) ... "full of light", B3: 60
Gethsemane, P1: 36
"God is spirit, to be worshipped in spirit and
    in truth", B3: 112
God-Man, B2; 160; C4: 51
God's Onely Begotten Son, P1: 82
harmless ... as a dove, yet ... wily as
    serpents, DD: 56
His crucifixion, P1: 77
His disciples, B2: 82
historical, B3: 118
"I am the Door; no man comes to the
    Father but by me", P1: 129
"I am the Way, the Truth and the
    Life" (Jesus), B4: 30, 68, 71; P1: 34, 73-75;
    P2: 53, 68, 74, 84
identification ... with the totality of all
    beings, B4: 80
"In as much as you do this to the least of
    these, you do it to me", B4: 80
in the desert, B1: 93
Incarnate Logos, C4: 119
incarnation, B4: 4; C3: 14, 28
incarnation of truth-to-oneself, C3: 63-64
Is it not written, Ye are Gods?, DD: 57
Kingdom of Heaven, B1: 31, 40
life-story, B4: 13
Love one another, B2: 112, 125
MANUAL OF POWER, C3: 123

Master dialectician, P2: 122

Messiah, C3: 8

most conscious human being, P1: 128

"My father works and I work", B1: 134; B4: 106, 154

"My judgement is just, because I seek not mine own will, but the Will of the Father which hath sent Me", P1: 20

One Supreme Source, B4: 111

origin of all beings, RS: 52

our Anchor, CA: 34; P1: 82

"Pantherion", B3: 134

parables, B1: 36

paradigm of perfect freedom, C4: 35

Perfect Man (Messiah), B3: 119-120

perfect Yogi, B4: 164

Ratio ... Word ... incarnate, P1: 19

"rejected stone", B3: 83

resurrection of, B4: 70

return to his heavenly Father, B4: 19

rod (took a), DD: 56

said "God is Spirit", B1: 4

Satan, B1: 20

seamless garment of, B4: 12

Self-consistency of, P1: 81

self-sacrifice in Golgotha, CA: 44

separativity ideas, B4: 80

suffered on the cross, CA: 39

Supreme Paradox, C2: 34

teachings, B1: 148

temptation, B4: 11-12

the Being condition of, B4: 73

The Jesus Prayer, C3: 96

the Way, P1: 74

The Way, the Truth, and the Life, B4: 30, 71; P1: 34, 73, 77

"Two fight three, and three fight two in one house", B3: 78

"turning the other cheek", B2: 47

way of, B2: 171; B4: 15

"What the Father does in secret, that I do openly", B4: 111

"Who has seen me has seen the Father", B4: 111; EG: 18

"Work while it is light, for the night comes when no man can work", B4: 154

" ... words that I speak unto you ...", P1: 2

Jesus Christ

& Virgin Sophia-Mary, C3: 13

"all things to all men", B3: 81, 133

embodied ... secret of sacrifice, CA: 92

entered into a ... physical body, CA: 31

eternal Spiritual Being, CA: 31

eternally conceived Logos-Self, C3: 14

fore-runner, C3: 64

forshadowing ... death of, CA: 89

incarnated, CA:26

is a Fish, CA: 34

is our Anchor, CA: 34

LORD JESUS CHRIST HAVE MERCY on me a sinner, C3: 96

Mark Man, C3: 83

Messiah, C3: 8

relation with God, P1: 82

relationship with mankind, P1: 82

true significance of God's incarnation, C3: 28

vindicated (crucified), C3: 26

Jewel

immediate ... of the soul, B2: 100

Jew(s)

& captivity, EG: 65

& Jewish Liberation Force, C4: 21

& the Messiah, B3: 118

individuated people ... suffered, CA: 21

looked backward in Time, B4: 68

Nietzsche had studied the, EG: 84

Jijimuge

& Logos, C3: 59

Japanese Buddhism, C4: 89

language, C3: 59

Jivan-mukhta

"delivered in life", C2: 88

Jina

& origin of all beings, RS: 52

Jesus, Buddha, Mahavira, Lao Tse, Zarathustra, Socrates, RS: 52

Job

see B4: 101

John

Gospel of, EG: 22, 77

Joy

& God, B1: 144, 147; EG: 11

conscious free-willed affirmation, B1: 146

is a more active word, B2: 127

our highest, P1: 156

present when we affirm, B2 : 127

Judaism

affirmation of analytical products and procedures, C2: 37

Christianity derives from, EG: 8
Law (Torah), C2: 12, 102
Judge
  & Correct use of terms, C1: 71
  & pre-, B3: 171
  self-, C2: 11
Judgment
  & choice, CA: 57
  & conscience, C4: 19
  highest, C4: 74
  Last, C2: 48, 74
  of Jesus, P1: 20
  see C2: 42
  self-judgment, B2: 111; C2: 11
  three elements, C1: 74
Jugglers
  ye word, DD: 8
Jupiter
  & conscience, C1: 101
  & CURE & reversal of the Fall, C2: 117
  & Manual of Power, C3: 123
  & Mercury, C2: 56, C4: 17, 38-39, 60, 69
  & Philosopher's Stone, C4: 38
  & Samson's riddle, C4: 63
  & Saturn, C1: 100-101; C2: 33-34, 56;
      C3: 69; C4: 17, 27, 38-39,
      60,68-69, 111; CA: 48
  & trine process, C4: 38
  centre, C1: 101
  decompression, C4: 68
  Deo-Pater, CA: 48
  dissolution process, C2: 99
  expanded state, C4: 66
  expansion, C3: 69
  opposite of Saturn, CA: 48
  paradox of the free and the domed, C4: 60
  posits Saturn, C2: 56
  Saturn/Jupiter/Mercury, C4: 38
  Saturn-Jupiter-Saturn (continuance of the
    Eternal), C2: 33
  see C2: 99, 117; C3: 6-7, 101, 123
  (see diagram), C2: 109; C3: 7
  sonic alterations, C2: 33-34
  source of true conscience, C1: 101
Jury
  self-, C2: 11
Justice
  no … in this world, DD: 29
  perfect, CA: 86

Justification
  of the Works of God, C2: 100
  self-justification, C1: 92

K

K
  & function, C2: 59
  see English gematria, C3: 19-20, 84-88
Kali
  & magical energy, C3: 79
Kama
  Hindu Eros, C2: 113
Kant
  Ding an sich, C3: 23
Karma
  & one's own desires, C4: 17
  action-reaction law, B1: 147
  Hindu concept of, C2: 113
  intuited, C4: 65
  is constitutive, C4: 17
  (karma-rupa) (functional-form), C2: 59
  Law of, B3: 46
  see B3: 46-47
Key
  of life and destiny, B3: 174
  secret, DD: 63
Khalif
  one measures … for God, EG: 17
Khepira
  breaks the lock of Nut, DD: 9
Kierkegaard
  & Buber (Martin), C2: 31
  state of "first immediacy", B1: 25
  The Devil is sheer spirit, C2: 106
Killer
  & a judge, C1: 71
King
  & sage (CHINESE WISE MAN), C3: 127
Kingdom
  of heaven is *within*, B2: 103
King Kongs
  men are all, C2: 129
Kinodynamic process
  & mind, C2: 91
Know
  & "K" function, C2: 59
  & *feel*, B2: 117
  & knowledge, B2: 117

Knower
 finite (body-identified Observer), C3: 118
 infinite (God), C3: 118
Knowledge
 -pursuer, B1: 131
 -pursuit, B1: 128
 & Islam, C2: 102
 & Logos of God, P1: 85
 & sentience B4: 178
 & Sufism, C2: 103
 & Wisdom, B1: 52, 124-125; B3: 163; B4:
  23; C2: 145; DD: 19
 basis of all, B4: 178
 capacity to sense changes, B4: 178
 counter-, B1: 127
 for its own sake, B1: 128
 God's wisdom, B1: 52
 is specialistic, C2: 145
 is *for the sake of its possessor*, B1: 128
 key to control, C3: 71
 nature of, B1: 48
 necessarily finite, B1: 131
 pain sought, B1: 128
 self-knowledge, B1: 5; C4: 17
 Tree of, B1: 23, 47-48; B3: 69; CA: 19;
  DD: 42
 "unconscious", CA: 83
 without a knower, B1: 128
Kong
 inner, C2: 129
Kongscious
 & primal power, C2: 129
Kosmic
 Universal Master-tool, C2: 46
Kosmohexon
 & HIHU, Infinite Intelligent Power,
  C2: 115
Kosmos
 & last judgment, C2: 74
 Builder, C3: 121
 His Great Work, C3: 14
Kronos
 & Rhea, C2: 75
 & Mammon, C2: 75, 83
 & Time, C2: 75
Kyriosity
 & Lord (Kyrios), EG: 17
 curiosity is, EG: 17

L

L
 & The Real, C4: 95
 sameness, C4: 95
 see C2: 2
 (*see diagram*), C4: 95
 see English gematria, C3: 19-20, 84-88
La
 La donna e mobile, TC: 10
 "La ilaha illa llah", C4: 120; EG: 16
Labour(s)
 division of, B2: 5, 7
 fruits of my, DD: 34
Labourers
 & Kingdom of Heaven, P1: 110
Lack(s)
 & desire, B3: 47
 & Eros-love, B1: 139
Ladder
 & Jacob, B2: 176
 of life, B4: 39
Lambda
 -Light, C3: 32
 Light, C3: 40
Lamech
 headstrong, B1: 91
Language
 & "Babel", B2: 54
 & sense of hearing, P2: 69
 & words, C3: 77
 = linkage; Christ's seamless Logos garment,
  C2: 15
 common, B2: 52
 communicate, C3: 59
 communication, C3: 104
 development of, B3: 116
 differences, B4: 190
 different, B4: 190
 forces of evolution, C3: 59
 one original natural, B2: 53
 problems of, B3: 116
 secret, B2: 53
 sign, C4: 72
 SIGNALS, C3: 76
 spoken, C3: 103
Lao Tse
 & Hillel, C3: 93
 & Jesus, Buddha, Mahavira, Jina,
  Zarathustra, Socrates, RS: 52
 "He who first sees the pity of battle will

triumph", C4: 16
"Honour and shame are the same", B2: 82
origin of all beings RS: 52
Laodiceans
& indifference, CA: 54
& lukewarm, CA: 54
So speaks God to the, CA: 54
Larynx
= The Law of Yes and No, C4: 119
Laughter
& Isaac, B2: 138-140, 147, 153
of acquired power, B2: 138-140, 147, 153
two kinds of, C2: 135
Law(s)
-conformability, B3: 73
-Makers, B2: 12
& energy, B1: 28
& Judaism, C2: 102
& natural world, B3: 73
& Nature, C2: 101
& physical universe, B1: 29
& St Paul, P2: 130
& the absolute man, RS: viii
as we sow, so shall we reap, B1: 7
basic, B3: 113
Cain ... forgot *The Great*, CA: 87
chemical, B1: 30
constant uniform stimulation ..., C2: 146
Cosmic, B4: 100
God's, CA: 43
inverse square, C3: 98
"Law in the flesh", P2: 111
material, B1: 66, 70
mechanical, P2: 93
of action and reaction, B2: 124; B3: 46;
CA: 79
of Being-Encapsulation, C2: 106
of cause and effect, B1: 7
of change, C4: 73
of chemistry, B3: 39
of Christ, P2: 135
of Creative Love, CA: 79
of electronics, B3: 39
of Fang and Claw, P1: 24
of gravity, B3: 39
of KARMA, B3: 46
of Love (God's), CA: 37; P1: 25;
P2: 95, 131, 134
of Moses, P2: 130-132
of Persistence of Error, RS: 57

of polarisation, TC: 13
of proportion, P1: 4
of Reality (principles), B3: 113
of resonance, B2: 182
of Sorcery, C4: 33
of talent development, B1: 120
of the AFFIRMATION OF ALL
NEGATIONS, DD: 70-71
of the Hexon, C3: 101
of Time, B1: 124
of Yes and No conflict, C4: 119
Sacred, C4: 80
The Great Law of the Seamless Garment, CA: 87
the great ... of the Infinite Sentient Power,
DD: 70
whole universal, P2: 134
Lead
signifies the Intellect, C4: 90
Saturnine metal, C2: 72
Leaders
intelligent, P1: 148
Learning
& survival, C2: 136
Leben
to live & "lieben", *to love* / "leib",
body / "loben", *to praise*, B1: 7
Leib
body & "leben" *to live* / "lieben",
to love / "loben", *to praise*, B1: 7
Leibnitz
vindicated (monad), C3: 26
Left
half (brain), C3: 82
vices, C3: 101
Left-handed
& cowardICE, C4: 5
Legal
rights, TC: 41
Legs
& bureaucrats, C4: 69
Leo
[*Zodiac sign*] *see* C3: 113; C4: 31-33
& individuated will, C4: 31
& solar energy, C4: 32
& *will* (Sol), C3: 113
Let
"ananda" of Hindu philosophy, C4: 12
"Fiat!", C4: 41
"Let go and let God", B4: 118
"THERE" ... "BE" ... "LIGHT",

DD: 9-10

Letter(s)
  & words, C4: 22
  A E I O U, *(see diagrams)*, C4: 30
  unvoiced & sounded, C4: 97
  key to world forms, C1: 95
  P and M, C4: 97-99
  see English gematria, C3: 19-20, 84-88

Leucotomy
  see C2: 50

Level(s)
  & free will, B3: 105
  & still centre of our being, B3: 107
  animal, B3: 104
  fifth, B3: 105
  five, B3: 81
  Leveller, Great, P1: 113
  hexonic, C2: 44
  higher, B3: 111
  of being, B3: 103-105; P2: 3
  of pure consciousness, B3: 106
  parahexonic, C2: 44
  rationally self-controlled, B3: 104
  volitional, C2: 44

Liar(s)
  & the devil, B4: 194
  and deceivers, B3: 112

Libra
  [*Zodiac sign*] *see* C3: 113;
  & abstract ideational investigation, C3: 113

Library
  see DD: 85

Lie(s)
  & memory, P1: 65
  & Truth (Picasso), C3: 21
  father of, B2: 24
  Prince of, P1: 32

Lieben
  to love & "leben" *to live* / "leib", *body* /
  "loben" *to praise*, B1: 7

Life
  -capacity, B3: 47
  -energy, B4: 35
  -force(s), B1: 97; B2: 142, 183, 184; B4: 81;
    C1: 48; C2: 71; P1: 31; P2: 2; 2;
    TC: 7
  -forms, B1: 122
  -story, B4: 13
  -Three-fold, B4: 68-69
  -way, B4: 31-35, 96

  & Christ, P2: 84
  & *communication*, CA: 88
  & death, B1: 70; P2: 83
  & East-West axis, *(see diagram)*, C4: 66
  & essence of, C3: 55
  & Evil, B2: 32
  & extra-ordinary, P2: 61
  & feeling, B2: 117
  & Fire-fighting rules, C4: 71
  & form, B2: 110
  & Incarnate Logos, C4: 91, 119-120
  & intelligent power, B2: 84
  & Kirkegaard ("first immediacy"), B1: 25
  & *meaning*, C4: 73
  & meaningless, B1: 66
  & purpose, C1: 6
  & *relationship*, CA: 92
  & & right motive, B4: 63
  & self-preservation, TC: 23
  & solidarity of all being, C4: 112
  & survival, CA: 23
  anti-, P1: 42
  Book of Life (Logos), C4: 91
  Divine love at work P2: 14
  Elixir of, C4: 38
  enemy of, C4: 49
  energy, C4: 15
  eternal, B2: 84; P1: 44
  "Fires of ...", CA: 28
  function of love C1: 7
  Great ladder of, B4: 39
  great ocean of, B1: 97
  human (essentiality of), CA: 88
  "I am the Way, the Truth and the Life"
  (Jesus), B4: 30, 68, 71; P1: 34, 73-75;
    P2: 53, 68, 74, 84
  is full of difficulties, B4: 63
  is Love embodied, B1: 7
  is *relationship*, CA: 92
  is simple, B4: 63
  "leben", B1: 7
  "LET" ..."THERE" ... "BE" ..., DD: 9-10
  lose, CA: 92
  love of, B4: 117
  meaning of, P2: 46
  of pure joy, B1: 145
  On earth, B3: 30
  orderly, B4: 58
  preserve, CA: 92
  Real, B1: 115

relational interactivity, B2: 73

responsibility, B2: 96

see English gematria, C3: 20

sensuous, C4: 56

tree of, B1: 47, 63

Two threads weave our (Teilhard de Chardin), C4: 60

ultimate meaning of, B1: 1

vibrates, C3: 56

"water of Life" which Christ offers to mankind, (Christ), P1: 143

Way of True, B4: 73

wheel of, C3: 4

Lila

Divine, C3: 95

Light

-power, B1: 20

& darkness, B4: 27; C1: 106; C3: 57

& lens system, P2: 68

& Logos, C3: 40

& Lucifer, B1: 19-21, B4: 27

& narrow beam, P2: 68

& "night", B: 154

& the half-sleepers, DD: 13

body ... "full of light", B3: 60

consciousness, B2: 97; C4: 28

Eternity, C2: 76

excess of, B4: 27

Eye, C3: 107

generation of, B1: 21

God is, C4: 35

I said the word "LIGHT", DD: 10

"If thine eye be single, thy whole body is full of light" (Jesus), B3: 44, 50, 60

intelligence, B1: 22; B3: 60

Lead, kindly, C2: 9; C4: 36

"Let there be light", B4: 191

see "Fiat Lux", C3: 56

Son of, C3: 57

symbol for consciousness and understanding, B4: 191

symbol of consciousness, P2: 69

symbolises consciousness, B2: 97

true, C3: 55

understanding, B1: 22

uninterrupted motion, C1: 86

"Work while it is light, for the night comes when no man can work" (Jesus), B4: 154

Light-bearer

Lucifer, B1: 17; B3: 180

Likes

& dislikes, CA: 69; P2: 63

Lila

Divine, C3: 95

Limb

phantom, B4: 123

Limit(s)

& feeling, C1: 38

& knowledge-pursuer, B1: 131

application of terms, C1: 83

one's conceived, C2: 81

Limitation

of form, C1; 105

Limited

our power is, B1: 33

Line

time-, C3: 29

Linear

mind, C2: 76

separation ... Time ... Temptation, CA: 49

sequence, CA: 47

Linkage

& language, C2: 15; C3: 59

Lion

"lion-man", EG: 74-75

Listening

& subtle body, C4: 24

Little

Gods, EG: 34

Live

= VEIL = LEVI = EVIL = EL-VI, C2: 14

"leben" *to live* / "lieben", *to love* / "leib", *body* / "loben", *to praise*, B1: 7

Living

body, C1: 18

Loben

to praise & "leben" *to live* / "lieben", *to love* / "leib", *body*, B1: 7

Lock(s)

-breaker, DD: 19

Christ ... break the locks of heaven and hell, DD: 55

of Nut, DD: 9

Logic(s)

& "*Truly* human", B2: 165

incarnation of this (Jesus), B4: 4

THREE, C3: 102

True, B4: 4

Logo-logic

& Logos-God, C2: 44

Logologic
   logic of the Logos, C3: 102
   short way into life, C4: 119
Logos
   -Christ C2: 6, 18
   -energy, EG: 26
   -form, EG: 26
   -God, C4: 7: EG: 26
   -Infinity, C2: 15
   -Mind, C2: 76
   -Self, C4: 106
   -Truth, C2: 6
   -word, EG: 26, 78
   & Cour-age, C4: 7
   & Dialectic, C4: 35
   & Faith and True Reason, C2: 114
   & Gospel of John, EG: 22-27
   & incarnation (Christ), C4: 63
   & jijimuge, C3: 59
   & language, C3: 59
   & linkage, C3: 59
   & *Muthos*, C3: 94
   & Mythos, C4: 84; EG: 23-24
   & Nama-rupa, C2: 16
   & phenomenon, C3: 1
   & Pleroma, Cosmic, C4: 59
   & Sin, C2: 15
   & Son of God, C4: 34
   & THE FATHER (WILL), C3: 111
   & The World, C2: 125
   & Truth, C4: 35
   & Unity, C2: 15
   Almighty Word, C3: 120
   Book of Life, C4: 91
   Christ-, C2: 9
   Christ's body, B4: 142
   "Concept", C4: 84
   divine "Word", P2: 46
   master concept, C4: 27
   NOUS-SOUN, C3: 33
   of Eternity, C2: 82
   of St John's Gospel, RS: 34
   One Cosmic Book of the, C4: 70
   onely begotten Son, C2: 27
   ordering principle, EG: 24
   Ratio of all Reality, C4: 119
   Ratio, P1: 3, 19
   Rational-Word, EG: 24
   real power, B3: 53-54
   "Reason-Word", B3: 54; EG: 23

   seamless garment (of Christ), C2: 15
   Second Person of the Holy Trinity, C3: 32
   see P2: 46
   self-opposing sentient power, C4: 27
   Supreme, C2: 108
   True knowledge of, C2: 128
   Truth, C2: 126; C4: 35
   VICTORY OF, C3: 39
   Voice, C2: 111
   Vortex-motion (formulator), C1: 106
   WHEEL OF BEING, C3: 40
   Will of God, C4: 91
   Will of, C3: 28
   Word-God, EG: 34
   Word, B3: 53; P2: 46
   WORD=VV-ord, C4: 118
Looking
   Time-Way, B2: 120
LOOSE
   light gained in play, C4: 80
Lord
   & eleusinian octave, DD: 35
   & thirteenth tone, DD: 35
   "Fear of the Lord is the beginning of
      wisdom", C2: 145
   spirit's voice, DD: 35
   the Lord said unto my lord, DD: 41
Lords
   of the earth, B4: 152
Loss
   & our freedom, B3: 75
   of awareness of the *wholeness*, B3: 60
   of consciousness, RS: 30
Lot
   & Abram, B2: 91: P1: 114
Love
   [*definition*], B1: 86, 111, 119, 132, 135;
      B3: 99; C1: iv, 7; C2: 35;
      P1: 25, 142, 153, 158; P2: 14
   -seed, B3: 34
   & Bluebeard's Last WifE (a play), C2: 67
   & Christ, P1: 143
   & Christianity, C2: 102
   & DOCTRINE of the will
      (ST AUGUSTINE), C3: 105
   & end … means, C4: 77
   & fear, P1: 97
   & Feeling, C4: 77
   & freedom, C4: 34
   & Great Law of Life, C3: 123

& hate, B2: 115; C2: 131-132; CA: 38

& integration, P2: 55

& Jesus, B2: 164: P1: 6

& Logologic, C4: 119

& one's neighbour, CA: 61

& our enemies, P2: 106

& passions, P2: 133

& Pleroma, C3: 35 & realm of absolutely
    true, B1: 114

& Taoism, C2: 103

& Truth, B4: 112

& Venus, C2: 99

act of, P2: 5

Agape / Agape-, B1: 136-141

blind, C2: 113

concreteness, (in its), C3: 59

Divine power at work, B1: 135

divine, B1: 150; B2: 160; B3: 99

embodied, CA: 95

embodied (love-seed), B3: 34

Eros / Eros-, B1: 136-139

essence of fruitful human relation,
    CA: 94-95

eternal, B1: 142

Eternity dialectic, C3: 69

for the underdog (Nietzsche), EG: 68

Fruit of God's spirit, P2: 135

God is, B1: 32, 86, 115; B3: 99; CA: 56;
    EG: 52; P1: 117; P2: 5, 121-122

God's, B1: 140; B3: 175; CA: 43; P1: 145

good motive, B1: 113

highest of all relationships, P1: 158

indefinable powers, B1: 132

infinite, P1: 153

infinite, intelligent power, B1: 132

Interest is a form of, B1: 135

is God, B3: 174; C2: 36

is the only power, C2: 132

Law of, CA: 37; P1: 25; P2: 95, 98, 131

Law of Creative, CA: 79

"lieben", B1: 7

"lost", C4: 77

"Love one another", B2: 112, 164

meanings (in English ... wide range),
    B1: 136

Ocean of, C2: 42

of God, C2: 75; P2: 5

of life, B4: 117

of Reason, CA: 86

Perfect, B4: 143; C2: 35-36; C4: 7; CA: 84;

DD: 49; P1: 97

power, B1: 86, 132; B3: 99; P1: 153

Power of the Spirit working, P2: 14

power that (works / acts / operates), B1: 86

Principle of, B2: 124

raising ... level of interaction, P1: 158

reality's "coherence" force, P1: 142

solution, the only real, B3: 40

state of being, P1: 158

"Those I love, I chasten", B1: 123

true, B4: 196

Universal law, P2: 134

universal, B2: 189; B3: 40; P2: 56

unrequited, C3: 113

will to act for the development of all beings,
    B3: 99

*will to work for the development of the best
    potentialities of being*, P1: 25

will to work for the development of the
    possibilities of being, B1: 111

work for the development of the functional
    potentialities of being, infinitely, C1: iv

working for the development of beings,
    C2: 35

working for the development of the hidden
    possibilities of all beings, B1: 119

working for the development of the
    potentialities of being(s), B1: 132; P2: 14

working for the development of the
    potentialities of non-being into
    being ..., C1: 7

Lover

The Lord thy, C1: 65

Low

frequency responses, B2: 133

Lozenge

Eternal Feminine, C3: 26

Lucifer

& assembled ones, DD: 24

& common source, DD: 23

& excess & "enough", B4: 27

& excessive power, B1: 20

& God, B1: 19-21

& infinite power, B1: 128

& Light, B1: 19-21; B4: 27

& zeal, C3: 19

beloved son, DD: 36

bright day-star, DD: 67

bright morning star, DD: 7

Bright Star of the Morning of Creation,

B4: 184
brother, DD: 16, 28
committed to the long course, DD: 48
Diabolos, the hurled-down one, DD: 30
fall of, B1: 17, 20-21
first inventor, B4: 26
first of Time's Scapegoats, B4: 27
Golgotha sacrifice, DD: 4
"Light-bearer" B1: 17; B3: 180; B4: 184
my friend, DD: 55
presumptive act, B1: 20
Satan, B1: 20; B4: 26
Satanic world, B1: 21-22
stone rejected by the builders, C4: 17
Sun of the Morning, C4: 12
willed to become brighter, B4: 6

Luciferan
Pride, B4: 26

LUDO
LU-DO Way of Play, C4: 80

Lukewarm(ness)
& indifference, CA: 54
So speaks God to the indifferent, the,
   CA: 54
"... spew thee out of my mouth" (God),
   CA: 54

Luna
& CURE & reversal of the Fall, C2: 117
& twi-light (see diagram), C4: 73
phasic reflectivity, C2: 99
see C2: 99, 117; C3: 6-7, 101, 123
(see diagram), C2: 109; C3: 7

Lunar
life of slavery, C3: 99
sacrifice, C3: 80

Lustration
of Error, C4: 80

Lux
& Fiat, C3: 3
& VOLUME OF THE SACRED LAW,
   C4: 80

M

M
& concept of "substance", C4: 97
& P, C4: 97-101
& Universal Matter, TC: 44-46
& vowel "O", C4: 98-99; DD: 19

& wisdom, DD: 19
see English gematria, C3: 19-20, 84-88

Machine(s)
-existence, B1: 67
& man, B1: 67; C4: 26; P1: 55-57
& materialistic identification, CA: 33
& our own existence, B1: 66
& The "dead", B1: 144
have no freedom, B1: 67
neither wake nor sleep, B1: 68
not a person, B1: 145
perfect, B1: 143

MADE
substance divided, DD: 28

Magazine
HERM, C2: 126

Magic
act of Will, C4: 65
key to, C4: 65
magician, C3: 129

Magical
Mary, TC: 44
PROCEDURE, C3: 126, 132
ritual, C4: 33
sincere prayer is, B3: 142

Magician(s)
& Exercises in consciousness convergence,
   C2: 63
& life-principle, C2: 92
& Pentagram symbol, C3: 81
& women, magicians and hagicians, even
   of nagicians, C2: 92
see the operant, C4: 33
way of the, C4: 20

Magna Mater
Great Mother, TC: 35
Universal Matter, TC: 35

Magnetic
electro-magnetic systems, B1: 30

Magnetism
enerhy phenomena, C3: 97

Mahavira
Jesus, Buddha, Jina, Lao Tse, Zarathustra,
   Socrates, RS: 52
origin of all beings, RS: 52

Mahapurusha
Cosmos, C2: 1

Maithuna
ceremonial sex-union, C3: 79

MA

substantial power, C4: 42

MAKE

THE Primordial Appetite, C4: 45

MakroKosmos

Tree of Life, C3: 16

Male(s)

-female bi-polarity, C4: 99

& female female, C4: 72

& female, C2: 108; C3: 33;
    C4: 93, 95-96, 100

& monocells, C4: 82

& rape, C2: 108-109

ancestors, C4: 70

elements, TC: 3

Honour, C4: 7

initiative and ideation, TC: 3

intellection-initiative, C4: 74

P component, C3: 128

rise of, C3: 80

see B2: 2, 4, 9, 12; C3: 17, 30

seriousness, C2: 108

spermid, C3: 110

Malkuth

Melekh-Tau, the crucified God-Man,
    C3: 31

Malleable

Mary, the universal ocean, TC: 45

Mammon

-diabolism, P1: 27

-mechanism, P1: 6

-mind, B4: 153

-thinking, B4: 144

-worshippers, B2: 162; B3: 30

& Kronos, C2: 75

& Rhea, C2: 75, 83

& Time, C2: 75

is finite, material evaluation, C2: 75

Rhea's son, C2: 83

son (of Rhea & Kronos), C2: 83

world of, B4: 53, 194

worship, B1: 53

worshippers of, DD: 64

your god, DD: 65

Man('s)

& absolute power, B3: 179

& Adam, C4: 96

& Agape-love, B1: 140

& ancient world, B2: 5; CA: 81

& Ark of Noah ... Structure of Truth,

B2: 51

& articulate speech, B4: 41

& consort, necessary for the development of,
    TC: 43

& Creative Evolution, B3: 14

& Crux Ansata, C3: 17; C4: 92

& Death, C3: 31, 38, 43

& discrimination, B1: 142-143

& Divine God-Man, B2: 162

& divine intelligence, B3: 15

& divine Son, B2: 158

& Emanuel, B3: 15

& ethical ideas, C4: 93

& first wrong choice, B1: 149

& God, C4: 3; CA: 11

& "Golden Age", B3: 12

& *human will,* C2: 148

& inclination-determined actions, RS: 23

& *initiative,* B3: 78

& Love of God, P1: 153

& magician, C2: 63

& material things, B2: 108-109

& Noah's Ark, B3: 134

& parable of the Talents, C2: 47

& peace, C2: 73

& polarised relations, TC: 38

& Problems of Salvation, C2: 92

& rape, C2: 108-109

& rapist, C3: 127

& reflexive self-consciousness, TC: 43

& relation with woman, TC: 43

& sense of guilt, B2: 37

& sin, B1: 106

& "Spirit", B2: 15

& state of innocence, P2: 102

& Temptation, B4: 15

& the Absolute, TC: 42-43

& the Absolute and the Prime Matter,
    TC: 38

& the Bible, B4: 195; C4: 70

& the hunt and war, B2: 11-13

& THEOSIS, C3: 96

& three basic functional possibilities, B2: 52

& time, B3: 2; C2: 76; P1: 140

& Trinity, EG: 51

& universal Truth, P2: 19

& woman, C3: 127

& world of Mammon, B4: 194

"A man cannot go to heaven without a
    wife", TC: 50

a small mirror, C4: 117
Absolute awareness, C1: 112
acceptance of … restraints, C4: 93
afraid, DD: 47
aggressive, P1: 92
alienated, C2: 92
animal instincts, P1: 147
Anchor-Man, CA: 34
and other "creatures" react, C4: 38
ANSWER to all problems, C4: 1
anti-Christ impulses in, P1: 45
appetite negated by fear, C3: 83
as a creature, B1: 130
as a mediator, P1: 128
average, C2: 80
banished from the community, CA: 81
becomes Ma(g), C2: 63
BEING OF, C3: 9
body-identified Observer, C3: 118
cannot become *infinite*, B3: 51
capacity for freedom, CA: 86
capacity for inner re-assessment, B3: 19
child of Saturn … or … of Jupiter, CA: 48
CHINESE WISE MAN, C3: 127
choice, CA: 48; P1: 8
civilised, C4: 93
Cosmic, C2: 1
Counting and keeping of records of
    behaviour patterns, C3: 91
counting process, C3: 90
covenant, B2: 21
created being, B3: 52
creativity (original), B3: 19
departure of … spiritual centre, B1: 67
devious, B1: 86-87
direction of development, P1: 146
disintegration (capacity to resist), B2: 108
does not desire the painful, C2: 66
ego - man, B3: 59
egotism, B1: 125; B3: 59
embody, B3: 52
ENLIGHTENED, C3: 94
Eternity-aware, B2: 19
evil, P1: 54
existent visible being, B1: 53
external modes of consciousness, C4: 86
fall from grace, B2: 171
Fall, B2: 164; B3: 12-16, 19, 60
Fallen, B2: 32, 160
FIELD OF SENTIENT POWER, C3: 44

finds himself married, TC: 41
first, B1: 60; B4: 165
first created … state of innocence, P2: 102
forces of the unconscious mind, P1: 108
free, B3: 77
free choice, CA: 66, 86
freedom, C3: 89
frightens himself, C2: 67
glory of, B2: 166
God-Man, Man-God, EG: 13-15
God immanent in, C1: 34
God *"repented that He had made man"*, C3: 19
God's creations, P1: 12
God's high purpose with, B2: 22
God's Spirit, DD: 41
"Good" and "Evil", C2: 66; DD: 42, 49
"He knew what was in man" (Jesus Christ),
    B3: 81
Highest Act of Will, C4: 103
his capacity for self-study, P1: 30
his "own executioner", B1: 88
his own weakness, B1: 92
"If God is dead, it is man's duty to take His
    place" (Nietzsche), CA: 11
Ill-equipped, P2: 69
Impulsive … state of "first immediacy"
    (Kierkegaard), B1: 25
Incarnate God-, C2: 74
indebtedness (forgets), B3: 56
Individuation, C3: 104
infinite debt, C2: 69
Infinite Will of the Eternal Spirit, C4: 104
inner disunity, B3: 61
intellectually well-developed, P1: 62
intelligence, B1: 10; B2: 26
is a battlefield, B1: 26
is a Noah's Ark, B3: 135
is formed of thy ground and my spirit,
    DD: 48
Jesus accepted, B3: 134
Jesus Christ is the … first, P1: 128
Jesus Christ gives us a picture … of, CA: 34
judgments, C4: 19
Justification of the works of God, C2: 100
knowledge, B1: 124
Kosmic, C3: 122
last, B4: 191
life of God (same source), C2: 57
little Beast (man, the individual), C3: 45
love-seed, sown by God, B3: 34

machine, P1: 56
material body of, C1: 18-19
materialism, B1: 29
materialistic view of the world, B3: 13
mediator, B4: 185
Mercury & Saturn & Jupiter, C4: 39
microcosmos, P2: 105
mirror & *(see diagram)*, C4: 117
modality of sentient power, DD: 69
Mystical Marriage, P1: 141
not a computer, CA: 71
not mechanically determined, C4: 3
of faith-in-spirit, B2: 84
of private purpose, B1: 88
of spirit, B3: 77-79
on the treadmill, B3: 9
one of God's actualisations, P1: 137
One of God's creations, P1: 12
opposes God's will, B1: 147
original creativity, B3: 19
original source-power (seek to know),
    B3: 122
Perfect, B3: 119-120
Phases of Development, C4: 91
phenomena cluster, C4: 107
"play the devil", C2: 75
PO-WER: POWER-MAN, C3: 50
potentiality, P1: 139
power to choose, B2: 89
precipitated by ASP, C3: 126
PRINCIPLE (P), C3: 116
purged with my (God's) fire, DD: 48
reads only one book, C4: 70
"redemption", B3: 19
reflexively self-conscious, RS: viii-ix
rich young, B4: 1, 7
sacrifices, B2: 152
search for ultimate satisfaction, C2: 140
self-alienation, B1: 53
Self-deceiving Animal, DD: 49
self-image, B2: 113
self-justification, P1: 88
self-perfecting being, B4: 25
self-possession, C4: 51
self-produced C4: 107
sheep, wolves, serpents and doves in,
    B3: 134
simplest and most valuable things, C1: 4
Six is the "number of the Beast and of
    Man", C4: 69

Snake = Man, C2: 112
special being, B4: 176
special kind of being, P1: 25
spiritual being, P1: 91
spiritually-minded, CA: 6
"still small hours of the night", TC: 41
SUFFERING, C3: 105; B4: 162
There he built a city (Enoch), B1: 9
things of the universe, C1: 83
three greatest problems, B3: 124
time-creature, C2: 75
Time's offering to, B4: 15
TRAPPED into external modes of
    consciousness, C4: 86
triple gift, B2: 88
two worlds, stands between, P1: 140
unenlightened mind of, P1: 63
Unfallen, B2: 33
unfree, B3: 77
verbalised goals, C4: 58
vessel of intelligence, B3: 135
was God's reply to, B1: 21
will of the Absolute, C4: 63
will, P1: 55
woman (pregnancy), C4: 55
world (a man's), B2: 2; C4: 82
zone of threefold action, B2: 87

Manas
Mentation, C2: 10
Mandala
3-D being, C3: 120
function, C3: 52
Manipulation
& "unconscious" mind, CA: 80
Mankind
& Art, C4: 80
& Bible, B1: 1; B3: 38
& divine Son, B2: 158-159, 161
& evolution, B1: 105
& God's plan, B2: 27
& intimate interactivity, B2: 190
& Jesus Christ (died on the cross), CA: 91
& life-story of Jesus, B4: 13
& two minds, B1: 58
& universal love, B2: 189
articulate speech, B4: 41
camouflage, C3: 62
common origin ... goal, P1: 119
diseases, C4: 10
fall of Satan and, B2: 22

Fear, CA: 84
future, B3: 119; P2: 20
great heroes of, B1: 121
hidden divinity, B4: 128
hypnotised by ideas (Nietzsche), EG: 67
incessant misrepresentation, C3: 62
is made ... of Spirit and Matter, B3: 38
lower nature, B2: 26
misused ... valuable gift, CA: 6
"Our Father" ... has a plan for, CA: 99
PROLIFIC, C3: 82
rescue ... from ... slavery, CA: 39
well-being, P1: 145

Mantra(s)
3 Ms (Mandala, Mantra, Mudra), C3: 120
Indian, B3: 142
Mantra-Yoga, B3: 142
Sound structures, C2: 62

Manual
OF POWER, C3: 123

Manure
time-manure, C2: 32

Manvantara('s)
& THE BAKER, C3: 12
ectropy, C2: 47

Many
"many are called, but few are chosen", P1: 7
people, would die for Him, B2: 162

Map
of all Time-possibilities (Eternity), B4: 96

Mark
God placed a mark upon him (Cain),
    B1: 126
"miss the mark" (sin), B1: 106

Marriage
fittingness, P1: 138
mystical, P1: 132, 135, 141
of spirit and matter, P1: 130

Married
man finds himself, TC: 41

Mare
& Mary, C2: 86
Mare, cosmic ocean, C2: 86

Mars
& CURE & reversal of the Fall, C2: 117
action tendency, C2: 99
see C2: 99, 117; C3: 6-7, 101, 123
(see diagram), C2: 109; C3: 7

Martyrs
behaviour of ...at the stake, RS: 30

Marx
& true dialectic, C4: 9

Marxism
CULTURE, C4: 58

Marxists
& atheists, C4: 115

Mary
& divine Son, B2: 161
& hunger-spirit, DD: 16
& Roman Catholic Teaching, C2: 85
M1 & M2 & M3, TC: 44-46
Magical, TC: 44
Malleable, TC: 45
Mare, (Ocean / Sea) C2: 86; TC: 44
Melancholy, TC: 44
sacrifice, B2: 161

Masculine
CONSCIOUSNESS, C3: 80
formulating process, C4: 100
"masculine-protest", TC: 35

Mascprot
semi-females, C3: 18

Mask
"Through-sounder", C2: 111

Mass
-inertia, TC: 17

Master
concept, C4: 27
Each ... willed to be its own, C2: 115
Fabricator, C2: 47
Grand Architect, C2: 47
Universal Master-tool, C2: 46

Master Fabricator
see C2: 46-47

[Master Symbol]
[the cross in the circle, interpreted],
see diagrams, C2: 142-144, 106; C3: 4, 32-33,
    48, 99, 122; C4: 17, 23, 66-67, 117-118
see C2: 46-47

Mater-ial
& mother principle, TC: 21

Material(s)
& H.Q. = Hierarchical Query *(see diagram)*,
    C3: 49
bodies, RS: 5, 42
body, B2: 109; C1: 18-19; C4: 62
elements of a living body, C1: 49
embodiment ... veiling process, TC: 39
energies, C4: 62
events, B1: 61

existence, P1: 45

expression of vibrant energy, B4: 179

incarnation, B3: 109

knowledge, B4: 173

M = the Material or Mother principle, Substance, C3: 12

man-built platform moving amongst the stars, B3: 30

(mother) principle, C4: 109

objective techniques, C4: 48

particles, CA: 4

survival, B3: 30

things, B1: 41, 65; CA: 67

things ... "anchors" for consciousness, B1: 44

universe, B1: 65

world, B1: 43, 54, 61; B4: 36, 53; C2: 95, 129; C4: 76, 98; CA: 22; P1: 39, 63, 111

Materialism

energism, B3: 36

extroversion of consciousness, B1: 30

notion of, B1: 29

pure, C1: 19

state of externalised, B1: 64

Materialist(s)

& mechanistic behaviourists, CA: 22

& Nietzsche, CA: 10

blood brother, B3: 35

Cain was a, B4: 173

world of external handleable hardware, B2: 110

Intelligent, C1: 19

man, B3; 13, 31

mind of the, B1: 11

naive, CA: 4

non-belief, B3: 35

physical survival, B3: 30

pure, B4: 43; CA: 6

schizoid behaviour, B3: 36

scientist, B3: 17, 77

unintelligent forces, B1: 12

views man as a body of reactive matter, B4: 42

Materialistic

Humanist, Rationalist, Materialistic Atheist, C2: 1

notions, B3: 35

science, B4: 42

scientist, B3: 17, 76-77

thinkers, C1: 49

world-view, B4: 2

Materiality

& spirit, B3: 109

gross, B3: 109

significance, B3: 109

Matriarch

& absolute and arbitrary power, C3: 17

Matriarchal

authority, C: 17

& patriarchal societies, TC: 11

Matriarchy

& the coward, C4: 5

overthrow of, C3: 8

Matter

& Creation, B1: 6

& energy, B1: 72; B2: 104; P1: 122; P2: 2

& forms of energy, B3: 20

& "Mind", B3: 20

& "Mystical Marriage", P1: 132

& Mother, TC: 32

& resistance, C4: 97

& spirit, B3: 76

& Universal Substance, TC: 32

Absolute, TC: 34, 42

atoms B2: 130; B3: 17

behaviour of energy, P1: 84

behaviour pattern of spirit, B4: 181

behaviour-pattern of ... power, B4: 6

bound, inertic, apparently non-sentient mass, C4: 13

cyclic behaviours of power, B1: 15

discrete parts of motion, C1: 98

ecology of spirit, B3: 71

energy-mass, C1: 19

formless, C2: 72

Great Mother, TC: 35

HORIZONTAL, C3: 86

inertia, P1: 121

letter M, C4: 97

Magna Mater, TC: 35

mere, B4: 45

mind and, B3: 20

"physicality", C4: 97

Prime, TC: 32, 43

Satanic, B1: 21

see B3: 76

slavery to inertia, C2: 123

slaves of, P2: 14

spirit-matter problem (solution of), C4: 17

"substance", C4: 97

substantial rotation within Consciousness,
  C1: 81
Time and, B1: 15; B4: 69
Time-, B1: 13-14, 21
Universal, TC: 34-35, 43
wheeling or rotation process, B1: 14
Ma-world
Mother-world, C4: 98
Maya
& Lucifer, DD: 17
cosmic allusion, RS: 19
of imagination and feeling, C2: 89
Meaning
belongs to sentience, C2: 4
civilised people, C4: 73
of words, B3: 116
teleology, C2: 55
"what is the meaning of meaning?", B1: 66
Means
& ends, C4: 85
Mechanical
brain, CA: 10
interchanges, B4: 78
laws, B1: 65; CA: 33; P2: 93, 95
level, B4: 77
reactions, B1: 113
reactivity, P2: 60
Mechanicality
see C1: 11
Mechanics
law of, P2: 94-95
Mediating
position (man), P1: 45
Mediation
& meditation, C3: 120
Mediator
man, B4: 185, P1: 128
Meditation(s)
& God's Truth, B1: 92
assimilation, C2: 62
discursive process, B1: 16
interconnections of all ideas, B3: 102
serial process, B3: 103
yogic, B3: 101
Melancholy
& frustration, RS: 50
Mary, TC: 44
Melchizedek
King of Salem, B2: 92
priest of the most high God, B2: 92

Melekh-T
Crucified King, C3: 15-16
Melekh-Tau
crucified God-Man, C3: 31
Member
community (ancient world), CA: 81
Memories / Memory
& soul, B3: 127
& vibratory motion, C4: 90
a "Golden Age", C4: 90
food-tube's, C3: 77
forms of, C4: 109
of painful diseases, CA: 80
of the people, B1: 121
pain, C4: 56
protoplasmic, B2: 176
repetitive patterns, B4: 29
self-comforting, B4: 78
suppressing unpleasant, B3: 127
Unconscious, B4: 113, 116
unpleasant pain-, B4: 105
Men
& Hysteria, TC: 13
COUNTERS, DD: 63
"dead", B3: 9
few … can long endure isolation, CA: 82
first human ancestor, B3: 33
great, B1: 121; P1: 47
great men & "chain of the prophets",
  B1: 121-122
inner & outer, C4: 11
interfunction with women, B2: 5
"men loved darkness rather than light
  because their ways are evil", P1: 107
of power and wealth, P1: 45
two kinds of, B4: 44; C4: 11
Menstruation
& Maithuna, C3: 79
& Weiberbunde, C3: 81
Menstruum
lunar sacrifice, C3: 80
Mental
breakdowns, C3: 63
condition, B1: 64
disorders, RS: 41
incapacities, P1: 113
inertia, B4: 77-78
life, CA: 73
pain, B2: 72, 73, 75
processes, C2: 57; CA: 63, 72

"space", C1: 23

Mentality
slave, EG: 82

Mentation
MANAS, C2: 10
process, B2: 13, 119
(serial thinking and ideas), C4: 50
serial, C4: 87
thinking, B2: 13; C4: 50
Time-thinkings, B3: 78

Mentational
process (The "encircling gloom" is the),
     C2: 9

Mercury
& benefit, C4: 17
& CURE & reversal of the Fall, C2: 117
& Hermes, C4: 39
& Jupiter, C2: 56, C4: 17, 38-39, 60, 69
& Manual of Power, C3: 123
& Philosopher's Stone, C4: 38
& Saturn, C2: 56, C4: 17, 38-39, 60, 69
& Saturn and Jupiter, C4: 17, 111
& Tehuti, C4: 39
& the half-sleepers, DD: 12
& trine process, C4: 38
cyclic nature of things, C2: 99
Messiah, C3: 6; C4: 39, 60
paradox of the free and the domed, C4: 60
Saturn/Jupiter/Mercury, C4: 38
see (diagrams with symbol ☿), C3: 4; C4: 118
see C2: 99, 117; C3: 6-7, 101, 123
(see diagram), C2: 109; C3: 7
Sol and, C2: 117
spin, C4: 39
state, C4: 69

Mercy
& God, C2: 17
& the righteous, DD: 29
& severity, DD: 29
act of mercy (God's creative act), B1: 4
act of mercy we do two things, C2: 49
free intelligent response, P2: 99
release C3: 91

MERIT
signifies, DD: 21
What is this MERIT?, DD: 15

Merriment
& male C2: 108-109
& rape, C2: 108-109
& seriousness, C2: 108-109

IS Female, C2: 108

Messenger
"angel", B1: 17

Messiah
-Hermes functions, C3: 8
& assembled ones, DD: 58
& embodiment, B3: 109
& Jewish boys, C4: 21
& (Mercury), C4: 39, 60
& Saturn & Jupiter, C4: 39, 60
& zone of ... conflict, C4: 111
believe (Christians & Jews), B3: 118
for all lost beings, C2: 139
heart of God, C3: 10
Master of all Dialectical Oppositions, C3: 8
Messiah–Hermes, C3: 8
True, B3: 109

Metamorphosis
of certain insects, C2: 14

Metanoia
& repentance, C4: 108
change of mind and heart, P2: 125
moment of, C4: 108
Occurs, C2: 11
re-thinking, C4: 67

Mikrohexon(s)
& HIHU, Infinite Intelligent power,
     C2: 115

Mikro-Kosmos
& Tree of Life, C3: 16

Mind(s)
& body, B3: 17; CA: 89
& "brain processes", C2: 91
& consciousness of our spiritual origin,
     B1: 64
& convergence of energy, P2: 80
& fall, C1: 87
& great flood, B2: 46
& history (period of), C3: 74
& ideas, B2: 19; B3: 66
& Imagination, B1: 43
& inside and outside worlds, C3: 119
& introspection, B3: 39
& "matter", B3: 17, 20
& nuclear missiles & risk, B2: 188
& "scientistic" education, C4: 26
& space, C1: 23
& the retina, C3: 119
& timing in the Theatre, C2: 41
& "well knit", B4: 141

& "wool gathering" & "wooly", B4: 141
19th century, C3: 74
alienated, CA: 89
anxious, CA: 50
captivated, B1: 64
child-, B4: 4
concentration of, P2: 80
condition our, CA: 53
confused, C1: 69
conscious, B1: 57-59; B2: 34
content, CA: 72
content of consciousness, C1: 25
critical, C4: 26
defensive, CA: 89
defining "mind", C2: 4
divide his mind, B1: 52
divided, B4: 105
ego-bound, B3: 7
energy, B1: 72; B3: 20
Eternal, C2: 76; CA: 51
evaluates, C2: 4
'fine', P2: 72
free our … from misinterpretations,
    B4: 193
"higher …", CA: 51
human, B2: 7, 34
ideation function, TC: 16
insulated & isolated, CA: 89
linear thinking, CA: 51
Logos-Mind, C2: 76
man's, C2: 92
master-tool, of the consciousness or self,
    C2: 46
meeting place of two worlds, CA: 72
"No Mind", C1: 23
of Cain, B1: 74
of Christ, B3: 16; CA: 51
of God, B3: 181; B4: 143, C1: 25
on guard, CA: 89
One-pointed, B4: 164
open, B3: 171
quiet, B1: 54
rationality, TC: 16
stillness of, B2: 19
Super-focussing, P2: 73
Time, C2: 76; CA: 51
two, C4: 8
unconscious, B1: 57; B2: 46, 75, 178;
    B3: 136; B4: 63; 116; CA: 74-75;
    P1: 93, 103

unenlightened, P1: 63
wake up & risk, B2: 188
Mindless
& Matter, P1: 121
Mineral
compacted centre of intellectual pride?,
    C1: 104
intelligence, C1: 104
Minerality
Satanic condition, B1: 21
MIPO
& PIMO, C4: 99
Miracle
breaking of the law of matter, C1: 70
Mirror
& attention of the observer, C4: 117
& Man, C4: 117
& reflection / reflexion, C4: 117
set before you, DD: 11
Misery
& unhappiness, EG: 60
Misinterpretations
free our mind from, B4: 193
Mis-representation
necessities of survival, DD: 1
Mistake(s)
& evolutionary plan, B3: 4
"deliberate", B3: 90
ego, C4: 24
inevitable, B3: 96
Mithraic
lodges, C3: 17
Mob
Mentality, EG: 72
mob-man, EG: 72
Modalising(s)
Continuum, C4: 76
Modalities
& phenomena, C4: 106
& totality of phenomena of all worlds,
    C1: 25
of a continuum of power, C2: 93
of God, C3: 75
of the motion, C1: 25
of the ASP, C2: 53
of the sixth principle, B3: 78
parts are, C4: 9
Model
the embodied God, B3: 52

Moment(s)
  & spirit of man, B3: 79
  Jupiter-, C4: 69
  now-, B3: 79
  of our life, CA: 37
  re-posit his awareness, B3: 79
  Saturn-, C4: 64, 68-69
Money
  Changers, P1: 100
Monism
  & Non-dualism, C2: 68, 101
  & RIGOROUS LOGIC DENIES, C3: 25
  an attempt to grasp ... that which is
    unknowable, C2: 101
  implies circumscription, C2: 101
Monocell(s)
  -consciousness, C3: 18
  & aggressive initiative or
    quicker reflexes, C3: 110
  & INTIMATE RELATIONSHIP, C3: 18
  & self-balancing reaction, C3: 62
  & solar energy, C3: 109
  spermiform, C4: 82
Monsters
  & unenlightened beholders, CA: 8
Moon('s)
  & cyclic changes, C3: 111
  & protoplasm, C3: 67
  moon-pull tides, C4: 82
  Pitriyana (moon-path), C2: 77; C4: 81
  swear not by the inconstant moon, C3: 7
Moon-worshippers
  oovids, C3: 110
Moral
  position & sacrifice, B2: 136
Morality
  collection of rules, B3: 94
  new, EG: 65
  "slave morality", EG: 82-83
Mortal
  & immortality, B3: 126
Moses
  Tau (& The Anchor), C2: 65
Mot
  "Parole", EG: 24
  "word", EG: 24
Mother
  & Father & forms, TC: 35-36
  & Father Principle, TC: 36
  & Holy Spirit, C4: 109

  & polarity, TC: 32
  & substantialisation, TC: 35
  & Trinity, *(see diagram)*, C4: 108-109
  Cosmic, C4: 109
  Infinite Sentient Power, C4: 108
  Magna Mater, TC: 35
  material, C4: 109
  (of) Invention, C2: 135
  Prime Matter, TC: 32, 36
  Sophia, Cosmic Wisdom, C4: 110
  substance, C3: 5
  suitable, B2: 160
  total cosmic information, C4: 110
  Universal Matter, TC: 34-35
Mother-god
  & gynocrats, C4: 99
Motion
  -pattern(s), C1: 41-42
  & "Solid God", EG: 9
  & field, C1: 41
  & Infinite Continuum, C2: 62
  & matter, C1: 98
  ENERGY IS FIELD MOTION, C3: 97
  quality of the, C1: 74
  spherical, B1: 46
  THREE KINDS, C3: 75
  translating and rotatory, RS: 13
  Uninterrupted ... IS Light, C1: 86
  vibratory, C3: 57; C4: 90
Motivation
  & our deepest problems, B3: 28
  deepest, CA: 37
  in human beings, P2: 66
  innermost, P2: 121
Motivational
  Research, RS: 17
Motive(s)
  & ATOM-MOTA, C4: 63
  & Lucifer, B4: 62
  & ordinary man, C2: 36
  & our deepest problems, B3: 28
  & phenomenon, B4: 59
  acquired, B1: 111
  act of choice, B4: 61
  bad, B1: 112-113
  basic, B1: 110-111; B3: 28
  God's, P1: 142
  good, B1: 113
  hidden, B4: 63; P1: 107-108

Mountain
& problem of Reality, C3: 107

Mouth
"I will come and fight against them with the
sword of my mouth" (Christ), P1: 44

Movement
appearance of, B4: 103

Mudra
3 Ms, C3: 120

Muhammad
see C2: 100, 105

Murder
& prisoner in the dock, C1: 71
& *TO kill*, C1: 71

Murderer
see B1: 126-127

Music
& child, B2: 56-57
Music of the Past, C2: 94
"the type of the arts", B4: 108

Musicians
& sacrifice & training, CA: 92

Muslim(s)
& hidden mystery, B2: 155
& *unity of being*, C2: 101
La ilaha illa llah, C4: 120

My
"I", B4: 182

Mysterious
power, B3: 48-49
presence, B3: 48
somewhat ("God"), B3: 141
Will, B4: 61

Mystery(ies)
& Mithraic male lodges, C3: 17
fall, B2: 35
Great, B2: 169
hidden (God), B2: 155
Intelligence is a, B3: 124
of mysteries, B3: 54
of the seed, C4: 62

Mystical
Marriage, P1: 130, 132, 135, 139, 140, 141
Meaning, B3: 135

Mystics
"God needs me as much as I need Him",
EG: 8

Myth(s)
ancient world, C1: 5
MUTHOS, C3: 94

Mythos
& "Concept", C4: 84
& Logos, C3: 94; C4: 84; RS: 53; EG: 23-24

N

N
see English gematria, C3: 19-20, 84-88

Naga
-snake, C3: 51

Nagician
& basic life-principle, C2: 92
& (function), C2: 92
& women, magicians and hagicians, even of
nagicians, C2: 92

Nakedness
Noah & covering, B2: 28, 32

Nama
formative sound, C3: 118

Nama-rupa
(Name-form), C2: 16, 43, 53
inseparable double term, C2: 16

Name(s)
"Jesus" means, B2: 170
& Form, C2: 16
& image, B2: 43
& Man's intelligence, B2: 26
& *naming*, C2: 60
& *power*, B2: 27
& the last man, B4: 191
& three sons (Noah's), B1: 100; B2: 25, 26
attached to ideas, C3: 3
bad, B1: 108-113
bring order into the world, B1: 101
Divine C2: 99
giving of, B2: 42
"Good ..." (Shakespeare), B1: 107, 110;
B2: 100
Hebrew, B2: 25
of persons ... meanings (Bible), B4: 189
original (hexonic), C2: 17
"Shem function", B2: 42
structuralising agent, C2: 16
verbalisation, C2: 59-60

Naming
function (Shem), B2: 43
Revocalisation, B2: 42-43
see B2: 42-43; C2: 16-17

Narcissus
& Choice ... meaningless, TC: 16
Narrow
path, B4: 129
way, P2: 52-57, 68, 73
Nations
& Abraham, B2: 94
& external war, B1: 38
Natural
world, B3: 73
Nature
& "Na" and "Tura", C2: 101
& the pantheist, C1: 31
conceived of as the zone of being, C1: 33
God Creative in, C1: 34
is in God, C1: 34
of God, B2: 169
people of good, P1: 54
TO THE ELIZABETHANS, C3: 75
Nauta
SAILOR, C3: 130
Nay
& Yea, DD: 30
Nazarene
"Who has seen me has seen the Father",
    B4: 111
Nearer
signifies not *Greater*, DD: 20
Need(ing)
& Eros, B1: 137
& mystics, EG: 8
Negate
is to say "No", B3: 144
Negation(s)
AFFIRMATION OF ALL, DD: 71
"thing", C4: 103
Negative
& Expectancy, C4: 79
& the Balance place between blood and
    nerve, C4: 74
& Sushumna (Twilight), C4: 74
and positive, C4: 74
feeling, B3: 144
Neighbour
"love one's ...", CA: 61
Nerve
& blood, C4: 74
Nervous
energy, B4: 116
system, B1: 39

Neurosis(es)
& disorder in man, B2: 54
& stress disorders, B3: 61
cellular, EG: 15
New
"A new commandment I give unto you
    ..." (Jesus), P1: 6
Jerusalem, C2: 139
Nexus
& particles, EG: 32
Nietzsche('s)
('s) answer, CA: 12
& "beyond man", EG: 83
& Eternal Recurrence, RS: 38
& fear, EG: 82
& *Genealogy of Morals*, C2: 128
& Greek philosophers, C4: 31
& Jewish Redeemer, EG: 69
& Superman, EG: 83
& Ubermensch, C2: 128; EG: 83
Answer, CA: 12
"God is dead", C2: 128; CA: 11
God Is Not Dead (EH), EG: 62
"God is not dead [*first line - error: should read
    "God is dead". Ed.*], EG: 62
see CA: 10-12
slave, EG: 82-83
terrible dilemma, EG: 96
"The snake will one day coil affectionately
    around the eagle's neck" (Nietzsche),
    C3: 117
"the will to power", C1: iii
"What joy ... if you had not me to shine
    for", P1: 116-117
Night
-hungers, DD: 18
& "light", B4: 154
negation of power, DD: 9
"Work while it is light, for the night comes
    when no man can work" (Jesus), B4: 154
Nightmare(s)
& our body-object, C1: 61
ride by and befrighten, DD: 18
riding, DD: 10
see C1: 61; DD: 10, 18
Nirguna
Brahman, C1: 81
No
Great Rota, DD: 11
Satanic spirit, B4: 186

"Yes", B4:186

Noah
-principle, B1: 105
& Ark, B2: 48; B3: 134-135
& concealment & veil, B2: 28, 32
& covering ... nakedness, B2: 28, 32
& intelligence, B1: 94, 99, 103, 105;
    B2: 28, 30, 32, 38, 41, 48-50
& noetic principle, C3: 34
& the Flood, B2: 46
drunk, B1: 103; B2: 28, 49
"drunk with the Spirit", B2: 41
grace, B2: 25
modern, & nuclear war, B2: 31
three sons, B1: 100; B2: 25, 31, 48, 54, 59

Noetic
family, B2: 48
principle or Nous, B3: 135
principle, C3: 34

No Mind
Buddhist doctrine, C1: 23

Non-accident
& accident, C2: 1-2
(rationally determined capacity for
    self-evolution ..."), C2: 1-2

Non-being
& "Being", B2: 67
beyond all binding contours, C1: 28

Non-communication
is death, CA: 91-92

Non-dual
infinite continuum, C4: 57
polarisation C3: 76, 128
reality, C3: 23, 35
the non-dual Real, C2: 82
ultimate reality, C4: 100
view of the origin of the universe, B3: 58

Non-dualism
& Monism, C2: 68, 101
Advaita, C2: 68
Non-pluralism, C2: 101

Non-existence
incomprehensibility does not mean, P1: 126

Non-intelligence
Absolute, B1: 12

Non-materiality
& of the reflexive Self, RS: 40

Non-rational
& AN, C4: 1
female, C4: 92-93

sensuous ... aspect, C4: 1

Non-reason
& Reason, C2: 87

Non-reflexive
thinking is dangerous, B3: 65

Non-rotating
motion, RS: 6

Non-Self
& night, B1: 68

Non-serial
simultaneity of power ("Eternity"), B1: 16

Non-words
"Nothing", C2: 22
pseudo-words, C2: 22

North
Pole, C3: 33

NOS-SON
intelligent child of infinity, C3: 33

No-thing
& beginning, DD: 8
& little self, B2: 67-69
& Spirit, C4: 32
= "not-a-negative" = "pure positivity" =
    infinite power, C2: 22
God was that, DD: 8

Nothingness
& infinite sentient power, C4: 103
& True Self, B2: 68
Alphatheos, C4: 57
fear of, B4: 69

Noumena
& phenomena, C3: 95; EG: 11

Noumenal
world (Plato), C3: 97

Nous
Noetic principle, B1: 97; B3: 135; C3: 34

NOUS-SOUN
God's voice, C3: 33

Now
& repentance, B2: 191
great ... Eternity, B1: 125
Heaven, C4: 103
"Here-Now", CA: 47
Infinite & Eternal, CA: 45, 47
moment of initiative, C4: 16
N - VVV, C4: 16
of God, CA: 47

Now-moment
initiative, B3: 79

Nuclear
-threatened world, B3: 53
& Cain, B1: 129
& matter is … energy, B2: 70; B3: 17
& minds … wake up, B2: 188
& Noah, modern, B2: 31
& radio-active materials, B3: 69
bombs, B4: 87
E=Mc2, B4: 87
fear of … war, B2: 34; B3: 144
fission & power & matter, B4: 6
forces & planetary system, B3: 178
Hiroshima and Nagasaki, B4: 87
inter-neuronic battle, B3: 40
inter-stellar nuclear warfare possibilities,
    B3: 111
missiles, B2: 188
 "Nuclear Free Zone", B2: 188
power, B1: 129
processes, B3: 69
research, B3: 17
risk, everyone at, B2: 188
submarines, B1: 129
War, B2: 187
war, fear of, B2: 34; B3: 144
war, threat of, B2: 187-188, B3: 40
war, world-wide, B2: 31
warhead & "trigger" situations, B3: 178
weapons, B2: 70, P1: 116; P2: 73
Nucleus
& spirit-field, C4: 36
Number(s)
& Pythagoras, C4: 31
& the assembled ones, DD: 20
Nut
& Geb, C4: 37
"Nut-case", C4: 37
The Goddess, C4: 37
the lock of, DD: 9
Nux vomica
first "Nut-case", C4: 37
megalo-cosmic primary condensation,
    C4: 37

Omega and Omicron, C4: 28, 118
ORIGINAL VOID, C3: 103
Sacred Place, C3: 122
see English gematria, C3: 19-20, 84-88
total field, C4: 30
Obedience
simple, P2: 103
to cosmic law, B4: 100
to the rules laid down by the Mark Man),
    C3: 83
to the Trinity Law, C3: 92
Object(s)
-identification, RS: 28
& consciousness, B4: 171
& content of consciousness, C1: 97
& creative power, B4: 174
& feeling, C1: 39
& goal, C4: 85
& Observation, C3: 89
& widdershins cycle, C3: 112
body-, C1: 60
centre of reference, C1: 59
forces, C1: 58
form, C1: 53
forms of motion, C1: 40
located sphere of energy, C3: 61
of consciousness, RS: 4
receives this action, C1: 56
subject-, C1: 85
zones of turbulence, C1: 84
Objectivation
& alienation of the self, C4: 52
Objective
& "things", B2: 155
& unfulfilled purposes, CA: 76
fear, CA: 2
God-worshippers, EG: 31
god, EG: 29
Observer(s)
& reflexion, C4: 117
& watcher, RS: 15
body-identified, C3: 118
Eye-ness, C3: 43
Eye-Time-God = Divine Incarnate, C3: 13
I-ness, C3: 43
Great Cosmic, B4: 166-167
knows only the modifications of the, RS: 3
IS NOT THE OBSERVED, RS: 1
two kinds of, B3: 177-178

O

O
A E I O U, *(see diagrams)*, C4: 30
Absolute centre of Wunder-Auge, C3: 112

Observers-for-God
& ecologists, B3: 178
see infinities of interrelating powers, B3: 177
Observing self
& consciousness, RS: 14
Occidental
"oriental", C2: 54
Ocean(s)
& the universe, C4: 116
& woman, C4: 92
appetival, C4: 92
infinite life-, B4: 81
Mare, the cosmic, C2: 86
of light, C1: 86
of sentient power, C2: 93
Reality, C4: 120
within oceans, C2: 118
OI
"reduction of power", C3: 104
Olfactory
mating stimuli, C3: 78
Olive
Branch, P2: 49, 51
Olympic
athlete, B2: 107
OM
sacred syllable, C4: 98
Omega
-Substance, B3: 6
& Omicron, C4: 28, 118
Alpha-, B3: 5
Alpha-Light-Omega-Body of God, B3: 6
Alpha-theos, C4: 56
Omicron
& Omega, C4: 28, 118
Omnipotence
cannot cease to be, EG: 1
Omnipotent
God is, EG: 1
Omni-present
God is, EG; 1; P1: 159
Omniscience
God's, C2: 73
One
-pointed Mind, B4: 164
& The Good Fight, B1: 34
Cosmic Law, C4: 70
Cosmic Book of the Logos, C4: 70
god, DD: 57
Man, the Divine God-Man, B2: 162

original human blood, B2: 176
Supreme Power Source, B2: 189
Supreme Source, B4: 111
turn ("Universe"), B1: 46
"Two walk better than one" (Paul), TC: 41
Universal Energy, B4: 80
worthwhile object of worship, B3: 43
Onely
-Begotten Son, P1: 82
Oneness
& Christ, P2: 96
& harmony with whole creation, P2: 105
greatest principle, B2: 124
of Eternal Being, B1: 21
One-pointed Mind, B4: 164
Only, B4: 146
power and intelligence, B3: 62
sense of, CA: 41
True, B2: 108
Unity, P1: 27
One-pointed
Mind, B4: 164
Oovids
moon-worshippers, C3: 110
Opacity
& spiritual health, B3: 136
Opening
strange power, B4: 40
Opinions
& self-definitions, B4: 5
Opposite(s)
& type-figures, B1: 79
mutually defining, C4: 9
pairs of, B1: 51; P1: 46
polar, C4: 119
TRUE DIALECTIC, C4: 9
Opposition(s)
between Pneuma and Soma, C4: 112
contradiction, C4: 110
Master of all Dialectical (Messiah), C3: 8
means of discovery, DD: 71
of Saturn and Jupiter, C4: 39
"Opposition is true friendship" (Blake),
    C4: 120; DD: 1
Psyche solves, C4: 112
to God's will, B1: 147
Oppugnancy
Energy of Conflict, C3: 6
opposes the intention of the Divine Love,
    C3: 6

Optimum
Unique ... in any field of action or theory
    would mean, C3: 67

Oracle
& *orientation of one's will*, C3: 129
Delphic, B3: 37

Orbit(s)
& chaos, EG: 25
& planets, B3: 169

Order
& Chaos, C4: 29
& Logos: Word = VV-ord, C4: 118
& phenomena, B4: 58
& things, B3: 169
cyclic presentation, C1: 85
degree of, B1: 38
Divine, C2: 98
forces of, B3: 118
maintains, B1: 38
new (Satanic world), B1: 21
ordering force, EG: 25
ordering principle, EG: 24
original, B2: 55
Principle of, B1: 39
rescues us, B3: 117
systems of (inside our bodies), B1: 37
work, B1: 123

Ordinary
thought, C4: 26

Organic
being(s), C4: 64, 86
body, living, C1: 18
compounds, C1: 52
control, C4: 26
existence, P2: 127
form, C3: 24
inter-relationships, P2: 42
processes, C4: 18, 25, 87
self-control, C4: 25
substances, C2: 84

Organise
& goal, B1: 123

Organising
intelligence, C4: 61

Organisation
function of life (body's), C1: 48
is a necessity, P1: 118

Organism(s)
finite, C3: 41
human, B4: 5

our, B4: 6; P1: 106

Organ(s)
"brother", B2: 2-4
co-operate, B2: 3
outer sense-, B2: 131
special sense-, B2: 131; B4: 130

Oriental
"occidental", C2: 54

Orientation
& ORACLES, C3: 129
act of will, C2: 140
Expectancy, C4: 79

Origin
& final goal, C3: 34
& Spiritually minded human beings, CA: 5
& THEOSIS, C3: 96
common, CA: 41; P1: 115, 119
cosmic, B3: 122
divine, B4: 25, 47, 111
embodied in us, B4: 111
of all things, C1: 93
of evil, P1: 28
of sin, C4: 53
one, B2: 189
spirit-, C1: 89

Original
anxiety, CA: 16
Cause, C4: 85
perfection, CA: 65
Sin, B2: 77; CA: 85
unity, P1: 115

Originating
Energy, P1: 125

Oscillation
doubleness of nature, B1: 93
MOTION, C3: 75

OTHER: OT
wheel of power, C3: 4

OTHERNESS
OF THE ABSOLUTE, C3: 67

Our Father
& Sanity, C2: 64

Outer
& inner world, B1: 72; B2: 116, 131
"Effect" really means "outer fact", C1: 44
men, C4: 11
physical system, C4: 86
responsibilities, C4: 25
world, B1: 39, 72; B2: 24, 116, 131;
    B1: 72; B4: 8

Outshining
  Lucifer, B1: 17-18
Outside
  the infinite field of sentient power, C1: 44
  of things, B1: 31
Overseer
  "bishop", B2: 6
Over-view
  Eternal-Way, B2: 123
Oviforms
  & moon-flux, C4: 82
Ovo
  Omne vivo ab ovo, TC: 6
Ovum
  close to original life form, TC: 6
  egg, CA: 29; TC: 6
  Omne vivo ab ovo, TC: 6
  primary centre of reference (fertilised),
    C4: 104
  sphere of protoplasm, CA: 29
Owe
  & "own", B2: 141; B4: 54
  & source power, B2: 141; B4: 54
Owl
  BAKER'S daughter, C3: 12
Own
  "owed" to the infinite power, B4: 54
  see B2: 141

P

P
  & I, C4: 98
  & (positing) function, C4: 101
  & related vowel "I", C4: 98
  & SP function C3: 128
  see English gematria, C3: 19-20, 84-88
  unvoiced letter, C4: 97
Pain(s)
  -avoiding, B4: 114
  & avoidance, B2: 65
  & "eye" (Ayin), C3: 105
  & experience-records, B4: 117
  & fear of, B4: 120
  & fear, B2: 71; CA: 39
  & His (God) freedom, C3: 89
  & many levels of existence, B4: 34
  & memory(ies), B4: 78, 120
  & ORIGINAL APPETITE, C3: 36

& our own imperfections, B2: 102
& our will, CA: 41
& pleasure, B1: 25, 114; B2: 65, 89; B3: 92;
    B4: 105, 113-114, 123; C3: 105, 123;
    C4: 2; CA: 7, 8, 20, 40, 67; P2: 17,
    20, 23; RS: 16, 17
& rational aspect (WER), C4: 2
& response-capacity, B3: 93
& Saturn-moments, C4: 69
& self-awareness, C3: 89, 105
& sensuous life, C4: 56
& stimulus-assimilation capacity, RS: 17
& the Absolute, C1: 76
& the soul, CA: 101
& truth, B2: 75
avoidance of, RS: 16
creational, C3: 89
dislike, B2: 71
excess, C4: 48
EXPERIENCED BY GOD, C3: 89
impedes circulation, B4: 123
impedes the free flow of blood, B3: 170
life-protective, CA: 39
mental, B2: 72-73, 75
no-saying, DD: 44
painful situations, C2: 112; C3: 90
"phantom limb", B4: 123
pleasure-pain problem, P2: 23
physical, B2: 72-73
refusal of experience, B4: 122
Remembered, B4: 121
repressed, C4: 47
spur to self-examination, C2: 95
Unhappiness, misery, ..., suffering, EG: 60
we can block, B4: 122
Painters
  & interrelatedness ... significance, C4: 113
Pairs
  of opposites, B1: 51; P1: 46
PaMa GOD
  Hebrew ... Tetragrammaton, C4: 95
Pantheism
  see EG: 5
Pantheist
  see C1: 25, 31
Pantherion
  Jesus, B3: 134
Papyrus
  & RUS, C3: 117

Parabrahman
see C4: 52; RS: 46
Parable(s)
of the talents, P1: 8
waken our consciousness, B1: 36
Parachuter
free-fall, B3: 132
Paraclete
& Islam, C2: 10
Paracosmic Will
"God the Father", C2: 147
Paradigm
Jesus Christ, C4: 35
man crucified, B4: 110
Paradise(s)
means, C2: 88
two (the Quran), C2: 87
Paradox
& "dialectic", P2: 56
Non-dualism (Advaita), C2: 68
Supreme, C4: 32
Para Hexon
Ecclesia, C3: 45
Ekklesia, C3: 32
Parahexonic
(divine) level, C2: 44
Parapara
= Beyond the Beyond = The Incarnate
Infinite, C4: 52
Parents
& autistic children, C4: 72
& laws of heredity, B1: 23
Parmenides
& The One Alone exists, C4: 31
Parole
idea of rationality, EG: 24
"mot", EG: 24
"word", EG: 24
Parontic
sentient power, C2: 60
Parontos
beyond Being, C2: 60
Particle(s)
& atomism, C2: 4
& The Supreme Power, B1: 32
& unconscious mind, B1: 60
assumed, B1: 60
functions of, force, EG: 32
non-sentient, C2: 4
seed, B1: 31

ultimate, B1: 60
Particular
God ... focus ... thing, CA: 45
Partless
continuum, B1: 32, 60; C2: 93; C4: 78
ocean of sentient power, C2: 93
Supreme Spirit, EG: 4
Parts
& atom, B1: 60
& pattern, CA: 77-78
& Reality, B4: 129
& the Narrow Path, B4: 130
"integrate", B4: 130
modalities, C4: 9
phenomena, C4: 75-76
relation ... to a whole, CA: 77
Passive
& INNER FEELING, C3: 92
mode, C2: 11
pleasure reception, B2: 127
Passivity
& metanoia, C2: 11
& slavery, B4: 161
yogi ... free himself from, C4: 87
Past
& determinists, C2: 148
& present, C2: 148
Path
hard and narrow, B4: 129
of true self-development, B1: 85
Suryayana and Pitryana (sun-path &
moon-path), C2: 77; C4: 81
Patience
infinite, B3: 45
Patient
"agent", C2: 52
"disease", C2: 52
Patriarchal
& matriarchal societies, TC: 11
Pattern(s)
-comprehending mind, CA: 51
-makers, C2: 115
& God's mind, B3: 183
& HiHu, Infinite Intelligent Power, C2: 115
action, C4: 86
comprehension, C4: 91
essence of, CA: 77-78
Eternal, C2: 33
infinite, CA: 70
infinity of, C1: 46

of life, CA: 77
of Reality, B3: 183
of Truths, P1: 64
telic, C4: 85
total, C4: 48
underlying ... off anxiety, CA: 77
value-stressed, C1: 39

Paul
pleroma, C4: 99
see also St. Paul
"Two walk better than one" (Paul), TC: 41

Pay
the price of what I will, C4: 6

Peace
& Christ, C2: 73
& universal love, B3: 40
Inner wholeness, B3: 40
of mind, P1: 64
"peace that passes understanding", C2: 33

Pearl
inside us, C3: 74
Process, C2: 6

Penis
developed clitoris, C3: 80

Penny
drop, C4: 42

Pentacle
feminine, C3: 80
(see diagram), C3: 81; C4: 30, 32-33

Pentagram
magical ritual, C4: 33
see diagrams, C3: 81; C4: 30, 32-33
symbol, C3: 81

People(s)
& one language, B2: 54
& lost faith, CA: 22
& mental "darkness", B2: 98
nearly saved, CA: 22
of all nations, B2: 54
of good nature, P1: 54
view themselves ... as machines, CA: 22

Percept(s)
act of perception, RS: 44
& concept(s), C2: 114; RS: 44

Perceptions
Gross, C4: 76

Perfect
freedom, B3: 101
"His worship is perfect freedom", C4: 34-35
internal harmony, B2: 101

love, C2: 35; CA: 86; DD: 49; P1: 97
machine, B1: 143
man, B2: 103; B3: 119-120

Perfection
& the fall, B3: 68
"Be ye perfect, even as your Father in
        heaven is perfect", P1: 23
final destiny, B2: 102
of God, CA: 55, 65
pre-fection, C4: 51; CA: 70

Perfumes
& TANTRISTS, C3: 79

Periphery
non-dual infinite continuum, C4: 57

Persistence
Rotation is the cause of, EG: 6
"Law of the Persistence of Error", C4: 69
of symptoms, C4: 79

Person(s)
& infinite intelligent power, B3: 175
& machine, B1: 143, 145
& source power of the universe, C4: 115
& things, C1: 96
response-able, P2: 113

Persona
"mask", C2: 111
"Through-sounder", C2: 111

Personal
Gethsemane, B4: 117
God, B1: 11
individual integration (post-analytic), C3: 35
universal power, B1: 7

Personality
& Mystery of Christianity, C2: 111
individual, P2: 70

Persuasion
name "Japhet", B1: 107

Phallopolemics
useless ...; *(see diagram)*, C4: 16

Phallos
Is born, C3: 36

Phallos-Pharos
Light of the World, C3: 33

Phantasy
of separativity, RS: 35

Phantom
limb, B4: 123

Pharisees
& Christ's Truth, P1: 60
& Scribes, P1: 61

PHASES
OF DEVELOPMENT OF MAN, C4: 91
Phenomenon(a)
-complex, C4: 107
& Absolute Sentient power (ASP),
C3: 124-125
& act of will, C2: 63
& consciousness, B4: 57
& continuum, C2: 93; C3: 2
& Divine Lila, C3: 95
& intelligent persons, B4: 60
& Logos, C3: 1
& Maya, C2: 89
& resistance, C1: 103
& will, C3: 21
eternal noumenal, EG: 11
external, B4: 59
field-force, C3: 98
intensification of an eternal function, EG: 10
Logos verbalisation, C4: 119
"modalisings" of the continuum, C4: 75-76
modalities (of God), C3: 75
modalities of consciousness, C1: 85
of rest, C3: 61
of suggestion (auto- or hetero-), C4: 25
"schizophrenic", C2: 58
Self-created, Self-initiated, Self-determined,
C4: 106
universal, C4: 112
Phenomenology
see ORIGINAL APPETITE, C3: 36-37
Pheromones
ECMs (external chemical messengers),
C3: 78
Philogeny
& Biogeny, C2: 127; C4: 84
Philosopher(s)
biassed, B1: 144
DOUBT, C1: 98
FORKED-TONGUES, DD: 62
Greek, C4: 31; RS: 4
Greek & Nietzsche, C4: 31
in Ancient Greece, C2: 87
pattern of local self-intensification, EG: 11
Solid God, EG: 11
Philosopher's stone
& Elixir of Life, C4: 38
& Saturn/Jupiter/Mercury, C4: 38
Stone, C4: 38

Philosophy
& attempt to define things, C1: 83
& centred consciousness, C2: 138
chief problem of, C1: 105
Christian, P1: 1; P2: 85
of Divine *Will*, P1: 47
science and art, C4: 87
Physical
activities, B1: 76
body, B1: 26, 30, 61, 72-73; C3: 99; C4: 76
CA: 4, 9, 26, 64, 67; P1: 38; P2: 1, 28
contact, C4: 76
continuance, B1: 41
experiments B1: 74
existence, B1: 41
force, CA: 7
laws, B1: 29
mental, B2: 72, 73, 75
pain & mental pain, B2: 73
pain (At the physical level), C2: 95
pain (fear of), B2: 71
pain (which has a limit) B2: 73
physical, B2: 71, 73; C2: 95
processes, CA: 63
sense organs, B1: 74
survival, B3: 30
world, B1: 40; B3: 30
Physicality
& resistance, C4: 97
"matter", C4: 97
outermost expression of spirit, B3: 109
resistance, C4: 97
"substance", C4: 97
Pillar
& Tree of Life, C4: 71
PIMO
& MIPO, C4: 99
joint principle of male-femaleness, C4: 99
Pingala
& THREE PHASES: PUSH, PULL,
BALANCE, C3: 30
Pisces
[*Zodiac sign*] *see* C3: 114
emotional expression, C3: 114
Pitriyana
& reincarnation, C2: 77
& Suryayana, C2: 77; C4: 81
Pity
-for-others, EG: 68
"Beware of pity" (Nietzsche), EG: 68

Self-, EG: 68
Place
  & space, C1: 98
  circumscription of a zone, C1: 78
Plan
  Cosmic, P1: 99
  God, CA: 24, 99
  God's, B4: 97
  the Great, B1: 16
Plane(s)
  & Yod, C3: 29
  2-D, C3: 98
  FOUR, C3: 99
  of being, C3: 82
[Planetary symbols]
  [*interpretations*], *see diagrams*, C2: 109;
    C3: 4, 6-7, 49, 80-81, 99, 101, 123;
    48-49, 122; C4: 73
Planets
  seven C3: 101
(Planets, their functions)
  see C2: 99, 117; C3: 6-7, 101, 123
  (see diagram), C2: 109; C3: 7
Plants
  & principle of self-development, B4: 40
  "self", B4: 40
Plato
  & "Eros", B1: 137
  noumenal world, C3: 97
Play
  & culture, C4: 58
  LUDO or LU-DO, the Way of, C4: 80
Pleasure(s)
  -preferring, B4: 114
  -world, P2: 57
  & desire, B2: 125
  & pain, B1: 25, 114; B2: 65, 89; B3: 92, 170;
    B4: 105, 113-114, 123; C3: 105, 123;
    C4: 2; CA: 7, 8, 20, 21, 40, 67; P2: 17, 20,
    23; RS: 16, 17
  bait, CA: 9
  good functioning, P2: 12
  "joyfulness", B2: 126
  non-rational sensuous satisfaction-seeking
    aspect (AN), C4: 1
  not the purpose of life, P2: 12
  Passive reception, B2: 126
  pleasure-pain problem, P2: 23
  Saturn-moments, C4: 69
  see P2: 12

sensuous life, C4: 56
water-body, CA: 30
Pleroma
  & jijimuge, C3: 59
  & language, C3: 59
  & Logos, C3: 59
  Body of Christ, C4: 63
  Cosmic, C3: 59
  universal love, C3: 35
Plotinus
  Can things in time be causes?, C1: 94
  "take the flight of the alone to the alone,"
    B1: 131
Pluralisation
  man ... suffering, B4: 162
Pluralism
  RIGOROUS LOGIC DENIES, C3: 25
Plurality
  & One-pointed Mind, B4: 164
  at the periphery of being, B4: 162
Pneuma
  -somatic, C3: 25
  & psyche, C2: 87
  & Soma, C4: 112
  & two paradises (Quran), C2: 87
PO
  -WER, C3: 50
Poet(s)
  & forms of being, C4: 113
  & sonic structures of vowel and consonant,
    C4: 113
  maker, C2: 20
Poetry
  Archetypal (hexonic), C2: 5
  is dangerous, C2: 5-6
Point
  & "PLANES" OF BEING, C3: 99
  "concentrate", C2: 142
  Yod, C3: 28
Poisons
  & excess materials, C4: 77
Polarisation
  & H.Q. = Hierarchical Query, C3: 49
  law of, TC: 13
  life forms, TC: 9
  non-dual, C3: 128
  of spirit(S), C4: 1
  relational differences, TC: 8
  self-opposition, C4: 96
  "Sex", B2: 46

Polarised
    mode of reproduction (polarised & non-polarised), TC: 4
    pre-polarised state of energy, C4: 74

Polarity
    non-dual ultimate reality, C4: 100
    of Absolute Power & Universal Mother, TC: 32
    of Father and Mother, TC: 32
    of the sexes, TC: 32
    original, TC: 32

Pollution
    & science & technology & economics, B1: 100

Position
    & social hierarchy, B3: 26

Positive
    & Expectancy, C4: 79
    & Sushumna (Twilight), C4: 74
    and negative, C4: 74
    thinking, B2: 105

Positivity
    & pattern of events, B3: 144

Possibility
    error, CA: 86

Potential(s)
    hidden actuals, C2: 13
    of divine sonship, B3: 24

Potentiality(ies)
    & eternal power of God, B1: 3
    & Love, C1: 7
    of non-being, C1: 7

Potentised
    Homoeopathy remedies, C4: 77

Power(s)
    -intelligence & glory & danger, B4: 25
    -intelligence-all-presence, C2: 47
    -MAN, C3: 50
    -pursuit, B1: 130
    -SENTIENCE, C2:138
    -systems, B3: 67
    & concretion, B1: 134
    & Culture, C4: 14
    & DIFFICULTY, DD: 25
    & disintegration, B1: 134
    & divine love, B3: 99
    & Egotism in man, B3: 59
    & ETHICS OF THE *CONTINUUM*, C4: 75
    & first act of Creation, B1: 5

    & Free Will, B3: 106
    & God the Holy Ghost, EG: 49
    & ideas, B3: 64
    & invoked, C4: 41
    & IO, C3: 104
    & knowledge, B1: 128
    & laughter, B2 138-140, 147
    & love, P1: 117
    & Love of God, P1: 141
    & Men of private ambition, B3: 179
    & names, B2: 27
    & OI, C3: 104
    & Space, EG: 38-49
    & sub-atomic world, B1: 133
    & "substance", C4: 96
    & the scientist, EG: 38
    & things in the universe, P1: 135
    & total reality, B3: 174
    & Trinity Law, that Form-function-power, C3: 92
    & Truth, Beauty and Goodness, P1: 43
    & two-fold tendency, B1: 134
    & universe, B1: 8; P1: 135
    & value, B4: 35
    & world's greatest men, P1: 117
    absolute … fundamental to all things, B3 : 50
    acquired, B2: 138-140, 147, 153
    all-originating, B3: 141; P1: 127
    blissful self-fulfilling, B4: 185
    clarity gives, C3: 72
    consciousness is, B3: 66
    conservation of, C4: 106
    creative activity, C4: 88
    developmental, B4: 35
    differentiation of, B4: 148
    divine, B3: 179; CA: 101
    divine intelligent, B4: 22
    effective cause, B3: 47
    embodied, B3: 4; B4: 111
    embodiment of … spiritual, B3: 109
    "enlargement of …", C3: 104
    evolved, B1: 12
    exercise of His inherent, B1: 13
    faith is, B4: 7
    first beginning of all beginnings, B1: 2
    game, P1: 63
    generative, B3: 41, 140; C4: 67; CA: 14, 23-24, 99
    goal of knowledge-seeking, B1: 128

God, this Absolute, is, B2: 47

gradient of, B1: 32

Heaven (Balance of Power), B2: 36;
    C4: 75, 103

higher, P1: 127

human soul is a, CA: 102

Imagination, B1: 43

in names, B2: 27

Incarnation of Christ, CA: 15

incomprehensible originating, P1: 126

Infinite, B3: 124; B4: 47; CA: 13;   C4: 67

infinite, & infinite intelligence are not
    separated, B4: 21-22

infinite continuum, C1: 42

Infinite intelligent sentient, B3: 174: 56

infinite power & The real God, C4: 56

Infinite Sentient, DD: 70

Initiative and Ideational, TC: 34

inner self-teaching, B3: 14

Intelligence, B1: 10; B2: 147

intelligent, B3: 42, 124

intelligent creative, B4: 98

invisible, B1: 31

laughter of acquired, B2: 138-140, 147, 153

loss of, CA: 54

"MANUAL OF POWER", C3: 123

modalities of, B1: 133

"mysterious", B3: 48-49

NON-DUAL infinite continuum of sentient,
    C4: 57

nuclear, B1: 129

of the Universe, B3: 125

"personal", B1: 7

play of energy, CA: 13

positing, C4: 97

POWER-MAN, C3: 50

pre-polar, B2: 46

PRIMAL, C3: 121

private ambition, B3: 179

Pure, P2: 4

pursuit of infinite, B1: 130

"reduction of ...", C3: 104

reflexive, B3: 65

relating, B1: 8

Resident in all things, B1: 31

seats of, P1: 63

see DD: 36; EG: 37-50

self-aware ... self-knowing, B2: 185

sentience, property of, C3: 125

sentient power, BENEATH ALL

PHENOMENA, C3: 2

sentient & feels, C4: 14

Sentient, B4: 91

shows a two-fold tendency, B1: 134

Source-, B3: 62, 140; B4: 21, 46; CA: 23

Spirit is, B4: 35; EG: 37

spiritual, B3: 99

substance of reality, B4: 6

substance of the universe, P1: 135

"substance", C4: 96

"superstance", C4: 96

Supreme Being, B3: 59

The Supreme, B1: 32

tortoise, P1: 101

ultimate, P2: 5

universal, B1: 9; B2: 143; P1: 125

What is Power?, EG: 37

which evolved the universe, B1: 12

Within man are two, B4: 185

world *is*, B1: 133

Praise

"loben", B1: 7

the Lord, EG: 19

will-power, intelligence and sensitivity,
    B4: 46

Praising

"Praising is raising", DD: 5

Pralaya

& entropy, C2: 47, 77; C3: 64

& THE BAKER, C3: 12

Hindu philosophy, C4: 100

Prayer

see B3: 142-143

Precipitation(ing)

crystal, C4: 59

Luciferan, B1: 21

Pre-creational

Anxiety, CA: 25

Predicament

& mankind, CA: 84

Preference

for Truth, P1: 93

God's Way, B3: 34

Prejudice(s)

fear, B3: 171

mental and emotional levels, B3: 172

see B3: 171

Pre-polar

polarisation, B2: 46

Presence
mysterious, B3: 48
of God Himself, CA: 47

Present
& past, C2: 148
situation (& Determinists), C2: 148

Preservation
& continuance of inertias, P1: 123
self-, C1: 14

Pressure
& body-object, C1: 60

Prey
& energy of particular living beings, C4: 105

Price
pay the ... of what I will, C4: 6

Pride
& Jewish people, EG: 84
dividing fire, DD: 13
Luciferan, B4: 26
of position, B3: 26
of the man, EG: 88

Priest(s)
Four castes, C3: 65
high & GOAT & BEARD, C4: 72

Prima-materia
& Inertia, TC: 30
& the Absolute, TC: 30, 36
of Philosophical schools, TC: 30

Primal
origin, B3: 41
POWER(AL), C3: 121
religion, C2: 84

Prime Matter
& Absolute Power, TC: 32
& Mother, TC: 32
& Universal Substance, TC: 32
see TC: 31-32, 36-37

Primordial
power, B3: 41

Primrose
The Primrose (John Donne), C3: 81

Prince(s)
& brother Lucifer, DD: 13
of Lies, P1: 32

Principle(s)
& Bible, B2: 44
& governing concept, CA: 77
& (governing concepts, pattern, comprehension), C4: 50
& relationship between S and P, C3: 117

basic, B2: 47
central, B3: 78
embodied, B2: 47
first things, B2: 44
governing, B2: 48
knowledge of, B2: 45
MAN IS, C3: 116
Name =, C3: 128
of Reality (laws), B3: 113
ordering, EG: 24
realm of fixed, C3: 130
see C3: 130
Sensuality and, C3: 117
totality of all, P2: 46
true, B2: 48; P2: 46
whole pattern of our action, CA: 77

Private
aim(s), B3: 19, 148
purpose(s), B1: 88; B3: 150; CA: 40; P1: 118-119
deprived of relationships, C4: 67
thinker, C4: 67

Privation
OF LIGHT (DARKNESS IS), C1: 106

Problem(s)
& mutual helpfulness, B3: 70
ANSWER TO ALL, C4: 1
forced into man's consciousness, RS: 1
how to relate science and faith?, C4: 56
human beings, B1: 8
of power, B3: 48
origin of evil, P1: 28
our deepest, B3: 28
pleasure-pain, P2: 23
solution of all our, B3: 70
spirit-matter, C4: 17
three greatest, B3: 124

Procedure
& formal control factor, C3: 95

Process
reflexive, C3: 35

Process(es)
& Allopathy, C2: 121
& continuum of power, C2: 93
& "mind", C2: 4
& organism, C2: 121
& protoplasm, C2: 92-93
& sublimation, C2: 131
apparently separating, C2: 93
Assembling and dissembling, RS: 1

being-, C2: 21
body, CA: 63:RS: 35; P2: 44
brain, C2: 91; P2: 39
chemical, CA: 63
conscious/consciousness, B1: 59; C1: 54;
    RS: v, 24
cosmic, C2: 1
creative, P2: 41
cycles [i.e. cyclic] ... not cyclic, P2: 40-41
destruction, P1: 123
electrical, CA: 63
electronic and electro-magnetic, P2: 39
emotional, P2: 64
feeling, P2: 64
finite(ing), RS: 37-38
growth, RS: 49
human psyche, P1: 144
ideation(al), RS: 37, 58
illusory, RS: 51
inhibitive, C1: 77
inner, CA: 63
inner(most), C2: 110, 121, P1: 104, 144;
    P2: 38, 41
life's, P2: 81
logical, C1: 87; C2: 104
mechanical, RS: 37
mental, C2: 57; CA: 63; P1: 12, 24;
    P2: 19, 64, 66
organic, C4: 18, 25, 87
physical, C2: 83, 87; CA 63
physical, affective, mentational,
    comprehensional, volitional and
    episcopal, C4: 50
preservation, P1: 123
body, CA: 63
psychical, CA: 63
psychological, P2: 38, 39
repetitions of, P2: 40
spiritual, C2: 87; CA: 63; P2: 39
subjective, C2: 87; P2: 38
temporal pattern, RS: 1
Time, P1: 140
trine ... Saturn/Jupiter/Mercury, C4: 38
unconscious, B1: 59

Procrastination
creates clutter, C3: 53
explanation of, B4: 161

Prodigal
Son, B1: 85, 130; C3: 29, 58, 117;
    C4: 67, 90, 103; DD: 36; P2: 122;

RS: ix

Prodigality
evils, C2: 131-132

Profit
-pursuers, B3: 177
-seeking individual, B3: 176-177
-seeking materialists, B3: 177

Proof
methods of, C4: 115

Property(ies)
& human race, B4: 51-52
essential(s), B4: 51-52
inherent ... of God, B4: 91
what truly belongs to a being or thing,
    B4: 49

Prophecy
& speech, B4: 41
great men & link between past and future
    prophets, B1: 121
power of, P2: 72
Star-Wheel ... occasion of, B2: 121

Prophets
mouths of the, DD: 50
murder of the great, C3: 64
"the chain of the prophets", B1: 121
unwelcome truths ... persecuted, B2: 27
way of Eternal-looking, B2: 121

Proportion
Unity of God ... Ratio, P1: 4

Proprium
= ownness, C2: 113

Protopathic
aggressive reactivity, B2: 63

Protoplasm
& ancestor's records of bad conscience,
    B2: 180
& empirical ego, C3: 55
& record, P2: 111
& water, CA: 29
not ... merely chemical elements, B2: 183
"first plastic substance", CA: 29
one original, B2: 176
perfect recording material, C3: 77; CA: 85
substance of living beings, CA: 29
two basic properties, P2: 76
water-bound life, C3: 67

Protoplasmic
ancestral ... line, B2: 181
depths C4: 45
evolution, RS: 24

memory, B2: 176
records (unconscious), B2: 177
responses, C3: 54
sensorium, C3: 55

Proud
violence, C2: 103

PSI
is the KEY, C3: 116

Psyche
& anima, C2: 87
& finite zone of sentient power,
    C4: 46
& Greek sages, B1: 136
& interaction of pneuma and soma, C3: 25
& pneuma, C2: 87
& Pneuma and Soma, C4: 112
& Two Paradises (Quran), C2: 87
& Twilight, C4: 73-74
empirical ego, C2: 87
frightened, C4: 46
Greek word (for the soul), B1: 13
human, C2: 95
"psychological atmosphere", B4: 179

Psychic
atmosphere, B4: 179
RELEASE, C4: 46

Psychoanalysis
& *self-awareness*, C4: 80

Psycho-analytical
procedures, RS: 23-24

Psychologists
& anxiety, CA: 2
modern, C2: 83

Psychological
atmosphere, B4: 179

Psychology
Modern, B1: 95; B2: 46; P2: 49
vocabulary of, C2: 83

Psychosomatic
human organism (psycho-somatic unity),
    C4: 77
response, C4: 48

Psychotherapy
& anxiety, CA: 2

Pull
positing by the Alpha, C3: 35

Punishment
& the community, CA: 81
self-imposed, B1: 88

Puppet(s)
-handler, DD: 32
void of free will, B3: 45

Pure
"Blessed are the pure in heart" (Jesus),
    B1: 137
operation, C4: 41
will, C2: 78

Purity
& doubt, C4: 42
"Purity of heart is to will one thing",
    C4: 14; 33, 45

Purna
identity (infinite), C2: 58-59

Purpose(s)
& art, C4: 84
& association of ideas, C2: 59
& Intellect, B2: 61
& intelligence, B2: 22
& man ... All other creatures, B2: 152
& pain, CA: 39
& trinity of will, form and process, EG: 51
& unconscious mind, CA: 74
& value, C4: 58
& Will, EG: 51
All-Power, Supreme Intelligence, and
    Infinite Compassion has a, B3: 51
Divine, B3: 33
God's one, EG: 52
loss of, CA: 54
many ... willed at once (man), EG: 51
of life, C1: 6
other's, CA: 83
private, B1: 88; B3: 150; CA: 40;
    P1: 118-119;
unfulfilled, CA: 76
Unity of, P1: 119
universal, B3: 150
unrealisable, CA: 77
volitional, B4: 43
What is ...?, C3: 125

Pursuers
of knowledge, B1: 129, 133

Pursuit
knowledge-, B1: 128
of infinite power, B1: 129-130

Push
& universe (in presence of), C3: 35
positing by the Alpha, C3: 35

Pythagoras
All qualities are quantities (Numbers), C4: 31

Q

Q
& cowardice, C4: 5
& Logos-God, C4: 7
guard & not guard, C4: 5-7
see English gematria, C3: 19-20, 84-88

Qabalah
definition of Tiphareth, C4: 40

Quality
& Quantity, C2: 55-56
in the feeling, C2: 55
state of our will, CA: 37

Quantity
& Quality, C2: 55-56
ignores reality, C2: 117
in the intellect, C2: 55

Quantum
law, C2: 33

Quarrels
& unity of the communal group, CA: 82

Queen
Bee, C3: 18

Quick
& "dead", B1: 144; B3: 10-11, 22-24;
CA: 92; P1: 24; TC: 7
able to respond, C4: 75
alive and conscious, B1: 144
seizes, C4: 17

Quicken(eth)
see P1: 17, 23

Quiet
& Truth, B3: 148-149
faith, CA: 51
mind, B1: 54
quietest depths of our mental life, CA: 63
quietly watch the inner processes of
our being, P1: 104
voice, B3: 148-149

Quieten
ourselves (to discover ..., B3: 183

Quran
Two paradises, C2: 87

Quranic verse
see C2: 105

R

R
& The Real, C4: 95
difference, C4: 95
see C2: 2
(see diagram), C4: 95
see English gematria, C3: 19-20, 84-88

Race
human, B4: 51; P1: 115

Radiesthetic
sense, C1: 26

Radio waves
high frequency, B2: 133

Rage
& frustrated evil will, B1: 83

Raising
of Cain, B1: 125, 132

Ram
[Zodiac sign] see C3: 114
-power, B2: 150
& Abraham, B2: 151
& sacrifice, B2: 150
& salvation, B2: 153
caught in a thicket, B2: 145-146, 150;
DD: 10
energy(ies), B2: 149-150, 153; C3: 114

Rape
& male & female, C2: 108-109
& MERRIMENT & seriousness,
C2: 18-109
BY THEOS, C3: 127
(by the right man), C2: 108-109
of the Sabine women, C4: 100; TC: 11

Rapist
& woman & man, C3: 127
efficient, C3: 127

Ratio
"Logos", P1: 3
"reason", C1: 79
Unity of God ... proportion, P1: 4

Rational
aspect (WER), C4: 2
attempt to control, B4: 6
expression & Women, C4: 70
form, C1: 68
formulations & freeing ... from, C4: 70
mind, C3: 27
non-, C4: 1, 92-93

Rationalist
Humanist, Rationalist, Materialistic Atheist,

C2: 1

Rationality
& order, EG: 24

Reaction(s)
& energy, B3: 79
& physical body, B2: 65
adequate powers of, RS: 1
KARMA, B3: 46-47
"law of action and reaction",B2: 124;
     B3: 46; CA: 79
mechanical, B1: 113
self-defensive, CA: 93
"to every action there is an equal and
     opposite reaction", P1: 85

Reactive
Behaviour, P2: 112

Reactivity
& *tendencies* to, CA: 84
unwilled, C4: 50

Real
& contradiction, C4: 95
& sensuality and principle, C3: 129
= R + L, C2: 2
battle inside us, B4: 6
life, B1: 115
Power, EG: 71
Self, C4: 107

Reality
& Humanist, C2: 1
& Beyondness, B3: 130
& clarity, P1: 151
& God, B1: 124
& intelligent power, B3: 141
& Love, P1: 142
& Mercury, C4: 39
& *Power*, B4: 6
& Time, B4: 12
& Truth, B3: 112; B4: 31; C3: 21
& voidity, B2: 69
& whole consciousness, C2: 87
Acceptance of, CA: 36
Ahriman's statement, C2: 41
an ocean, C4: 120
attitude to, CA: 38
discrimination and relationship, C3: 103
division of, B1: 60
electro-magnetic and bio-magnetic studies,
     B4: 166
energy-behaviour system, B4: 89
infinite ocean of energy, B4: 81

infinite, C2: 80
inner world ... and outer world, B1: 41;
     B3: 173
garment & Reality, B4: 11-12
laws or principles of, B3: 113
multi-planar, B3: 31
non-dual, C3: 23, 35
of the Universe, B4: 100
perpetual change, EG: 77
problem of, C3: 107
reposited, C2: 33
Sound, C3: 51
substance of, B4: 166
total, B3: 129
ultimate, B3: 67; C2: 97; C4: 21, 76
whole, B3: 129, 173; C4: 39

Reason(s)
& Infinity, C1: 79
& non-reason, C2: 87
& *perfect justice*, CA: 86
& the average man, C2: 80
A POSTERIORI, C2: 125
A PRIORI, C2: 125
Divine, B3: 53
Faith and true, C2: 114
fear, C2: 132
intention of the will, C2: 147
Love of, CA: 86
mesh of pure eidetics, C2: 125
Principle of, P1: 4
PURE, C3: 75
"Reason-Word", B3: 54; EG: 23
two kinds, C2: 82
twofold, C2: 125

Re-assessment
"Redemption", B3: 16

Rebellion
& Lucifer, B1: 128

Rebellious force
Satanic energies, B1: 25

Recall
& vocabulary, C2: 18
At the Recall each being is caught in the
     net, C2: 18

Reclamation
of fallen men, B3: 33
of the fallen spirit, B4: 184
religious teaching, B4: 184
special role (For man), B4: 185

Re-cognition
   re-membering, C2: 60
Reconstitution
   & Reincarnation, C2: 77
   of the form, C2: 77
Record(s)
   & ancestors, B2: 179
   ancestral, C4: 87
   biomagnetic field, C4: 47
   experience, B4: 114
   library, B2: 180
   our bodies, P2: 50
   PAINFUL or unpleasant, C3: 47
   pleasant, B3: 94
   protoplasmic, C3: 55
   replaying, CA: 86
   totality of the, B4: 121
   unconscious, B2: 179
Recreation
   act of creation, EG: 15
Recurrence
   necessity for "eternal recurrence", C4: 78
Red One
   Adam, DD: 10
Redeemer
   Nietzsche, EG: 68
   is one who re-assesses ..., EG: 68
Redemption
   inner divine consciousness, B3: 16
   inner re-assessment, B3: 19
Reductionists
   vitalism, C2: 84
Reflection
   photon bounces, C4: 117
Reflexion
   act of, RS: 41
   attention of the observer, C4: 117
   of will, C4: 52
   power of, B3: 65
Reflexive
   -awareness, TC: 18
   & attainment, C3: 90
   & non-reflexive thinking, B3: 65
   & resistance, C4: 81
   "bent back upon itself" (thinking /
      consciousness), B3: 65
   consciousness, B3: 65
   intelligence, C3: 106
   non-reflexive energy, C3: 106
   process, C3: 35

see Reflexive Self-Consciousness
see Book RS
   self-aware, C2: 24
   Self-Consciousness, C1: 84; C2: 11, 64;
      C3: 45, 90; C4: 108
   self-determinable, C4: 14
   self-reflexive awareness, C3: 101
   self-will, C3: 113
   volitional, C4: 104
   will, C4: 15
Reflexive Self-Consciousness
   & act of will, RS: 43
   & METANOIA, C2: 11
   & self-responsible, C2: 11
   abbreviate to "resec", RS: 1
   act of, RS: 29, 45
   attainment of, C3: 90
   back-flow of consciousness, RS: 46
   beginning and the end of the journey into
      time and particularity, RS: ix
   key to man's freedom, RS: 46
   consciousness identified with itself, RS: 37
   distinction (passive mode / active mode),
      C2: 11
   Epistrephein, RS: 38
   essential to freedom, C1: 84
   evolutionary movement towards,   C2: 64
   free from the law of mechanical
      action-reaction, RS: 37
   freedom from object- identification, RS: 58
   gain and retain, RS: 43, 45
   highest possible form of awareness
   key to man's freedom, RS: 46
   lacked, C3: 111
   resec ... exercise, RS: 45
   return of the Self to the Self, RS: 45
   WORK TOWARDS, C3: 45
Reflexive(ly)
   aware, C2: 24
   centred, C3: 45
   establish, C3: 45
   recognised (pattern), C2: 33
   self-aware, C2: 24
   self-conscious, C1: 84; C4: 108;
      RS: viii-ix, 40, 58
   self-consciously, RS: vi
   self-determinable, C4: 14
   volitional field, C3: 45

Reflexivity
& self-examination, C4: 15
man to attain, C4: 15
Reft
Eye, C3: 107
Refusal
& inner balance, CA: 82
& pain , B4: 122
Regression
& pain, C4: 72
Reincarnation
reconstitution of the form, C2: 77
reincarnating self, C2: 107
Rejected
Stone, B3: 82-83, 109
Relation(s)
& emotionally starved, B2: 10
between anxiety and frustrated energies,
    CA: 77
contingent, C4: 12
man, TC: 20-21
new, C4: 110
reciprocal, B1: 115
tacit conspiracy, TC: 1
with God, B3: 126; C4: 61
woman, TC: 20-21
Relational
interactivity of sensitive beings, B2: 73
possibilities, RS: 9
tensiona and difficulties, TC: 22
Relationship(s)
& Eternity, CA: 46
& human development, CA: 82
& Jesus Christ, CA: 92
& language, P2: 69
& materialist, CA: 4
& other zones, C4: 54
& reality, CA: 36, 38
& techniques of life, CA: 104
& will, CA: 56
adequate ... with reality, CA: 36
between good and evil, CA: 40
between individuals, C4: 117
between pleasure and pain, CA: 40
cause-effect, C4: 1
contingent, C4: 108
Eternal Changeless and the Time-Matter
    world of change, B3: 3
false, B3: 165
free, B1: 115

harmonious, C4: 93
human, CA: 82; P1: 11, 22, 41, 50, 77
human interrelationship, P1: 158; P2: 12
interrelationship of all beings, C4: 115
interrelationship of Form, Function and
    Power, P1: 43
interrelationship ... of Truth, Beauty and
    Goodness, P1: 43
life itself is, CA: 92
materialist cannot ... be worried ... about
    his relationship to infinity ..., CA: 4
mutually educational, C4: 1
need in beings for, CA: 93
no ... except of individuals, C4: 9
[of] eye & ear, P2: 69
of Love (highest), P1: 158
of love or hate, CA: 38
of time and eternity, B3: 1
of universal love, P2: 56
other human beings, CA: 93
out of, CA: 93
out of, CA: 93
possibilities, C4: 108
privacy, C4: 67
real life, B1: 115
we cannot give up a ... without giving up
    also, CA: 93
with each other, CA: 104, P1: 51
with ... God, CA: 104; P1: 51
with ... reality, CA: 38
with Jesus Christ, CA: 104
Release
technique of psychic, C4: 46
Religion(s)
& centred consciousness, C2: 138
& interrelationship of all beings, C4: 115
& Nietzsche, CA: 12
& one human being, C3: 96
& science, CA: 12
other, B3: 52
patriarchal, C4: 96
Primal, C2: 84
real meaning, B2: 29
true hierarchical, C4: 87
Yoga, B3: 101
Religionists
dogmatic, C1: 67
Remedies
Homoeopathy, C4: 77

Remembering
& Forgiveness, B3: 97
re-cognition, C2: 60
Remembrance
Worship, C2: 39
Repeated experiences
cause and effect, B1: 7
Repentance
Metanoia, C4: 108
Now, B2: 191
Repetition
cyclic, C1: 69
Re-posit(ing)
form, C4: 110
Yourself, C2: 39
Reprisals
"stress disorders", B3: 152
Reproduction
polarised & non-polarised, TC: 4
sexual & non-sexual, TC: 4
vegetable, TC: 4
Reputation
building of a, P2: 77
RESEC
& consciousness, RS: 20
act, RS: 15
free self-determination, RS: 3
key to, RS: 3
WORK TOWARDS, C3: 45
Resentfulness
& retaliation, CA: 84
Resentment
& others' actions, B4: 28
re-feeling, B3: 97
Resistance
& awareness, C2: 56
& "field forces", C4: 76
& haptic experience, C4: 76
& infinite void, C2: 138
& "matter", C4: 97
& physicality, C4: 97
& "substance", C4: 97
experience of, C1: 103
inertia, C1: 103
physical weight-lifting, B2: 23
self-generated … more self-conscious and
    reflexive, C4: 81
spiritual weight-lifting, B2: 23
zone of encapsulation, C4: 97

Resonance
& Christ, P2: 83
law of, B2: 182
Respect
for ideas, B3: 64
Response
-able person, P2: 113
low level of, B2: 133
"Triple-F", B3: 29
Respons-ability(ies)
external, C4: 25
inner, C4: 25
man's real ability, P2: 41
of power, EG: 71
see C4: 25
spiritually free soul, P2: 112
Respons-ibilities
of power, EG: 71
see C4: 25
Responsibility(ies)
& actions, B4: 153
& man, B4: 185
& man of spirit, B3: 79
& Nietzsche, EG: 83
& power, B2: 147
accepting, B4: 151
collectively (world war), B4: 152
for inner/outer physical activities, C4: 25
for one's actions, CA: 87
for one's self, CA: 87
freedom implies self-, B3: 7, 79
heavy burden, B2: 95; B4: 152
high, P1: 8
human, B2: 25
individual, B4: 152-153
individual centres of, B4: 153
inner, C4: 25
liability, P2: 110
Life, B2: 96
outer, C4: 25
personal, P2: 35
see C4: 25
self-, B1: 6; B2: 65; B3: 7, 79; CA: 20, 62, 98
sense of, CA: 87
total, EG: 83
Rest
one of the phenomena, C3: 61
Restauration
pray for, C4: 36

Re-stauros
see C2: 79
Restoration
of the true interfunction, B2: 9
Resurrect(ing)
& self-consistency, P1: 77
power of Christ-love, CA: 96
Resurrection
of the body?, C4: 61
the caterpillar, B1: 135
Result
of our errors, B3: 92
Retaliation
anxiety, CA: 84
essence of ... embodied in us, P1: 35
Retrocognitive
Reflexion, C3: 71
Revelation
Book of, B1: 79
divine self-, P2: 87
of Sacred Truth, C2: 114
Revenge
counter-revenge, CA: 83
Revolutionary
impulse, B1: 67
Rhea
& Kronos, C2: 75
& Mammon, C2: 75, 83
& Saturn, CA: 47
Rhythms
& of Time, B4: 95
Rib
taken out of Adam, DD: 45
Rich
young man, B4: 1, 7
Riddle
Samson's, C4: 63
Right
& TWO HALVES of the brain, C3: 82
& FOUR PLANES OF BEING, C3: 99-100
mind, P1: 108
Righteousness
fulfil all, B4: 14
Risk
minds, wake up, B2: 188
nuclear missiles B2: 188
Ritual
CEREMONY, PROCEDURE?, C3: 95
River
"No man bathes twice in the same river"

(Heracleitus), EG: 77
Roc
& Ruach, C3: 117
& Ruch, C3: n117
of Sinbad, C3: 117
Rod
Jesus took a, DD: 56
Roman Catholic
Teaching, C2: 85
Rota
Great, DD: 11; EG: 25
"NO", DD: 11
Rotate
exist, C1: 68
Rotation
& kind of motion, RS: 12
& "matter", B1: 14; C1: 81
around a centre, C3: 61
cause of persistence, EG: 6
corresponds with Form, C3: 75
motion, RS: 6, 12
position change, P2: 2
see middle diagram, C4: 118
turbulent or vortical, C1: 106
vortex, C1: 87
ROTEH
wheel of life, C3: 4
Routine
process ("Hell"), B3: 21
Rubbish
& realisation of purpose, C4: 43
Ruach
of the Hebrews, C3: 117
Ruch
of Islam, C3: 117
Rules
of behaviour, B3: 94
Rupa
& Knower, C3: 118
RUS
see P & R, C3: 117

S

S
& SP function, C3: 128
= Spirit, C4: 118
issuant spirit, C4: 28
see English gematria, C3: 19-20, 84-88

separative energy, C4: 67

Sabine
women, C4: 100; TC: 11

Sacred
& Christal Sphere, C2: 139
Chrism, C2: 139
LAW, C4: 80
Place, C3: 122, 131

Sacredness
(secret-ness) of certain concepts, C2: 13

Sacrifice
& Abel, CA: 87
& Christianity, P1: 121
& extraordinary persons, CA: 92
& training, CA: 92
Abraham's, B2: 142
animal, B2: 146
Christ, CA: 36
continuum of A.S.P. (self-eating), C3: 91
dialectic of the narrow way, P2: 57-58
elect themselves to live a life of, CA: 92
essential of all true religious teaching, B3: 52
evolutionary advance, B2: 150
first great *conscious* self-, CA: 95
God had to make a double, B2: 159
higher evolutionary levels, B2: 151
Law of Being, C3: 83
lunar, C3: 80
Mary, B2: 161
mystery of, CA: 86, 89
of oneself, B2: 136
our power, B2: 147
secret of, CA: 92
self-, B2: 136
Substitute, B2: 145
total self, B2: 164
unintelligently suppressive, B2: 152
"We sacrifice, but not forever", EG: 76

Sadism
& pleasure, CA: 40

Sage(s)
CHINESE WISE MAN, C3: 127
contemplation, B1: 16
ego-annihilation, B3: 24
"infinite transparency of the sage", B3: 132
provokes the female to self-discovery,
    C3: 128

Sagittarius
[*Zodiac sign*] *see* C3: 112-114; C4: 32-33
& FIBONACCI APPLICATION, C3: 112

Sagittarius 13, C3: 114

Saint
AUGUSTINE, C3: 105
Hermes: patron saint of rogues, *(etc.)*, C4: 75
self-crucified Observer, C3: 13

Salmon
Celtic Christianity, B2: 78

Salt
pillar of, B3: 25

Salvation
& material world, CA: 22
& Name (sound aspect of reality), C2: 16
& is ... being rescued, P2: 128
& Jesus, B1: 99
cease to sin, B4: 127
final freedom, B3: 77
"Jehovah is ...", B1: 99
our certitude of, C3: 40
Problems of, C2: 92
removal of all fantasies, B4: 4
released from alienation, B4: 127
washing away of ... unpleasant experience-
    records, B4: 117-118

Samsara
Hindu view, C1: 108

Samson('s)
& eye of his soul, RS: 53
riddle, C1: 94; C2: 105; C4: 63

Sand
grain of, EG: 17

Sanity
displaced by insanity, B3: 181
unshakeable belief, C2: 64

Sarai
& Abram, B2: 93
& choice, B2: 96

Satan
& principles of Mammon-diabolism, P1: 27
& synagogue of satans, DD: 28-29
desire to be a visible God, B4: 18
embodied superior power, B4: 18
fall of, B2: 22
incarnation of the desire to be a ..., B4: 18
Lucifer, B1: 20; B4: 26
The Adversary, DD: 7, 27

Satanic
diabolic demonstration, DD: 3
disgrace, B1: 128
dust, B1: 26
embodied superior power, B4: 18

energies, B1: 25
Fall-mass, B1: 21
forces, B1: 33
impulse, B3: 34
spirit, B4: 186
state, B1: 24
visible God ... essence of the, B4: 18
Satisfaction
"being full of being", B1: 111
SATORI
THE WAY of self-activation, C3: 117
Saturn
& CURE & reversal of the Fall, C2: 117
& his consort Rhea, CA: 47
& *in*tensity, C4: 68
& Jupiter, C1: 100-101; C2: 33-34, 56;
  C3: 69; C4: 17, 27, 38-39, 60, 68-69,
  111; CA: 48
& MANUAL OF POWER, C3: 123
& Mercury, C2: 56, C4: 17, 38-39, 60, 69
& (pain), C4: 68
& Philosopher's Stone, C4: 38
& Samson's riddle, C4: 63
& Seven Deadly Sins, C3: 101
& the Fall, C2: 117
& trine process, C4: 38
compression, C4: 68
contraction, C3: 69
Earth-Saturn-Satan, C3: 26
existential separativity, C4: 66
Footstool, C3: 20
innermost self-condensation, C3: 4
Jupiter posits Saturn, C2: 56
mythic colour of ... dark, CA: 48
opposite of ... Jupiter, CA: 48
paradox of the free and the domed, C4: 60
Saturn-Chronos, C2: 56; RSC: ix
Saturn/Jupiter/Mercury, C4: 38
Saturn-Jupiter-Saturn (continuance of the
  Eternal), C2: 33
Saturn-moment(s), C4: 64, 68-69
see C2: 99, 117; C3: 6-7, 101, 123
see diagrams, C2: 109; C3: 7
shorthand for formative process, C2: 99
sonic alternations, C2: 33-34
Temptation (Saturn-Chronos), C2: 56
urn of being, C1: 100
Saturnine
grip, B3: 86
Metal, C2: 72

"Saturnine Age", C4: 90
Saturn-Chronos
& the realm of, RS: ix
Saul
& Damascus road, DD: 18
Saved
What does it mean to be, B4: 7
Saviour
& phases of development of man, C4: 91
God as First Cause, C4: 85
Jesus, B1: 99
saviour-savour of self-realisation, C2: 139
Scapegoat(s)
Abel, B1: 78-79
first, B1: 78-79; B4: 27
Lucifer, B4: 27
type-figure, B1: 79
Scattering
Gathering and, B4: 49, 162-163
Schelling
& the Absolute, C2: 96
Schizoid
behaviour, B3: 36-37
Schopenhauer
& Nietzsche, EG: 63
Science(s)
& art, C4: 85, 87
& A.S.P. field, C2: 138
& centred consciousness, C2: 138
& Christian Philosophy, P1: 1
& faith, C4: 56
& God, EG: 20-21
& high-technology, B4: 99
& intelligence, B1: 99-100; B3: 124
& nature of Matter, B2: 130
& Nietzsche, CA: 12
& philosophy, C4: 87
& pollution, B1: 100
& religion, CA: 12
& Source-power of all things, B3: 62
achievements of, B2: 143
aims ... at power, TC: 40
can measure, P2: 44
depend upon, P2: 70
discovery of principles, B2: 45
divine, P1: 83
Empirical, EG: 20
knowledge of ends and means, C4: 85
materialistic ... the word "Will", B4: 42
materialistic, B1: 12; B4: 42; C4: 48; P2: 38

Modern, C1: 5m
physical, P2: 73
see B2: 45, 143
Scientific
advances, B2: 98
Mind, C2: 38
research, B2: 98
Scientistic
education & critical mind, C4: 26
Scientist(s)
& atom(s), B1: 59
& nature of consciousness, B4: 171
& Solid God, EG: 11
& will, B1: 65, 76
atheist, B4: 86
Atomic research, B1: 32
empirical, B3: 76
future, B4: 166
great men & link between past and future
    scientists, B1: 121-122
materialist, B3: 76; EG: 80
materialistic, B1: 43; C1: 67
ONES CRUCIFIED IN THE EYE,
    DD: 62
pattern of local self-intensification, EG: 11
seek knowledge of ultimates, B1: 133
Sci-tech
& history, B2: 12
Scorpio
[*Zodiac sign*] *see* C3: 112-113
& widdershins cycle (FIBONACCI
    APPLICATION), C3: 112
act of devotion, C4: 32
Scripture(s)
& rules of our divinisation, B4: 127
Our Bible, B1: 1
SCRYING BALL
of God, C3: 24
Sculptors
& The artist, C4: 113
Sea
of anxiety, CA: 13
Seamless
garment, B1: 32; B3: 165; B4: 10; CA: 87;
    C2: 15, 41, 100; C4: 57; P2: 4
garment & Reality, B4: 11-12
Supreme Spirit, EG: 4
Second
birth, C4: 108
death, B4: 142; CA: 26

Secrect(s)
& unconscious mind, P1: 102
languages, B2: 53
of sacrifice, CA: 92
Secrecy
& truth, C1: 71
Security
in the outer world, B4: 48
Seed
& Abram, B2: 93
CRYSTAL, C2: 51
embodied (love-seed), B3: 3
hate-, B3: 34
love-, B3: 34
mystery, C4: 62
of perfection, B2: 103
see C2: 51-52
symbol, C4: 5
Seek
"Seek first the kingdom of heaven, and all
    else will be added unto you", RS: 21
Seeming
and "being", P1: 67
Self
& contradiction, B4: 65; C4: 88, 110
& "death", B2: 111
& dream "self", C4: 83
& non-Self, B1: 68
& Original Cause, C4: 85
& phenomena, C4: 106
& RESEC, C3: 45
& SACRED PLACE of Sentient Power,
    C3: 131
Absolute, C2: 46-47
alienation, C4: 52
an encapsulated vibratory consciousness,
    C2: 48
"cellf", B1: 117
"conscious intelligent self response", B3: 29
contingent, C3: 45, 46
Continuum Self, C4: 106-108
dissolution of the, P2: 57
electing oneself, C4: 91
eternal, B3: 183
God within, B3: 44
human, C4: 43
individual, B1: 115; B2: 142
Infinite, C2: 26
is consciousness, RS: 2
large, B2: 66-68

little, B1: 118; B2: 67-68
only true, C4: 107
Our animal, B2: 148
outer, B1: 68
pure free-will consciousness, RS: 31
real Self of man, the human Soul, P2: 28
reincarnating, C2: 107
sacrifice, B2: 164
sinning, B2: 142
Spiritual, P2: 3
the only real, C4: 107-108
"To thine own self be true", B4: 192
totality of, C4: 14, 33
true value of self-hood, B1: 122
True, B2: 68
unique, B1: 119
waking, B1: 68

Self-
-abnegation, B3: 24
-accusations, P2: 24
-accuser, C2: 11
-action, C2: 46
-activating, B1: 2
-activation, C4: 53
-actualisation, B4: 24; P2: 115
-actualising, B4: 24
-admiration, B4: 3
-advantage, B2: 181
-aggrandisement, B2: 59; B3: 148
-alienated, B3: 59
-alienation, B2: 75
-analysis, B3: 122
-annihilation, P2: 57
-appreciation, EG: 11
-assurance, C2: 139; CA: 16
-attention, C2: 62
-aware, B2: 185; C2: 24; C4: 110; CA: 31
-awareness, C2: 24-25; C3: 106; C4: 80;
    CA: 20-21, 25, 31, 101; P2: 56; TC: 23
-balancing, C3: 62-63
-centred, TC: 23
-centring, C4: 14
-change, B3: 133
-choice, C2: 25
-chooser, C2: 25
-chosen, B1: 6; C2: 26
-comforting, B4: 78
-committal, C2: 25; C3: 57; C4: 7
-communication, CA: 90
-compacted darkness, B1: 20

-compaction, C2: 138
-condensed, C4: 63
-CONFIDENCE, C3: 122
-conscious, C2: 147; TC: 24,
    RS: viii-ix, 40, 58
-conscious player C2 1
-consciously, RS: vi
-consciousness, C3: 45, 109; C4: 81, 110;
    TC: 24-25, 40
-consistency, B3: 123; B4: 11, 33; CA:
    55-56; P1: 74, 78, 81
-consistent, B4: 136, 138-139; CA: 55
-consistent Being, P1: 77
-constitution, C4: 17
-contradicting, B4: 161
-contradiction, B3: 123; B4: 65; C4: 88
-control, B3: 132; C2: 49; C3: 76; C4: 14,
    25; CA: 20; EG: 86
-convergence, C3: 5
-created, B3: 83; C4: 106; EG: 9
-creating, C4: 108
-creation, C2: 26, 32
-creators, CA: 57
-crucified, B1: 20
-crucifixion, C3: 47
-deceit, B2: 141
-deceiving, B1: 107
-deception, B3: 70; C3: 57
-defence, B1: 127; B2: 63; P1: 36
-defensive, B2: 47; B4: 118
-definitions, B4: 5
-deprivation, C2: 34; C4: 67
-destroyers, C1: 6
-determination, B2: 62; C2: 25, 95; DD: 70
-determined, C1: 107; C2: 25; C4: 106
-determined direction, C3: 92
-determined pattern, C2: 33
-determining, C4: 108
-development, B1: 85; B4: 25, 40; C3: 29
-devotion, C2: 34
-devouring, C2: 147
-direction, C2: 1
-directive (active assumption of a), C3: 92
-disagreement, B4: 161
-disclosure, C2: 26
-discovery, B1: 6; C2: 32; P2: 54; TC: 23
-dishonoured, P2: 23-24
-effort, C2: 25
-election, C2: 25
-encapsulated, C4: 17

-encircling C3: 72
-enjoyment, EG: 11
-enlightenment, C4: 1
-*establishment*, B2: 62
-esteem, B2: 51
-evaluation, C4: 68; C4: 7
-evident, B3: 149; B4: 80
-evolving, B4: 26
-evolution, C2: 2
-examination, C1: 89; C2: 95-96; CA: 63;
    EG: 11; P1: 146-147
-excitation, TC: 5
-execution, C2: 11
-existence, RS: 29
-existent, C2: 52
-existentiated, EG: 12
-experience, C1: 40
-exploration C3: 28
-expressed, C3: 57
-expression, C2: 26
-fixated, C4: 17
-frustration, B1: 20; C2: 34; C3: 89
-fulfilment C4: 44
-generated resistance, C4: 81
-glorification, EG: 11
-ignition, C4: 7
-government, RS: 52
-holdings, EG: 9-10
-hood, B1: 122
-image, B2: 100-101, 107; B3: 151, 182,
    183; B4: 3, 75, 125, 127, 194; EG: 88
-imagery, B3: 182; B4: 194
-immersed, RS: 29
-immobilisation, CA: 62
-imposed B2: 38
-in-anxiety, C3: 73
-incarnated, C4: 17
-induced, EG: 9
-indulgence, CA: 30
-initiated, C4: 106
-initiating, B1: 115; C4: 50
-initiation, CA: 62
-inperienced, C4: 13
-insulation, CA: 91
-intensification, EG: 11
-intensified, EG: 12
-isolation, B1: 5; B3: 56, 182; CA: 91
-judge, C2: 11
-judged, C2: 18
-judgement, B2: 111; C2: 11

-jury, C2: 11
-justification, B1: 85; C1: 92; P1: 88, 90
-knowingness, C3: 76
-knowledge, B1: 5; B3: 133; C1: 90; C3: 76;
    C4: 17; TC: 40
-locomotion, B4: 182
-love, B4: 118
-made, C2: 69
-maintenance, C3: 63
-making, C4: 45
-manipulative appetival power, C2: 92
-mobile, B4: 183
-mobilisation, CA: 62
-modalisation, C4: 86
-modalised, C4: 85
-motion, C4: 90
-multiplying C3: 72
-Name (True), C2: 17
-objectified, C4: 52
-observation, B4: 74
-opinions, B4: 3
-opposing, C4: 27
-opposition, C2: 80; C4: 6, 27, 96
-*origination*, B2: 142
-out-standingness, C2: 24
-overcomer, C2: 139
-perfecting, B4: 25
-perspectives, EG: 11
-pity, B3: 97-98; B4: 28; C4: 45; CA: 84;
    EG: 68
-pluralisation, EG: 11
-poisoner, B3: 97
-poisoning, C2: 34
-positing, C4: 7
-possession, C4: 51
-precipitated, C2: 66; C4: 7
-precipitation, B1: 20; C2: 66
-precipitator, C2: 69
-preservation, C1: 14, 16-17; TC: 23
-produced, C4: 106-107
-profit-seeking, B3: 176
-projected, B3: 182
-protection, CA: 84
-rationalisation C3: 27
-realisation, C2: 139; EG: 11; P2: 55;
    TC: 18, 41
-realiser, C4: 52
-recriminations, P2: 23
-reflexive awareness, C3: 101
-refutation, C3: 89; C4: 1

-reliant, C3: 63
-renewal, B1: 135; CA: 62
-resistance, C2: 139
-responsibility, B1: 6; B2: 65; B3: 7, 79;
    CA: 20, 62, 98
-responsible, C2: 11
-retrocognition, C3: 71
-revelation, C2: 139; P2: 87
-rotation, C2: 147; C3: 44
-sacrifice, B2: 136
-same power, B2: 152
-satisfaction, C1: 88; C3: 130
-scattering, C4: 7
-search, C2: 131
-searching, P2: 21
-security, B3: 148
-seeking, C1: 88
-seized, C4: 17
-sensuality, C3: 91
-sentience, C3: 45
-sentient, C1: 8
-*separation*, C4: 53
-stabilisation, CA: 16
-*study*, P1: 30
-subsistent, C2: 52
-substantialisation, C2: 139
-sufferer, C2: 11
-superiority, B3: 182
-survival, B3: 148
-trapped, B3: 182
-tried, C2: 56
-variable, EG: 10
-will, C2: 27
-witness, B4: 182

Selfish
  & inter-relation, B1: 118
  private purpose, B1: 88
Selfishness
  "egotism" B1: 115
  Enlightened, C2: 78
Sensation(s)
  & Latin word "sentire", B2: 117
  & sense organs, CA: 73
Sense(s)
  -organ(s), C1: 109; C3: 76-77
  & Art, C4: 80
  organ(s), B1: 54-55; B2: 16, 131-132;
    B3: 108; B4: 74, 130; C1: 44;
    CA: 72; P2: 127
  see C1: 26

Senseless
  world, B1: 66
Sensitivity
  & intelligence, B1: 13
  & the serpent, B3: 92
  & the totally insensitive, B4: 46
  degrees of feeling, B4: 180
  feeling-, B4: 181
Sensuality
  & Principle, C3: 117
  & the female, C3: 128
  posits individuation, C3: 116
  SNAKE: Separative self-sensuality, C3: 91
  "The snake will one day coil affectionately
    around the eagle's neck" (Nietzsche),
    C3: 117
Sensuous
  & The rational aspect, C4: 2
  delights itself, C4: 2
  life loves pleasure, C4: 56
  NA: sensuous seeker of self-satisfaction,
    C3: 130
Sentience
  & capacity to feel, B4: 87, 181
  & elements of human being, TC: 3
  & female, TC: 3
  & motion, RS: 10
  & principle of all consciousness, C1: 2
  & Sensuousness, C3: 130
  & substance, TC: 33
  & substantiality, TC: 3
  & ultimate source of being, RS: v
  awareness, C1: 101
  concept of, C2: 4
  field of, RS: iii
  Inner *(see diagram)*, C3: 73
  power to feel, TC: 2
  properties of the Absolute, RS: 10
  property of power, C3: 125
  property of the Absolute, RS: 15
Sentient
  "sentient motion", C1: 43
  "sentient power", C1: 43
  & infinite continuum, C2: 62
  continuum of power, RS: 41
  energy self-modalised, C4: 65
  power, C3: 14
Sentient Power
  & "A thing" is a ... modality of ..., C4: 102
  & Christ's seamless garment, C4: 57

& continuum, C1: 8; C4: 57
& energy, B4: 91
& *ethics of the continuum,* C4: 75
& Expectancy, C4: 78-79
& fear, C2: 144
& Holy Trinity, C4: 108
& Logos, C4: 27
& matter, C3: 72
& "spirit", C4: 13
& the circle's binding contour, C1: 32
& true initiative, C4: 105
Absolute, C3: 72; C4: 53
BENEATH ALL PHENOMENA, C3: 2
Consciousness, C1: 62
eternal, C1: 9
eternally infinitely extended, C3: 95
evolution of awareness, C4: 12
field of, C3: 30; C4: 44, 46
free initiative, C4: 13
"God", C1: 9
Godhead, EG: 13
Infinite, C1: 9, 40, 42, 45; C4: 57, 108;
    DD: 70
infinity of patterns, C1: 46
is catalytic, C2: 101
man is a field of, C3: 42, 44
mind, C2: 4
motion-pattern, C1: 42
NON-DUAL infinite continuum of, C4: 57
"Only the Infinite Continuum of Sentient
    Power is, says Yadillah", C4: 120
parontic, C2: 60
pre-analytic origin of all created things,
    TC: 27
SACRED PLACE, C3: 131
see B4: 9, 73, 91, 155, 182
see C1: 2, 8-10, 12, 24-25, 31-33, 40-46, 52,
    62-63;
see C2: 1, 4-5, 7-8, 11, 21, 24, 26, 28, 30, 33,
    46-47, 52, 60, 66, 78, 81-83, 86-87, 93,
    101-102, 112, 118, 124, 126-127, 137,
    144, 147;
see C3: 2-3, 14, 21, 24-25, 30, 42-45, 47-48,
    61-62, 72, 75, 95, 98, 105, 114, 119, 121,
    125, 128, 130-132;
see C4: 1, 3, 9, 27, 29, 38, 43-44, 46, 57, 71,
    75-76, 78-79, 88-90
see RS: viii, 3, 10, 25, 38-40, 42-43, 48, 50,
    59
see DD: 69-70

see EG: 13-14, 16-18
see TC: 2, 23, 25-27, 33-34
self-experience of the infinite, C1: 40
Spirit, C1: 63
supreme knower, C2: 137
the real God, C4: 57
THREE PHASES OF, C3: 119
ultimate reality, C3: 128
ultimate substance, RS: 3

Sentiency
= field awareness, C1: 70
& ocean, C1: 84, 87

Separate
& ego-self, B3: 83
elements of serialised knowledge, B1: 124
events, B1: 124

Separateness
& self-evident truth, B4: 80

Separation
function-pattern, C4: 53
of the sexes, TC: 11
sin, C2: 7
substantial, C4: 33

Separative
energy, C4: 67
thinking, C2: 53

Separativity
& playing the devil, C2; 7
idea of, B1: 53
to believe in, B3: 61

Sephiroth
& Malkuth, C3: 31

Sequence(s)
action, B1: 15
-process, B1: 14
ideas, CA: 72
of events, B1: 13
see B1: 3-4
Time and Eternity, B1: 14
Time and Matter, B1: 15

Serial
& Absolute Sentient Power, C2: 47
Quantity is, C2: 56
sequential process, CA: 71
"serial causation", C1: 43
Time-matter process, B1: 16
"toothed", C2: 83

Serpent(s)
-force, C3: 33
& Adam, B1: 24

& Book of Truth, C2: 72
& (Dan (judgement), C4: 22
& Eve, EG: 55-59
& super-sensitivity, B3: 93
& translating motion, RS: 5
AN-CHOR: Serpent Hierarchy, C3: 49
"Be ye therefore as wise as serpents and as
    harmless as doves" (Jesus), B3: 134
divide the, C4: 22
harmless … as a dove, yet … wily as
    serpents, DD: 56
in man, B3: 134
in the Garden, EG: 54
Jesus accepted the … in man, B3: 134
painful to admit the …. within us, B3: 137
pinned *(see diagram)*, C2: 65
spirit, DD: 52
subtle, DD: 45
subtlety of a, P2: 51
symbolises our sensitivity, B3: 92
tail in mouth, C2: 147; DD: 10
type of subtle, sensual being, B1: 79
wily as, DD: 56
"worm that dies not", C4: 2

Serving
Observation, C3: 89

Seth
Eve (son), B1: 91
see B1: 91

Severity
and mercy, DD: 29
Pillar of the Tree of Life, C4: 71

Sex(es)
& English gematria, C3: 20
& Freud, B2: 46 polarisation of biological
    forces, B2: 46
is a polarisation of biological forces, B2: 46
of the sexes, TC: 11

Shabda Brahma
Logos, C2: 16

Shabdabrahman
cosmic sound, C2: 53; C3: 120
theory of, C2: 43

Shakespeare
"Good name in man and woman is the
    immediate jewel of their souls", B1: 107
"The play's the thing wherein I'll   catch
    the conscience of the king", B2: 39

Shakti
Shiva's, C4: 92

Sonoriferous Aether (Akasha), C3: 51

Shaman('s)
operations, C4: 74
Twilight, C4: 74

Shame:
"Honour and shame are the same"
    (Lao-Tse), B2: 82

Shape
"idea" & "form", B2: 17; C1: 35

Sheep
& goats, DD: 55
gathered together in the plains, DD: 55
"I send you out as sheep amongst
    wolves" (Jesus), B3: 134
in man, B3: 134
Jesus accepted the … in man, B3: 134
"My sheep hear my voice" (Jesus), P2: 48
seem harmless …but, B3: 137

She-He
hermaphroditic or bi-polar name, C4: 95-96

Shell
Silver, C1: 91

Shem
& Ham, B2: 43
& Japhet, B1: 103; B2: 43
descendants of, B2: 54
feeling sensitivity, … how to name things,
    B2: 39
function, B2: 42-43
Man of the Name, B1: 102
means "name", B2: 25
"Renowned Name", B1: 98

Shepherd(s)
good & bad, RS: 52
Good, P2: 51

Shift
apparent, EG: 10
of attention (motion), C2: 62

Shiva('s)
& third eye, RS: 19
Shakti, C4: 92

Shock
coming face to face, B4: 63-64
delayed, C4: 81

Sight
may deceive, C1: 109
sense of, P2: 69

Sign
of a fish, B4: 81

Signals
THREE PHASES of development, C3: 76

Significance
particular, general or universal, C1: 93

Silence
absolute, C3: 57
special, B1: 35

Silenus
& King Midas, C1: 29

Silver
shell, C1: 91
T-shirts, DD: 2

Similars
seed is the sum of, C4: 62

Similia
similibus (treat like with like / homeopathic
law), C2: 122, 124

Simplicity
of God's truth, B1: 86

Simultaneity
& Eternity, B1: 16
God's, CA: 70
non-serial, B1: 16

Sin(s)
& Chaos, C4: 29-30
& CONSISTENCY, C2: 107
& God, C2: 75
& identification, C2: 148
& The Logos, C3: 40
Adam's, B1: 24; B3: 89
against the Holy Ghost, C2: 18
against the Son of Man, C2: 19
alienation, B4: 74, 126
ancestral, C2: 69
Creation, C2: 19
"dead in their sins" B3: 19
Greatest, C2: 19
man's fall into, CA: 67
"miss the mark", B4: 126
non-sinning zones, C4: 54
of the flesh, B4: 74
Origin of, C4: 53
Original, B2: 77; CA: 85
past, P2: 112
private aims, B3: 19
separation from God, P2: 117
separation from the Source (the
Continuum), C4: 107
SEVEN DEADLY, C3: 101
"Sin is within itself a *consistency*

..." (Kierkegaard), C2: 107
state of deprivation, C2: 15
"The sins of the fathers are visited upon the
children", B1: 84; B2: 77
"to miss the mark", B1: 106
will to separation, C2: 7
willed preference for self-origination, B2: 142

Sincerity
& good-doing intentions, DD: 1

Single
choice, B3: 131
"If thine eye be single, thy whole body is full
of light" (Jesus), B3: 44, 50, 60
reality, B3: 67
"the single eye" (Jesus), B3: 60

Singleness
of being, B3: 44

Six
-legged ... bureaucrats, C4: 69
-petalled flower of the Hexonic Field,
C3: 101
directions, C3: 100
number of establishment, C3: 45

Skin
gross limit, C3: 44

Sky-watchers
& star-gazers, B2: 122

Slain
ye shall become Abel, when ye shall have ...
Cain, DD: 64

Slanderer
Accuser, C1: 87
devil, C1: 87

Slave(s)
& civilised values, EG: 65
slave mentality, EG: 82
slave morality (Nietzsche), EG: 82-83
of matter, P2: 13

Slavery
& Greek citizens, EG: 69
& Jews, EG: 65
condition of, CA: 39
"Fall from Grace", B4: 161

Sleep
-scattered wits, B2: 118
& Death, B1: 68
& dreams, B1: 58; DD: 18
& earth-men, DD: 18
& Kingdom of innermost essence, B1: 68
& kingdom of non-Self, B1: 68

& machines, B1: 68

& outer self, B1: 68

& the soul, CA: 16

"a little folding of the hands in sleep"
    (what it means), B4: 154

deep, C1: 60

deepest, B1: 68

dreamless, B2: 117

Sleepers

half-, DD: 12-13

see DD: 9-11

Sleeping

machine-operating-while-sleeping, B1: 143

Beauty, C1: 94

Smell

see P2: 69

Snake

& pain memories, C4: 56

& TOTAL KNOWLEDGE, C3: 90

& woman, C4: 55-56

= Man, C2: 112

AN (snake, sensual satisfaction seeking),
    C4: 1

Naga-Snake, C3: 51

*"The snake will one day coil affectionately around
    the eagle's neck"* (Nietzsche), C3: 117

Three phases of, C3: 49

Social

hierarchy, B3: 26

systems, EG: 89

Society(ies)

matriarchal & patriarchal, TC: 11

politeness, EG: 90

Socrates

Buddha, Mahavira, Jina, Lao Tse,
    Zarathustra, RS: 52

origin of all beings, RS: 52

(Conceptual essences), C4: 31

wife, TC: 50

Software

inner world, B2: 110

SOKUTAKU NO KI

see C3: 108

Sol

& CURE & reversal of the Fall, C2: 117

& Luna *(see diagram)*, C4: 73

& twi-light sunset *(see diagram)*, C4: 73

life, C3: 123

principle of triple illumination, C2: 99

see C2: 99, 117; C3: 6-7, 101, 123

(see diagram), C2: 109; C3: 7

will, C3: 113

Solar

-energy, C3: 110

life, C3: 99

system, EG: 46

Soldier

& marksmanship, B1: 77

Solid

God, EG: 9

Solidarity

of all being, C4: 112

Solipsism

& Absolute Subject, C3: 41

Solution

in the word*s* "perfect love casts out fear",
    CA: 84

of all our problems, B3: 70

saturated, C2: 51

Soma

& pneuma, C3: 25; C4: 112

& Psyche, C4: 112

Son(s)

& Father, *(see diagram)*, C4: 108-109

& First Cause, C4: 86

& Holy Trinity, B3: 113-114

& Holy Trinity, *(see diagram)*, C4: 108-109

& Mother, C4: 108

& the Father, C3: 111; C4: 86

(= the Form), EG: 18

beloved, C3: 70

Divine, B2: 162

God's, P1: 17

"He that honoureth not the Son honoureth
    not the Father that hath sent Him" (Jesus),
    P1: 18

His only begotten, C2: 76

the Logos, C2: 27

of God, B2: 158; B3: 24, 33; C4: 34;
        DD: 23; P1: 23, 82

of Light, C3: 57

of Man, C2: 19

of Noah, B1: 100; B2: 25, 28, 31, 54, 59

onely begotten, C4: 91, 106

Soniferous Aether

Shakti, C3: 51

Sonne (die)

see C3: 110

Sonship

divine, B3: 24

Sophia
 -Wisdom, C3: 24
 Cosmic Wisdom, C4: 110
 Heavenly, B4: 22
Sorcery
 Law of, C4: 33
Sorrow(s)
 "Sorrow must come; woe to him by whom",
  EG: 85
 "Way of Sorrows" P2: 15-16, 23
Soul(s)
 & Anchor, CA: 18, 21, 101
 & anxiety, C2: 64; CA: 17, 100-101
 & aware finite, C1: 102
 & body, CA: 14-17, 100-102
 & despair, CA: 17
 & disparity, CA: 17
 & Divine Spirit, B1: 6; CA: 4
 & efficacy of sounds, B3: 142
 & embodiment, CA: 17
 & familiar percepts and concepts, C2: 114
 & fear, C2: 64
 & first birth, C4: 108
 & God's will, B1: 81
 & health, CA: 99
 & Hinduism, C2: 102
 & identification, B1: 96
 & its spirit-origin, C1: 89
 & love, C1: 66
 & Materialistically-minded people, B4: 2
 & Modern psychology, B1: 95
 & physical body, B3: 126
 & plasticity (soul's), B1: 96
 & psychological harm, CA: 97
 & self-control, B4: 154
 & sleep, CA: 16
 & spiritual pains, P2: 23
 & suffering and pain, CA: 102
 & Truth of Certainty (in Sufism),
  C2: 103-104
 & uncontrolled emotions, B2: 45
 & Will, B4: 9
 Action originates in the, C4: 50
 at death, EG: 95
 cannot disintegrate, B3: 127
 centre of the human, B1: 63
 "Christ my anchor," CA: 21
 co-creator with God, B4: 156
 How do we condition our ...?, CA: 53
 cup functions like the, C2: 79

 destruction of its belief, CA: 10
 dream-condition, CA: 16
 duty, CA: 43
 easily disturbed ... shocked, B1: 96
 embody themselves, B3: 128
 ensphered zone of the spirit of God, B3: 121
 essentially a *feeling* being, CA: 54
 exist for God, C4: 63
 feeling awareness of the self, TC: 16
 first birth, C4: 108
 "Good name in man and woman is the
  immediate jewel of the
  soul" (Shakespeare), B2: 100
 human, B3: 121; C2: 110; C3: 10; P1: 145;
  P2: 28, 38
 inner-mostness, C4: 50
 innermost, B4: 68
 is eternal, P2: 123
 living, C3: 34
 "lost soul", P2: 34
 Man's, B1: 26; P2: 21
 of man, EG: 51
 original, CA: 16
 our Generative Power, CA: 14
 Our goals and aims model our, B4: 63
 primary, CA: 16
 real Self of man, P2: 28
 Rotating spirit, C1: 88
 self-initiating, C4: 50
 Sleeping Beauty, C1: 94
 soul-doctors, DD: 49-50
 source of the human, B1: 3
 Spirit of God in Man, P2: 33
 time-expression of the, B1: 3
Sound
 -energy, C2: 43
 -forms (Divine Names), C2: 99
 & breath, C3: 103
 & Indian Mantras, B3: 142
 compression/decompression moments,
  C3: 2
 creative, B4: 41
 form-principle of Reality, C3: 51
 NOUS-SOUN, C3: 33
 pattern(s), B3: 142
 structuralising principle of basic reality,
  C3: 120
 structures (mantras), C2: 62
 ultimate reality is, C2: 33

Source
-energy, CA: 23
-power, B2: 141; B3: 62, 122; B4: 21, 54;
    CA: 23
Apeiron (source of the world), RS: 4
ASP (ultimate source), C4: 53, 56
common, DD: 2, 14, 20, 23, 31, 37
contrariness (source of), B4: 112
death (source of), B1: 48
evils, B4: 82
external, C4: 13
"Fall", separation from the Source, C4: 107
God, B3: 56
Infinite Power, B3: 50
Infinite source-power, B4: 55
intelligence & divine source, B1: 94
life of God and of Man has the same, B2: 57
of all evils, B4: 83
of all things, B4: 21; P1: 136
of all visibles, B3: 61
of humility, B3: 130
of impedences, B2: 99
of intelligent power, & geniuses, B3: 42
of our *initiation*, CA: 30
of true conscience, C1: 101
Our Father (Jesus), B3: 41
power of the universe, C4: 115
"sin", separation from the Source, C4: 107
Spirit as ... Source of all being, C1: 47
Supreme, B1: 28; B2: 58; 189;
    B4: 81, 110-111
(the Continuum), C4: 107
totality of all energies, B3: 58
ultimate, of being / all things, C1: 47;
    P1: 136; RS: v-vi
South
North-South axis, C4: 66
Pole, C3: 33
South Pole
south-pole judgement, C3: 64
Space
& Bodies, CA: 14, 24
& consciousness, EG: 48
& infinity, C1: 78; EG: 9
& no-thing, B2: 67
& Power, EG: 38-49
& Time, B4: 95, 97; C2: 84
between objects or forms, C1: 36
Cause of causes, EG: 44
constant behind all variables, EG: 41

field force, EG: 33
God the Father, EG: 49
immanent and transcendent, EG: 42
inseparable from power, EG: 38
objects in, B4: 85
physical, C2: 64
see B4: 85-86; EG: 38-49
totality of all possible places, C1: 98
Spark
collective ..., a great consciousness, EG: 47
Speak
& fall, C3: 124
Speech
articulate, B4: 41
Sperm
-forces, C4: 38
specialisation of, TC: 6
Spermid
& monocell, C3: 109
sun-worshipper, C3: 110
Spermiform
initiating, C4: 82
"male", C4: 82
Sphere(s)
Christal, C2: 139
container, B1: 46
Great Sphere, B1: 47
Infinite Sphere of Being, C3: 133
self-precipitated hierarchy, C2: 70
self-precipitated zone, C2: 66
SUPERIOR, C3: 68
Spin
(Mercury), C4: 39
see EG: 32-35
Spine
"ladder to all high designs", C4: 4
Spinoza
"Adequate knowledge is activity; activity is
    happiness," ... "Inadequate knowledge
    equals passivity equals misery." (Spinoza),
    C2: 57
"God is substance", P1: 136
vindicated (non-dual substance), C3: 26
Spiral
loose, C3: 129
Spirit
& body, C3: 58; C4: 95; EG: 4
& ecology, B3: 71, 73, 75, 80, 82
& fire, DD: 8
& free spontaneous creativity, B1: 53

& infinitely intelligent purpose, P1: 99
& Logos, C4: 32
& matter, B3: 76
& material incarnation, B3: 109
& "Mystical Marriage", P1: 132
& non-materialistic people, B3: 31
& the Creator, B2: 15
& true Temple, B3: 83
& wholly living bodies, P1: 76
20th century, C1: 47
anima, C2: 87
as an absolute, Spirit as God, Spirit as
    Creator and ultimate Source of all being,
    C1: 47
"Behold! I make all things new", B1: 105
"born of water and of spirit", CA: 27
centre of initiative, C2: 104
"diverse gifts" DD: 4
Divine, B4: 111-112; CA: 16, 98; P2: 28, 40
embodied, B3: 4
embodiment, B2: 169; B3: 109; B4: 112
Eternal intelligent power, B3: 4
finest of all beings, B3: 108
free initiative sentient power, C4: 13
free, C4: 112
freedom of choice, CA: 98
God is Spirit, B1: 4; C3: 58; C4: 35;
    P2: 19, 40
God's all-knowing, B1: 54
Holy, C4: 108
(Immediate Creativity), C4: 35
impedances, C4: 2
incarnates in earth (Tauros), C4: 30
inner divine, B3: 5
"intelligent initiating power", B3: 111-112;
    B4: 36
intelligent power, B3: 2; B4: 35-36
invisible, B1: 53
issuant, C4: 28
soul is but a locus of divine, B3: 127
love, C1: 66
man's, DD: 52
of God, P1: 130; P2: 54
of my God, DD: 39
one, DD: 4
original, B4: 181
pleasure, C4: 2
polarisation of, C4: 1
power of self-locomotion, B4: 182
power of the, B2: 128

power, C3: 86
progress of, B1: 1
Satanic, B4: 186
see B3: 76
seeks a body, C4: 36
sensitive power, B4: 183
sensuality, C3: 116
sentient power, C1: 63
spirit-matter problem, C4: 17
Supreme Subject, C4: 23
"there is one spirit", DD: 4
What is Spirit?, EG: 37
wind, air, breath, vital force, C1: 48
Word-Deed, DD: 57
Spiritual
awareness, B1: 41; B4: 180
Being, CA: 31; P1: 91
birth, B4: 37
body, CA: 102; P2: 59
brothers, B3: 31, 35
"… creativity", DD: 70
death, B1: 53
ecology B3: 73, 75, 80, 82
evolution, B3: 4
fire-body, CA: 30
Heart, B4: 82
man, CA: 7
nature, B1: 64
origin, B1: 64
pains, P2: 23
problems, CA: 3
processes, CA: 63,
reality, B3: 17
self, P2: 3
truths, B3: 111
world, B1: 77; B2: 133; B3: 73;
    P1: 62, 79, 140
world (leaders of) P2: 24
Spirituality
axis of, P2: 27
essential, CA: 10
Spiritually
minded human being, CA: 6
lost, P2: 27
unenlightened mind, P1: 63
Spiritus
GOD, SPIRITUS, ANIMA, CORPUS,
    devil, C2: 126
pneuma, C2: 88
pure intelligence, C2: 89

Split

in the mind of Adam, B1: 57

Sportsman(men)

great men & link between past and future
sportsmen, B1: 121-122

ST (SELF-CRUCIFIXION)

precondition of all creaturely activity,
C3; 47

St. Paul

see also Paul

"strong meat" doctrine, C2: 105

Stable

reference centre, CA: 26, 100

reference of consciousness, CA: 26

Stability

& physical body, B3: 108

& the mind, B3: 66

Stage

life-stage, C1: 80

Stage fright

fear of opinion, C1: 67

Star

-gazers, B2: 122

-substance, astral light, C2: 63

-Wheel, B2: 121

& prophesy, B2: 121

of David, C3: 80

WE ARE COMPACTED star-substance,
C2: 63

State

Great Beast, C3: 45

of our will, CA: 37

Statements

made to us … check them for truth or falsity
(good practice), B4: 193

Steps

on our soul's journey, CA: 64

Still

"Be still, and know that I am God", B3: 154

centre of our being, B3: 107

our mind and emotions and impulses,
B3: 183

"still small hours of the night" & man,
TC: 41

Stillness

& CURE & reversal of the Fall, C2: 117

& eternal non-activation, B3: 131

absolute, C3: 50

dynamic state of self-contradicting energy,
C3: 61

of mind, B2: 19

To gain this, B3: 154

Stimuli

& pleasure & pain, B4: 53

& self-balancing re-action to, C3: 62

calls for response, C4: 63

contingent, C4: 90

external contingent, C3: 44

external, C4: 13

from … things, B4: 53

Passivity to, B4: 161

PHEROMONES, C3: 78

react mechanically to, B4: 53

strike upon us, P2: 54

Stimulation

continuous uniform, P2: 57

external B4: 92

Stimulus

-complex, C4: 107

energy input, C3: 123

outer contingency *(see diagram)*, C3: 73

record, C3: 1

sense-organ, C3: 76

Sting

of intensest compaction, C2: 138

Stone(s)

& bondage, B4: 40

& Jesus, B3: 83

& Temple of Truth, B3: 86

corner-, B3: 83

of the desert, B4: 16

Philosopher's, C4: 38

rejected, B3: 82-83, 109

"self", B4: 40

Story

& "spinning a yarn", B4: 141

Stress

disorders & neuroses, B3: 61, 152

value-stress, C1: 40

Excess of, C4: 78

Stupidity

or ill-will, C1: 68

Subject

& consciousness, C1: 55

& idea of a goal, C4: 85

& identification, C1: 74

& judgment, C1: 74

Absolute, C3: 112

doer of the act and the sufferer of its
consequences, C3: 94

SUBJECT-OBJECT thinking, C1: 85
Supreme, C4: 23

Subjective
experience, C1: 54
state (in dream and deep sleep), C1: 60
way, C1: 53

Subjectivity
three degrees, C2 89

Substance(s)
& "infinite power", P1: 136
& "matter", C4: 97
& mystery of Christianity, C2: 111
& "physicality", C4: 97
& reductionists, C2: 84
& resistance, C4: 97
& "Separation", C4: 53
& shape or form, P1: 132
& spiritual warrior, C2: 81
& "superstance", C4: 96
"Faith is the substance of things hoped for",
    B4: 6
God is, P1: 136-137
letter M, C4: 97
life's ... (Cancer), C4: 30
non-dual, C3: 26
of consciousness, C1: 97
of the Absolute, C1: 98
of the universe, P1: 135
of cosmos (Hinduism), C2: 102
Power, B4: 6; C4: 96; P1: 136-137
Prime Matter, TC: 32
resistance, C1: 103
standing under, C4: 96, 101
"substantial aspect", P1: 132
suffering, C2: 135
Universal, C4: 63, TC: 32
what stands underneath differences, C3: 60
world ... continuum of sentient power,
    C4: 57

Substantiality
& elements of human being, TC: 3
& female, TC: 3
& sentience, TC: 3

Success
success-complex, C1: 90

Sudden
impulse (south-pole judgement), C3: 64

Suffering(s)
& Tree of Knowledge, B4: 14
conscious of, B4: 121

prayer-sayer, C4: 59

Sufism
certainty, C2: 103
fikr (meditation) and *zikr* (invocation), C2: 8

Suggestion
(auto- or hetero-), C4: 25, 79

Suicides
& mental breakdowns, C3: 63

Super
-biogram, C2: 131
-saturated solution, C2: 52
-stress, C1. 40

Superficial
appearances & eye, P1: 144
thinking P1: 10
consideration, P1: 11

Suppression
capacity for, B4: 32

Supreme
Invisible, B3: 61

Sun
-beings, C4: 82
& ATMOSPHERE of the Earth, C3: 67
die Sonne, C3: 110
of the Morning (Lucifer), C4: 12
Sun-Son of God The Father, C3: 6
Surayana (sun-path), C2: 77; C4: 81

Sun-goddess
Die Sonne & Japanese, C3: 110

Sunyata
void, C3: 109

Survival
-need, B1: 41
& basic motive, B3: 28
& group, B3: 94
in our souls, CA: 25
learning, C2: 136
of physical death, CA: 23
problem of, C1: 14
rules, B3: 95

Survivor
sentient power itself, C2: 137

Surayana
& Pitriyana, C2: 77; C4: 81 reincarnation,
    C2: 77

Sushumna
Balance place between blood and nerve,
    C4: 74
see Three Phases (Push, Pull, Balance),
    C3: 30

Twilight, C4: 74
Suzuki
principle, C3: 43
Sweat
Chrism, C2: 139
Sword
"sword of the mouth", CA: 7
two-edged, C2: 18; P1: 44
Symbol(s)
[definition], C2: 68
[Master Symbol, the cross in the circle, interpreted],
see diagrams, C2: 142-144, 106; C3: 4,
32-33, 48, 99, 122; C4: 17, 23, 66-67,
117-118
Fish, CA: 34-35
mediates between the two orders of fact,
C2: 68
PHASES of development, C3: 76
see CA: 27, 28-29, 34, 35,
C2: 8, 68; 142, 144; C3: 17, 53,
76-77, 81, 99, 104, 123, 124,
142-144, 146, C4: 5, 97
seed (sym) of will (bol), C2; 142
super-symbol (A SYMBOL IS A SEED),
C2: 142-144
to understand a, C4: 5
Symbolism
of male and female, C4: 96-97
BEYOND SYMBOLISM (A book to be
written), C2: 68
Symbolise(s)
concept of substance, C4: 97
MANUAL OF POWER ... Great Law of
Life, C3: 123
inertia of the physical body, C3: 123
Symbolised
Archetypal forms, C3: 8
the speaker, the sound symbol, and the
think symbolised, C3: 124
of matriarchal authority, C3: 17
Symbology
& PRIMAL RELIGION, C2: 84
Bible (its own system of), B3: 38
Cosmic Body of God, C3: 79
System('s)
electro-chemical ... systems, B1: 30
electro-magnetic systems, B1: 30
of defences, C3: 44

T

T
see English gematria, C3: 19-20, 84-88
T-shirts
Letters of silver, DD: 2
Tacit Conspiracy
doctrine of, TC: 16
see Book, TC
silent agreement, TC: 1
Tactics
outer wars, B3: 159
(see diagram), C3: 49
Talent(s)
man of, B1: 121
parable of the, B1: 119; C2: 47; P1: 8
full development of one's whole being,
C3: 106
see B1: 119-123
special, B1: 119-120; B3: 55; P2: 20
will to develop a, B1: 123
Talk
FIGuratively, DD: 46
Tantrists
& PERFUMES, C3: 79
Tantrum
technique, C4: 91
Taoism
Way of the Valley Deep, C2: 103
Taoist
empty vessel, RS: 36
Taste
& our senses, C1: 26
Tau
Moses *(see diagram),* C2: 65
Templum Hierosalem, C2: 56
Tauros
& Spirit, C4: 30
material body, C4: 32-33
see also entries under: Taurus
Taurus
[*Zodiac sign*] *see* C3: 113
& Gemini, C3: 113
see also entries under: Tauros
Tears
"God shall wipe away all tears from their
eye", B4: 118
Teachers
& Man's condition, B1: 149
Technique(s)
of that (outer) war, B3: 158

tantrum, C4: 91
Technological
  advances, B1: 98
Technology(its)
  & intelligence, B1: 100
  & the atom, B1: 59
  new, B1: 59
  science and high-, B4: 99
Tehuti
  & Messiah: Mercury, Hermes, C4: 39
Teilhard de Chardin
  Two threads weave our life, C4: 60
Teleology
  & purpose & meaning, C2: 55
Telepathy
  resonance phenomenon, C2: 59
Telic
  pattern, C4: 85
  structure, C4: 78
  value, C4: 58
Telos
  arche is the, C3: 35
Temper
  & human father, B1: 148
  under test conditions, CA: 61
Temperaments
  TENDENCY of, B4: 106
Temple
  & "One on the White Horse", B3: 86
  & stone used in the building of, B3: 86
  false, B3: 85
  New, B3: 84
  "… not built with hand", B3: 84
  of Cosmic Truth, B3: 85
  of Eternal Truth, B3: 84-85
  of Innermost Truth, B3: 84
  of Solomon, DD: 63
  of the Living God, P1: 38
  of Truth, B3: 86
  of Universal Truth, B3: 85
  Truth-, B3: 85
Templum
  Hierosalem, C2: 56
Temptation(s)
  & "presentations of Time", P1: 140
  & TIME, DD: 45
  deliverance from, C1: 90
  in the wilderness, P1: 27
  of Jesus, B4: 11, 16-17
    Saturn-Chronos) … the contra-will of God,

C2: 56
  temporal presentation of action possibilities, CA: 49
  temporal phenomena, C2: 13
  three, DD: 53
  Time's offering to man, B4: 15
  Time-presentation(s), B4: 12; C2: 76
  Time-stimulus, B4: 97
  trial, DD: 53
Tendency(ies)
  -conservation (body), TC: 17
  & two-fold tendency (power), B1: 134
  & unconscious mind, P1: 102
  action (Mars), C2: 99
  animal instincts, impulses, B3: 135
  certain kind of, B3: 134
  Dark forces hidden as, P1: 103
  instinctive, EG: 67
  to fall into action (Inclination), RS: 22
  to reactivity, CA: 84
Tension(s)
  -relation, TC: 5
  destructive, B4: 117
  excess, B2: 9
  special function, CA: 31
Terms
  application of, C1: 83
  meanings of the, B3: 116
Test
  occasion for, B2: 171
  situations, C2: 64
Testes
  & tests, C4: 38
Teth
  & Book of the whole process, C4: 55
Tetragrammaton
  Name for God, C4: 95
  see B2: 106; C3: 25; C4: 95
Texut
  Texut-Thoth-Hermes - Mercury-Messiah,
    C3: 121
Thales
  & (Water), C4: 31
Theanthropism
  & Humanism, C4: 12
Theatre
  & persons in high places, B2: 39
  development of, B2: 39
  timing in the, C2: 41
Theism
  & humanism, B4: 25; C4: 12

Theme
Bible, B1: 11
THEOS
& RAPE, C3: 127
& THERAPY, C3: 127
& woman & man, C3: 127
THEOSIS
BECOMING GOD, C3: 96
THERAPY
& RAPE BY THEOS, C3: 127
& woman & man, C3: 127
THERE
said Lucifer, DD: 9
where my word went forth a place
   appeared, DD: 9-10
Thicket
ram caught in a, B2: 145
Thing(s)
& Infinite Power, B1: 15
& "intellect", B1: 50
& material world, B1: 55; B2: 23
& play of forces, B2: 156
& pre-creational state, B1: 3
& think, C1: 25
& this world, B2: 25
Absolute insulation of, B3: 137
AND Persons, C1: 96
behaviours of energy, B2: 155
define, C1: 83
dynokinetic process, B2: 156
Every created, TC: 28
fact of their existence, C1: 21
Father of all, B2: 157
God creates a, CA: 65
image, B2: 43
interfunction of all, B2: 171
interrelated, B3: 137
manifestation of spiritual forces, B2: 157
modality of Infinite Sentient Power, C4: 102
modifications of this Supreme Spirit, EG: 4
name for a, B2: 43
of Time and Matter, B4: 137
power resident in all, B1: 31
shape or form, B4: 134
Supreme Source of all, B1: 28
"thing-ness", C4: 103
vortices, C1: 111
Think
& thing, C1: 25
when we, P2: 53

Thinking
& Counting or evaluation, C1: 24
& danger, P1: 150
& disintegration, C1: 20
& feeling, B3: 69; C4: 77; P2: 60, 66
& human action patterns, P2: 66
& ideas, P2: 62
& means ... ends, C4: 77
& solving problems, P1: 149
& threefold life, B4: 68
becomes angry, C4: 77
can get lost, C4: 77
encapsulates, C4: 76
exclusivist way of, B1: 51
habitual way of, B1: 16
humanisation of our, B3: 117
is defining, B1: 132
is of two kinds, B3: 65
kind of, C3: 10
manipulating ideas, B2: 166
non-reflexive and reflexive, B3: 65
power of positive, B2: 105
presentation of ideas, CA: 71; C3: 10
rejects feeling, C4: 77
Separative, C2: 53
serial, C4: 50, 91
special zones in the brain, B1: 97
splitting of our feeling, action and, B3: 69
superficial, P1: 10
"Thinking is difficult" (German proverb),
   B3: 168
Thomas
& doubt, P1: 52
& "God created the heavens"
   (Quranic verse 65.12.), C2: 105
Thought(s)
& language, B3: 116
& separate functions of the human soul,
   B2: 8
astonishing, B3: 6
consumes energy, B4: 28
feeling and will, B2: 8
frightening, B3: 79
ordinary, C4: 26
stored unconsciously, B3: 145
Threads
Two (Teilhard de Chardin), C4: 60
Three
functions, B2: 55
"Life-Three-fold", B4: 68-69

LOGICS, C3: 102
Ms (Mandala, Mantra, Mudra), C3: 120
PHASES of sentient power, C3: 119
sons of Noah, B2: 54
trunks of the Qabalistic Tree, C3: 30
Whole Threefold Being, B2: 185

[Three-part diagrams]
[*related to three-part man / thinking / etc.*],
    (see diagrams), C2: 45; C3: 23, 36;
    C3: 121, 130, 133; C4: 40

Threenking
threefold thinking, C2: 45

3-D
existential individual, C3: 98
waking world, C3: 102

Thumetic nature
MUTHOS, C3: 94

Tides
moon-pull, C4: 82

Time
-beings, CA: 49
-commitments, B3: 80
-conditioned mind, B4: 108
-conscious man, B2: 19
-events, B4: 96
-life, P2: 123
-looking, B2: 121
-matter, B1: 7, 13-14; B2: 21, 192-193;
    B3: 3
-Matters, B2: 123
-moments, B4: 13; C2: 74
-possibilities, B4: 96
-presentation, B4: 12
-process (Akarana Zarvan), C3: 133
-process, B2: 16; B3: 3; CA: 49
-schedule, B3: 80
-sequences, B1: 14, 21
-stimuli, B4: 97
-things, B2: 16
-thinkings, B3: 78, 80
-units, B1: 14
-Way, B2: 120-123
-world, B2: 18
& dark (sable, Saturn), C2: 76
& eternal simultaneous content of infinity,
    C1: 72
& Eternity, B1: 3, 14; B2: 120-123; B3: 1;
    B4: 69, 95, 96, 103, 107; C2: 74,
    76; CA: 44; DD: 39; RS: 43
& first birth, C4: 108

& focussing attention, CA: 45
& God, C2: 57
& God's simultaneity, CA: 70
& granular interactions, C2: 82
& Infinite Power, B1: 3
& Linear mind, C2: 76
& linear separation, CA: 49
& Mammon, C2: 75
& matter, B2: 192; B4: 137; C4: 108
& Night (negation of power), DD: 9
& "Now", C4: 16
& one's choice, C2: 23
& partial existence, C2: 115
& reason, C2: 82
& repentance, B2: 190-191
& Saturn, C2: 76
& Scapegoats (Lucifer), B4: 27
& sequential activities of, B1: 5
& space, B4: 95; C2: 84; EG: 39
& suffering, B4: 14
& Temptation, B4: 15
& temptation, B4: 97; C2: 76: CA: 49
act of *creation*, B1: 3
"Bitty-ness", B4: 15
children of, CA: 48
creatures of, B2: 21
cyclic process, B1: 14
Egg of, C4: 38
events, B1: 4; B4: 132
in His existence in, CA: 4
Jesus wills to enter, B4: 15
Laws of, B1: 124
Luciferan precipitation, B1: 21
march of, B4: 132
marches on, B4: 94
mentational thinking, B2: 119
myth of Saturn, CA: 47
process & the eternal, C2: 108
product of change, EG: 2
"runningness", C2: 56
Satanic condition, B1: 20
scroll of, C2: 74
see CA: 44-52
see DD: 9, 25, 31, 35, 59, 61
sequential appearance of, C3: 95
series of events, B1: 3
serial work process, B4: 107
Things of, B2: 16
Time's offering to man, B4: 15
TIM-ID (Time-Form), C3: 50

"Time is the moving image of Eternity",
    B1: 3; B3: 2; B4: 96; CA: 46
we *generate*, CA: 46
within Eternity, CA: 44

Timing
    in the theatre, C2: 41

TIM-OV
    Egg of Time, Hiranyagarbha, C4: 38

Tiphareth
    Beauty = Balance *(see diagram)*, C4: 40

Tiredness
    last enemy, C4: 18

TO BE
    TO BE or NOT TO BE ... TO ACT or
      NOT TO ACT, DD: 62
    "to be or not to be" ... "to *do* or not to *do*",
      C2: 67

Tone(s)
    -values, C4: 113
    musical, C4: 113-114

Tongue(s)
    & control, B2: 27
    miracle of nervous organisation, B2: 27
    FORKED-, DD: 62

Tonic
    state, C1: 38

Tooth
    to grow a ("Dent"), C4: 22

Tora
    Scroll, DD: 11

Touch
    & motion of the absolute, C1: 110
    & vortex, C1: 111
    resistance of things, C1: 111

Touchstone
    and the Devil, C1: 111

Tower(s)
    & Sons of Noah, B2: 53
    and monuments to self-esteem, B2: 51
    Babel, B2: 53; B3: 179

Toxins
    & tiredness, C4: 18

Translating
    light-motions, C1: 107

Translating motion(s)
    & do not close, RS: 5
    & the excluded infinite, RS: 9

Translation
    corresponds with Will, C3: 75
    Motions of pure, RS: 8

of light, C1: 108

Transparency
    of the sage, B3: 132
    original spiritual, B3: 136

Treadmill
    & man, B3; 9

Tree
    & seed, B1: 31
    & three trunks of the Qabalistic, C3: 30
    & twig(s), P1: 104-105
    of knowledge of good and evil, B1: 23,
      47-49; B3: 69; B4: 14; CA: 19, 40;
      DD: 42; P2: 11
    of life, B1: 48
    of Life, C3:16; C3: 30; C4: 71
    see diagrams [of Life], C3: 30; C4: 74
    "To thine own self be true", B4: 192

Triad
    Truth, Love and Action, C3: 16

Trial
    & temptation, DD: 53
    by water and by fire, DD: 39

Triangle
    Eternal, C3: 30

Trinity
    & Absolute Sentient Power, C2: 83
    & anti-Christ or Devil Principle,   P1: 43
    & Father, *(see diagram)*, C4: 108-109
    & Holy Spirit, *(see diagram)*, C4: 108-109
    & Jesus, B4: 31
    & key to Unity, C3: 83
    & Mother, *(see diagram)*, C4: 108-109
    & Son, *(see diagram)*, C4: 108-109
    & trine relation of form-evaluation-power,
      C3: 91
    He-, C3: 50
    Holy, B2: 185; B4: 69; C3: 32; C4: 108-109;
      P1: 43; P2: 82
    incarnated in Jesus Christ, P1: 43
    Truth, Beauty and Goodness, P1: 43

Triple
    "Triple-F" response, B3: 29
    Tau, C2: 56

Triplicity
    God's, B2: 87

Trouble(s)
    & fall from grace, B2: 171
    humanity's, B1: 60

True
    & Beautiful & Good *(see diagram)*, C4: 40

& false relationships, B3: 165
Hermeneut, B4: 192
ideas, CA: 26
knowledge is power, B2: 128
self-development, B1: 85
Truth(s)
-lovers, B4: 144-145
-telling, C3: 22
-Temple, B3: 85
& an individual, C3: 37
& argument, C1: 102
& Astral Light, C3: 40
& Beauty and Goodness, C4: 40, 102,
    P1: 43-44
& body of the Eternal God, B3: 87
& Christ Himself, P2: 84
& Dialectic, C4: 35
& disobedience ... displaced the service of),
    CA: 21
& ego-self suppresses, B3: 86
& ego's self-defence process, B3: 85
& ENCOUNTER with nothingness,
    C4: 102
& falsity, P1: 30, 40, 64
& final sealing of the Crucified King, C3; 16
& fortress-temple of, B3: 86
& Jesus Christ's words, C4: 35
& Life, B4: 71
& Logos, C4: 35
& Love, B4: 112
& Marxists, C3: 21
& Mind of God, P2: 46
& Nietzsche, CA: 11-12
& "One on the White Horse", B3: 86
& our true life-way, B4: 34
& Perfect love, B4: 143
& Pilate, P1: 70
& Prodigal Son, B1: 85
& quiet voice within, B3: 148-149
& realm of eternal, B3: 113
& self-consistency, B4: 33; P1: 74
& spiritual bread, P2: 45
& Sufism, C2: 103
& the spirituality which God breathed,
    P1: 93
& the Veda, C1: 95
& tricky man, B1: 86
& Untruth, P1: 32
& unwelcome, B2: 27
& Word (embodied), B1: 102

& words of Truth and of Falsity, P1: 64
Absolute, B3: 120
anti-, P1: 42
battle of, ... against Untruth, B3: 167
Beauty, C4: 102; P1: 43-44
Body of Universal, B4: 142
confers peace of mind, P1: 64
Divine Truth of the Universe, B4: 143
divine, P2: 115
Each path is a separate *aspect* of, C2: 102
embodied, B3: 112; B4: 72
embodiment of the principle of, P1: 34
embody, B4: 74
essential spiritual, B3: 111
Eternal, B3: 86; B4: 143, 185; CA: 24;
    P2: 87, 114
final freedom ... ultimate, B3: 77
form of reality, B3: 112
Form of Reality, B4: 31
gives Oneness, B4: 146
God of, B3: 154
God's, B1: 86; B4: 143; CA: 38
Goethe has defined, C1: 6
Goodness, C4: 40, 102; P1: 43-44
guidance of the inner, P2: 51
Hidden, B3: 86
"I am the life", B4: 73
"I am the Truth" (Jesus), B4: 72; P1: 75
"I am the Way, the Truth and the
    Life" (Jesus), B4: 30, 68, 71; P1: 34,
    73-75; P2: 53, 68, 74, 84
in Religion or Philosophy, C1: 96
inner, P2: 51
Integrated pure, C3: 32
Kingdom of Universal, B4: 144
"know the truth and the truth shall make
    you free", B2: 128; P2: 42, 49
little Book of, C2: 72-73
(Logos, Dialectic), C4: 35
Logos is, C2: 126
mental pain, B2: 75
must be felt and willed, P2: 60
new, B4: 72
no Absolute, C1: 83
of God, P2: 45-46
of good book-keeping, B1: 87
of Logic, B1: 86
of the four-sidedness of squares, B3: 149
One ... Ultimate, B2: 66
pertains to the intellect, C4: 102

precondition of, B4: 193

principle either of Truth or of falsity, P1: 30

pure, B4: 10

pursuit of, C4: 102; P1: 41

quiet voice within us … speaks only
   Truth, B3: 148-149

Reality of the Universe, B4: 100

rejected stone of universal, B3: 84

revelation of sacred, C2: 114

seamless garment of pure, B4: 10

shortest path to the, B1: 85

simple, B1: 86-87

(Son) incarnate, C3: 111

statements … check them for, B4: 193

Temple of Truth, B3: 86

"that which is fruitful" (Goethe),C1: 6

to oneself, B4: 194

To tell the, B4: 192

Trinity of, P1: 43

TRUTH IS A LIE - Picasso, C3: 21

unalterable, CA: 24

Unific, B2: 66

Universal, B4: 30; P2: 48

voice dying away in the night, DD: 35

Volume of the Sacred Law, C4: 80

whole, P1: 71

Word of, B4: 142-143

word of, P1: 64

words of Truth and of Falsity, P1: 64

Tsadi

Rule as an emperor, C4: 54

Tum-land

Egypt, DD: 9

Turn

other cheek, EG: 66; P1: 35, 83

Twelve

Jesus … called, DD: 57

Twice-born

Kingdom of Heaven, C4: 108

Twig

"As the twig inclines, so grows the tree",
   P1: 104

Twilight

& Luna & Sol, C4: 73

imagination, C4: 73

Sushumna, C4: 74

two worlds, P2: 48

zone, P2: 45, 50

Two

"Two walk better than one" (Paul), TC: 41

Worlds, P2: 133

Type-figures

see B1: 79

U

U

& The Absolute, C4: 30

A E I O U, *(see diagrams)*, C4: 30

see English gematria, C3: 19-20, 84-88

Ubermensch

Nietzsche, C2: 128

Ultimate

& discontinuum, C4: 106

& experience(s), C4: 102

& Truth, B2: 66

Cause, B2: 58

dualism, B3: 141

God is the only, C4: 36

reality, B2: 86; C4: 21, 76

source, RS: vi

substance, RS: 3

Unconscious

& biograms, C2: 131

& mind, B2: 34

& modern psychologists, C2: 83

& Modern psychology, B2: 34

& sleep, B1: 58-61

at war, B1: 60

energies, CA: 75

interests, CA: 74

knowledge, CA: 83

memory, B4: 113, 116

mind(s), B1: 57, 61; B2: 46, 75, 176, 178;
   B3: 136; B4: 121; CA: 74-75, 80;
   EG: 91; P1: 93, 103

parts of the mind, B3: 93

protoplasmic records, B2: 177

realm, B4: 63

Unconsciousness

& sleep, B1: 58-61

& sub-conscious, RS: 33

"darkness", B2: 97

forces, B2: 34

objectless sentience, RS: 4

Understanding

conscious statement to oneself, C4: 101

door of, CA: 39

get, C1: 3

"Light", B4: 191

Undesirableness
& interference, C1: 76

Unfaith
Greatest, C2: 81

Unfallen
man, B2: 32

UNFINISHED
BUSINESS, C3: 27

Unhappiness
possibilities of, EG: 59
precondition of, B1: 83

Unique(ness)
nature of each individual, C4: 114
nature of each spirit, C1: 93
of individual beings, B1: 122
self, B1: 119

Unity
& essence of His divinity, B4: 160
& too many interests, B4: 162
& persons who pluralise, C1: 67
& sacrifice, C3: 83
lost, B4: 67
not homogenous sameness, C3: 91
of being, C2: 101
of God, P1: 4; P2: 4
of purpose, P1: 119
of spirit, P2: 58
of substance, C4: 117
of the human race, P1: 115
of will, B3: 60, 68; P2: 74
organic, C4: 65
original, B3: 60, 68; B4: 65, 161; P1: 115
perfect, B3: 60
principle, C1: 82; C4: 117
pure, C4: 116

Universal
& Pleroma, C3: 35
Being, B3: 126
evolution, B1: 122
MAN (COSMIC OR UNIVERSAL), C2: 1
Mass-Inertia, TC: 31
Power, B1: 9; B2: 143; P1: 125
purpose, B3: 150
Substance, TC: 32
truth, B3: 83
Master-tool, C2: 46

Universe
& activities of power, B1: 7
& intelligence, B1: 11-12

& interactionist view, B3: 58
& One Supreme Power, B1: 34
& purpose, C2: 55
& Principle of Reason, P1: 4
& reality, CA: 36
& spherical motion, B1: 46
& truth, B4: 100
a projection, C4: 98
an encapsulation, C4: 37
beyond our comprehension, CA: 36
continuum, C4: 112
Creator of the, B1: 11
"debris of prior universes" C4: 37
evolutionary movement, B1: 16
expression of energy, B2: 85
"God's Plan for His universe", B4: 97
God's, B1: 87
innumerable(ness), CA: 37
is rhythmical, B4: 154
mode of behaviour of energy, B2: 131
monistic & problems of evil, C2: 101
of active forms, B1: 8
of beings, B1: 23
Omega of Cosmic fulfilment, B1: 122
"one turn", B1: 46
play of energy, CA: 13
special modes of infinite power, B1: 8
teleology, C2: 55
things of the, CA: 37
vibratory energy system, C4: 67
whole manifest, P2: 129

Unjustified
& mercy, C2: 49

Unknown(s)
occasions for anxiety, B2: 128

Unpleasant
& pleasant records, B2: 180

Unrealisable
aims … are freely given up, CA: 77

Unsatisfaction
& *Dis*-satisfaction, C4: 68
& Saturn moments, most/least intense,
C4: 68

Untruth
& "One on the White Horse", B3: 86
& the prodigal, B1: 85
battle of Truth and, B3: 154

Urusalima
City of Peace, the New, C2: 33

Urgency
private aim, B3: 148
Uterus
sperm-eater, C3: 111

V

V
see English gematria, C3: 19-20, 84-88
Valley
Deep, the Way of the, C2: 103
Value(s)
-stressed pattern, C1: 39
& an individual, C4: 117
& One Supreme Source, B4: 110-111
& our affection, B4: 8
actual, C4: 116
developmental power, B4: 35
embodied, B2: 82
see (for definition), C4: 85
telic, C4: 58, 85
the child sees, B2: 57
will-stresses, RS: 19
Vandalism
& Cain, B1: 127
& suppressive forces, B2: 29
& wild ram-in-a-thicket energy, B2: 151
Vanity
"coming to nothing", B4: 132
Vav
& Yod, C3: 29,
Is the kinetic Yod, C3: 51
Drive, C4: 54
(see diagram), C3: 51
Tetragrammaton *(see Hebrew letters)*, EG: 14
Veda
Truth, C1: 95
Vegetable
reproduction, TC: 4
Vehicle
of experience, C1: 5
Veil
& concealment, B2: 28, 32
& Noah & covering, B2: 28, 32
of the Temple, C3: 33
Vengeance
& God's Law, CA: 43
Venus
& CURE & reversal of the Fall, C2: 117
& MANUAL OF POWER, C3: 123

& passive accepting love, C2: 99
& Samson's riddle, C4: 63
& sweetness, C4: 63
see C2: 99, 117; C3: 6-7, 101, 123
(see diagram), C2: 109; C3: 7
Verbalisation
of experience, RS: 33
can one know without, C2: 59
VERTICAL
(spirit power), C3: 86
Vibration(s)
& fear, C2: 144
& Saturn and Jupiter, C4: 38
& sound, C3: 2
& Spiritual world, B2: 133
alternation of compression, P2: 2
patterns of energy, B1: 72
posit-unposit alternation, C2: 20
unharmonious excessive, P2: 7
Vibratory
action, B2: 133; C3: 2
"being"-zone, C2: 48
motion, C3: 57; C4: 90
pattern of wave-clusters, C2: 77
system, C4: 68
Victory
Christ's (over the devil), P1: 38
View
continuum may be viewed as, C1: 98-99
evolutionary point of, TC: 23
observer's viewpoint, RS: 14
hedonistic, RS: 16
interactionist, B3: 58
non-dual, B3: 58
of a finite mind, RS: 48
[of} average man, TC: 14
of causation … oriental philosophies,
    C1: 43
of creation, C1: 77
of … cycle of birth and death, CA: 47
of himself (materialist), CA: 6
[of] material elements, C1: 50
of materialist(s), CA: 3, 33
[of] nature of matter, B2: 130
of Samsara, C1: 108
[of] space, C1: 99
of the universe, RS: 16
[of] universal prime matter, TC: 31-32
oneself, TC: 40-41
"overview" (eagle … symbol of the),

B2: 122-123
Samsara (Hindu), C1: 108
sexes … mutually exclusive, TC: 10-11
too simple, B2: 130
woman … has a different, TC: 21

Viewpoint
-locus, C2: 46
interest of sentient power, C2: 101
unique individual, P2: 70

Vindicated
Spinoza, Leibnitz, Jesus Christ, C3: 26

Vineyard
Kingdom of Heaven, P1: 110
Lord of the hired labourers, P1: 110

Violence
& Cain, B1: 90
& Taoism, C2: 103
counter-, B1: 127
inner, B1: 62
physical, TC: 14
Weapons of, CA: 7

Violent
Lamech, B1: 91

Virgin
see DD: 16, 22

Visible
& invisible power, B3: 62
God, B4: 18
world, B1: 53

Vision
two kinds oF, C2: 53-54

Visual
sense, C1: 35

Vitalism
Reductionists, C2: 84

Vocables
& Pearl Process, C2: 6
Misused, C2: 16

Vocabulary
Deficiency, C2: 16
educated persons, C2: 50
individuality, C3: 104
Japhet, B2: 43
of psychology, C2: 83

Vocal
Chords *(see diagram)*, C3: 103
cords, C3: 103

VOCARE
EST INVOCARE, C3: 1, 76; C4: 4

Voice(s)
& *urgency*, B3: 148
consciousness, C3: 76
God's, C3: 33
God-given … in our mind, B3: 148
in our mind, B3: 144-145
inner, B2: 105
Invoke, B3: 141, 144
of Eve, B1: 56
of God, B1: 35, 56; B3: 147
of our parents, relatives … [etc],
    B3: 145, 148
quiet … speaks only Truth, B3: 148-149
see P2: 48
still small, B1: 35; B3: 15, 148-149; B4: 47
The Logos, C2: 111
"To voice is to invoke", B3: 144
unique, innermost, B3: 148

Void
& freedom, DD: 8
formless, DD: 8
infinite, C2: 138
no THING, DD: 61
ORIGINAL, C3: 103
Satanic matter, B1: 21
SUNYATA, C3: 109
wisdom is a full, DD: 19

Voidity
& Cain, B2: 69
concept … notion, B2: 69
infinite vacuum, B2: 68
self-contradicting, C1: 11
space, B4: 85

Volitional
being, C4: 104
initiating of new action, C4: 91
level, C2: 44

Volume
of the Sacred Law, C4: 80
(see diagram), C3: 98
three-dimensional, C3: 29

VO-MIT
TIM-OV, C4: 38

Vortex
-centres, C1: 111
-light, C1: 107
-motion, C1: 106, 108
-zone, C1: 99
Crux Ansata *(diagram)*, C4: 92
empty centre, C1: 101

motion-interference, C1: 87

[Vowels]

A E I O U, (*see diagrams*), C4: 30

see English gematria, C3: 19-20, 84-88

Vox

= Box, C2: 16

Vulture

& eagle & hawk, B2: 122

symbol of the "over-view", B2: 122-123

Vulva

sealing of, C3: 80

W

W

(conation tends towards separation), C4: 67

see English gematria, C3: 19-20, 84-88

Walk

"Two walk better than one" (Paul), TC: 41

Want

& *Will*, C3: 102

"impulsive man wants what he wants when
  he wants it"(& Kierkegaard), B1: 25

IN ANIMALS, C3: 64

War(s)

& "a man's world", B2: 2

& ancient world, B2: 4

& beliefs, B4: 99

& espionage, B3: 153

& gap between male and female, C4: 100

& hunt, B2: 2, 12-13

& life of the spirit, CA: 30

& rape of the Sabine women, C4: 100

& survival, B2: 12-13

nations at war with each other, B1: 38

conflict between the force of good and …
    forces of evil, B1: 26

external, B1: 38; B3: 163

Greeks and Amazons, C4: 100

Inside man, B1: 25

man-made, B2: 172

nuclear, B2: 31, 34, 187-188; B3: 40, 144

outer, B3: 158

within ourselves, B4: 99

world & collectively guilty, B4: 152

Warrior

see I H S V, C3: 65

Spiritual, C2: 80-82

Washing

away of … unpleasant experience-records,
    B4: 117-118

WASPS

& towards spiritual realisation, C2: 103

God's method of maintaining human
    community on the gross material level,
    C2: 103

teach business procedure, C2: 103

Watch

see C4: 50-51

Watching

& Work towards freedom, C4: 50

feelings of liking and disliking, CA: 68

our mental processes, CA: 72

our processes, C4: 50

Water(s)

-body, CA: 29-30

-bound life in protoplasm, C3: 67

-filled bag or sac, CA: 32

-life, (Cancer) C4: 32

& birth, CA: 29; EG: 76-77

& cell-multiplication, C4: 81

& dual nature, CA: 32

& Four Elements, C3: 122

& Heaven (Balance of Power), C4: 75

& MONOCELLS, C3: 109

& movement of God's spirit, B1: 22

& Suryayana and Pitryana, C4: 81

& Thales, C4: 31

& universe as energy continuum, C4: 116

ancient symbol for plastic material
    substance, EG: 76-77

Bible symbol of plastic substance, CA: 27

"birth into water", CA: 29

"born of water and of spirit", CA: 27;

in the Bible B1: 95

of Thales (Hyle), C3: 13

of the fallen Satanic world, B1: 22

opposition to the monocell's movement,
    C3: 109

see (H20), C4: 32

symbol of material plasticity, CA: 29

eternal life, C3: 13

"water of Life", P1: 143

woman is as, DD: 45

Wave

-form(s), B4: 88: RS: 11

Way

& Christ, P2: 84

"broad way", P2: 53-57, 77

devious, B1: 85

exclusive & *inclusive*, B2: 178

Higher Way, P2; 75

His (God), B1: 85

"I am the Way, the Truth and the Life"
   (Jesus), B4: 30, 68, 71; P1: 34, 73-75;
   P2: 53, 68, 74, 84

"narrow way", P2: 52-57, 68, 73

of empirical science, C4: 20

of Jesus, B2: 171; B4: 15, 71

of Sorrows, P2: 15, 23

of the Magician C4: 20

of the Valley Deep, C2: 103

of the Woman, C2:103

Our Way of life, B4: 31

true, B2: 172

unstraight, B1: 85

We

In the mouth each one sai*d* "WE", DD: 13

"We sacrifice, but not forever", EG: 76

Weakness

must be overcome, DD: 43

Weapons

development of, B1: 127

of this world, CA: 7

sophisticated, B1: 127

Weaving

& language, B4: 141

Weiberbunde

(women's associations) … e.g. the
   Bacchanalia and Thesmophoria, C3: 81

Wellbeing

& human soul, P1: 145

& willed actions, B2: 10

God's love, P1: 145

West

W (+ *diagram*), C4: 67

What

WHAT, WHERE, WHEN, WHY, WHO,
   How and If / Else, C2: 89-91; C4: 71

Wheel(s)

& celestial Mercury, C4: 39

& the Messiah, C4: 39

anxiety-, CA: 84

cyclic, P1: 67

GREAT NEGATION, DD: 11

my … is turning, DD: 11

of fortune, P1: 46

of life, C3: 4

of the stars, B1: 22

ROTEH, C3: 4

"wheels within wheels" (Ezekiel's vision),
   B1: 14

When

WHAT, WHERE, WHEN, WHY, WHO,
   How and If / Else, C2: 89-91; C4: 71

Where

WHAT, WHERE, WHEN, WHY, WHO,
   How and If / Else, C2: 89-91; C4: 71

Who

WHAT, WHERE, WHEN, WHY, WHO,
   How and If / Else, C2: 89-91; C4: 71

Whole

& Reality, C2: 40-41

Holy Trinity, B4: 69

indivisible, B3: 126

Marx, C4: 9

ORGANISM, C3: 29

pattern of our action, CA: 77

Reality, B4: 129; C4: 39

relation … to its parts, CA: 77-78

Truth, P1: 70-71

Wholeness

& peace, B3: 40

& the Wilderness, B4: 15

Health, B2: 8; B3: 38

Holiness, B3: 82

inner, B3: 40

of Eternity, B4: 13, 15

state of perfect and complete integration,
   B4: 195

total self-consistency, B4: 11

Whore

of Babylon, C2: 18

Why

WHAT, WHERE, WHEN, WHY, WHO,
   How and If / Else, C2: 89-91; C4: 71

WICR

Worship Is Continual Remembrance, C3: 43

Widdershins

FIBONACCI APPLICATION, C3: 112

Widow

in a sea of weeds, DD: 17

sullen woman, DD: 17

Wilde, Oscar

"It isn't what you do …", B4: 63

Wilderness

Jesus is led by the Holy Spirit into, B4: 15

Will(s)

-power, B4: 46
-to-be, B4: 64
-to-be-something, C3: 61
& Bluebeard's Last Wife (a play), C2: 67
& "Gold", C4: 90
& "good" and "bad", B1: 75
& "security" of outer reason, C4: 26
& act of choice, B4: 61
& Cain, B2: 8
& desire, DD: 49
& eternity, C4: 87
& fear, DD: 49
& God-given capacity, B3: 99
& intelligence, B4: 46
& Jesus, P2: 60
& materialistic science, B4: 42
& mind, C2: 4
& MOTION, C3: 75
& original unity of, B4: 65
& Our real, divinely given, B3: 183
& Philosophy of the Divine, P1: 47
& reaction tendencies, C4: 48
& reconstitution of the form, C2: 77
& *self-consistency*, CA: 56
& separate functions of the human soul,
     B2: 8
& Spirit in man, C4: 33
& Spirit non-rotating, C1: 88
& Supreme Creator, P1: 76
& Suryayana, C2: 77
& the Self, RS: 32
& the soul, CA: 62
& TRUE SELF-CONFIDENCE, C3: 122
& Wish, Want or Desire, C2: 79
abandoned for the "security" of reason,
     C4: 26
absolute Ground of Being, C4: 20
act of, P1: 52
acts of, B4: 9
against a will, DD: 26, 49, 67
behaviourist psychologists, P2: 64
belongs to eternity, C4: 87
clash of, C1: 102
concepts (most mysterious of all), B4: 61
conflict, B2: 178
consciousness, C3: 45; RS: 32
contradiction or opposition, C4: 110
deepest (become able to see), B3: 183
DIFFICULTY, DD: 26

directed towards life or death, B1: 82
divine, C2: 148; P1: 18-19, 47
Earth, DD: 67
Empedocles, C4: 31
Enemy of Life is the will to death, C4: 49
Evil, B1: 83
faith, B2: 106; C2: 3, 113
FATHER (WILL) POSITS the Son,
     C3: 111
fire is the symbol of free, CA: 27
focus of our, CA: 37
free, B1: 30, 123, 146; B4: 45, 147, 161;
     C2: 134; C4: 20; CA: 24; P1: 161;
     P2: 20, 39, 42
freedom, B2: 160; CA: 21
God-given Unity of, B4: 64-66
God, C4: 91; P1: 76
God's, B1: 123; B3: 99; CA: 43; P1: 48,
     81-82, 137
"Gold" signifies, C4: 90
"good" and bad", B1: 75
group-, C4: 104
Hate and Love are states of our, CA: 38
Human beings, B2: 166
*"Impeccability of will; totality of self; no loose
     ends"* (Castenada's - Don Juan), C4: 14, 33
individual human, P2: 59
individuated, C4: 31
Infinite, C4: 104
initiative power, C3: 21
innermost state, B1: 76
Intellect B3: 78; C3: 71
intelligence and, P1: 123-124
is magical, C2: 140
is not Wish, Want or Desire, C2: 79
"It is My Will to do the Will of My Father"
     (Jesus), P2: 66
king of one's being, C3: 102
Leo, C4: 33
loss of inner centrality of the free, B4: 161
lost unity of, B4: 67
Love and do what you will (St Augustine),
     C3: 105
Magic, C4: 65
man of good or evil, B1: 76
man's highest act of Will, C4: 103
moments of, CA: 37
moulds our soul, B4: 63
movements of the, C4: 30

"My meat is to do the will of Him who sent me, and to finish His work", C4: 94

not definable, P2: 67

of the Absolute, C4: 63

of the mind, C2: 4

of the true Self, B3: 183

operation of, C4: 5

original divine causal power, B4: 61

pay the price, C4: 6

Philosophy of the Divine, P1: 47

power of self-initiation, CA: 62

pre-analytic wholeness of the, C3: 11, 60

problem of the human, B4: 166

projects itself, B4: 63

Pure, C4: 50

"purity of heart is to will one thing", C4: 14, 33, 45

reasoning, C2: 147

search for ultimate satisfaction, C2: 140

see B4: 61, 63; CA: 55-56

see quotes, C4: 6, 14, 45, 94; P2: 66

self-aware, C4: 11

self-centring on, C2: 41

Sol, C3:113

soul, C1: 88

soul self-initiating, C4: 50

spiritual power, B2: 106

stress of the, EG: 2

symbol is a seed of, C4: 5

to attain infinite power, B1: 128

to power, B1: 128

translation (MOTION), C3: 75

TRUE SELF-CONFIDENCE, C3: 122

truest (become able to see), B3: 183

Truth, P2: 60

unity of heart, mind and, B2: 8

universe comes into being by act of, B1: 13

willing, B2: 106

work of individual human, P2: 59

Willed

intention, C4: 50

Wily

"Be ye therefore as wise as serpents and as harmless as doves" (Jesus), B3: 134

harmless ... as a dove, yet ... wily as serpents, DD: 56

Wisdom

& folly, DD: 19

& God's spiritual universe, B1: 124

& knowledge(s), B1: 124; B3: 163; B4: 23;

DD: 19

& totality of all possible knowledges, B3: 163

& whole pattern of our life, B4: 23

Cosmic, C4: 110

Divine, B4: 22

"Fear of the Lord is the beginning of wisdom", C2:145

God's, B1: 52

here is, DD: 16

in eternity, DD: 19

intuits the continuum aspect, C2: 145

is a full void, DD: 19

sees the *pattern* of events,

B1: 124

Sophia, C4: 110

sophists, DD: 16

sphere of, P2: 8

true, P2: 9

Whole, B1: 125

Witchcraft

& menstrual cycle, C3: 81

Wit-to-Woo

virtue of, C3: 13

Woe

"Woe to you who are inheritors" (Nietzsche), B1: 84; EG: 73

Wolf

painful to admit the .... within us, B3: 137

symbol of appetite, P2: 47

"universal wolf which last eats up itself" (Shakespeare), C1: 94

Wolves

"I send you out as sheep amongst wolves ..." (Jesus), B3: 134; P2: 46

in man, B3: 134

Jesus accepted the ... in man, B3: 134

within us, P2: 51

Woman(en)

& "worm that dies not", C4: 2

& Adam C3: 70; DD: 45

& before the beginning, DD: 16

& behaviour of ... towards men, C4: 71

& CLAY, DD: 45

& Crux Ansata, C3: 17; C4: 92

& formal restraints, rejection of,C4: 93

& instinctive life, C3: 18

& moral restraints, C4: 93

& principle, C3: 116

& rational expression, C4: 70

& rational, TC: 12, 14

& rationality potential, TC: 14

& sentience (S), C3: 116

& Taoism, C2: 103

& The Absolute, TC: 49

& the Absolute and the Prime Matter,
    TC: 38

& THERAPY, C3: 127

& virgin, DD: 16, 22

basic life-principle, C2: 92

capacity for forgetting, C4: 70

child-bearing process, B2: 12

counting, C4: 55

enmity between thee and the, DD: 48

feeling-sensitivity, B2: 13

In the ancient world, B2: 5

is as water and earth, DD: 45

Mary, DD: 16

mother, DD: 22

power, non-rational, C4: 92

pre-occupation with changing fashions,
    TC: 10

Prime Matter, TC: 38

Queen ... chess-board, C4: 92

Queen Bee, C3: 18

rejection of formal restraints, C4: 93

see TC: 10

Severity Pillar of the Tree of Life, C4: 71

Shakti, C4: 92

snake, C4: 2

status of Goddess, C3: 17

sullen, DD: 16

Universal Mother, TC: 48

voraciousness, C4: 93

Way of the Woman (Taoism), C2: 103

Witchcraft, C3: 82

Woman's

noble sovereignty and courage, C3: 80

Womb

Holy Grail, C3: 80

Wonder-Eye

& absolute sentient-power field, C2: 33

Women

& women, magicians and hagicians, even of
    nagicians, C2: 92

Word(s)

"tunes" in the consciousness, C3: 1

-Deed, DD: 57

-garments, B4: 141

-impoverished, C2: 50

-manipulating, C2: 43

-poor, C2: 50

-power, C2: 50

-rich, C2: 50

-richness, C2: 50

& Infinite Intelligent Power, B4: 102

& "is", C2: 67

& letters, C4: 22

& *limits of its application*, C1: 21

& Shabdabrahman, C2: 43, 53

& the fourth Gospel, B3: 117

& *the* God, EG: 22-23

& the will B4: 42

& Whole Truth, P1: 71

all powerful, C3: 7

Bible is often called The, B1: 102

Christ's, P1: 14-15

Divine, P2: 48

"doing", C2: 67

embodied, B1: 102

formed sound, C2: 28

forms, C1: 24

"God", B4: 102

God's eternal, B1: 54

God's, P1: 68

In our minds are the records of

all the, B3: 151

"In the beginning was the Word ...",
    B3: 117, 167; B4: 41, 191; EG: 22

little, B4: 102

"Logos", B3: 53; C3: 1; C4: 118;
    P1: 3, 19

Mind of God, P2: 46

New, P1: 6

of finite application, P1: 71

of God, B3: 53

of Jesus, P1: 2, 5

of truth, B1:107

of Truth and of Falsity, P1: 64

ordering power, C4: 119

parts of the Logos-Ratio, P1: 5

power of, B1: 101

principle of Order, EG: 23

"Reason-Word", B3: 54; EG: 23

records of all the, B3: 151

represent forms, C1: 24

see P2: 46

see quote, B3: 117, 167; B4: 41

see VOCARE EST INVOCARE, C3: 76

"The words that I speak unto you, they are
    spirit and they are life", P1: 2; P2: 114

thought-tools, C2: 53

Trap of, C2: 79

"the Word made Flesh" (Jesus), B1:102

words of truth, B1: 107

[Word analysis methods]

see C3: 20

see diagrams, C2: 112

Work(s)

& animal and human, C4: 84

& *idea*, B3: 57

divinely appointed, B2: 22

Energy, B4: 105-106; C3: 61

Eternal, B4: 107

external or internal, B4: 106

faith, P2: 132

good, P2: 127

Marxism, C4: 58

"My father works and I work" (Jesus), B1:
   134; B4: 106, 154

new heaven and a new earth, B2: 22

of collective mankind, B3: 57

of God, C2: 100

of the individual human will, P2: 59

outer and inner, B4: 8

personal, P2: 59

Prayer is, B3: 143

"Work while it is light, for the night comes
   when no man can work" (Jesus), B4: 154

Workers

& four castes, C3: 65

World(s)

-court of all humanity, B4: 153

& contradictory forces, C4: 111

& *God*, C4: 88

& magician & hagician & nagican, C2: 92

& Paul's *pleroma*, C4: 63

& Principle of Order, B1: 39

& voices ... in our mind, B3: 145

ancient, B2: 5, 156

dangerous place, B2: 174

Dream, C4: 83

Eternal, P: 140

external material, B1: 35

externals of the, B4: 48

God so loved the world that he gave his onely-
   begotten Son, [i.e. one-ly], C4: 88

hygiene (problems of), P2: 119

infinite, P1: 140

inner, B1: 58, 72; B2: 16, 116

made by the Logos, C2: 125

man's, C4: 82

material, C2: 129; C4: 76, 98;
   P1: 20, 39, 111, 120, 140

nations of the, B3: 70

natural, B3: 73

new, P1: 12

next, B1: 71

of arithmetic, P1: 111

of ideas (Plato), B2: 17-18

of innermost being, B1: 71

of the spirit, DD: 58

outer, B1: 39, 41, 71-72; B2: 16, 24, 116;
   B3: 108; B4: 47, 53

outside (&) innermost, B1: 35

see diagram, C3: 68

soul, C1: 75

spiritual, P1: 140

sub-atomic, B1: 133

substance, C4: 57

substantialised or hypostasised concept,
   Begriff, C4: 17

super-stresses, C1: 41

"The world is a fiction made up of
   contradiction", (Blake), C4: 111

"The world is too much with us", B4: 48;
   P2: 127

this world and the next world, B1: 71

time-matter, B2: 21

two, P1: 44-45

VICTORY OF THE LOGOS, C3: 39

violence in the, B2: 31

war, B4: 152

WICR's, C3: 43

Worm

that dieth not, C3: 77; C4: 15

Worship

& Infinite Power, P1: 136

& WICR, C2: 118

A God is a proper subject for, B3: 125

act of free intelligence, P2; 117

act of training, B3: 112

continual remembrance, C2: 118

"His worship is perfect freedom",
   B3: 99; C4: 34-35

idol, B2: 59, 113

idolatry / idolator, B2: 58, 113

intelligent power, B3: 43

of God, P2: 131

supreme object of the, B3: 43

Worthiness
embodied truth, B3: 112
Writers
& sacrifice & training, CA: 92
& verbal stimulus, C4: 113
artists, C4: 113
of … the Bible, B1: 13, 16
Wrong(ly)
capacity for choosing, CA: 66
capacity for doing, CA: 66
motives, P1: 107
Wunder-auge
widder-shins cycle, C3: 112, 114

X

Y

Y
see English gematria, C3: 19-20, 84-88
Yadillah
says, C4: 120
Yantra,
function of a, C3: 52
Ye
"Is it not written, ye are gods?", EG: 11
Yea
& Nay, DD: 30
Yes
& "No", B4: 186
free spirit of God which says, B4: 186
Yggdrasil
myriad-branched tree, RS: 36
YHWH
see (Hebrew letters), EG: 13-14
Yod
& THE BIG SECRET, C3: 28
becomes Vav, C3: 29
kinetic, C3: 51
Primary Point, Yod of the Tetragrammaton, C2: 106
(see diagram), C3: 51
Yodh
"hand" or instrument of the A.S.P., C4: 55
Yoga
practices, C1: 56
Bhakti, C3: 93
Mantra-, B3: 142
"religion" B3: 101

"union", B3: 101
Yogi(s)
& Shiva, RS: 20
aims to fuse his consciousness, C1: 56
Jesus the perfect, B4: 164
Yoni
-Darkness, C3: 33

Z

Z
see English gematria, C3: 19-20, 84-88
The "whoreson Z", the "unnecessary letter", C3: 19, 88
Zarathustra
Jesus, Buddha, Mahavira, Jina, Lao Tse, Socrates, RS: 52
origin of all beings, RS: 52
Zen
Immediacy of Response, C2: 103
Zikr
& fikr, C2: 8
(invocation), C2: 8
[Zodiac]
(Zodiac signs of) see C3: 12, 112-114; C4: 30, 32-33
Zone(s)
& continuum, C2: 93; C4: 53
& formal content, C1: 74
& interest, C2: 93
"beings", C2: 93
encapsulation, C2: 61
energy, C4: 65
finite encapsulated, C4: 107
in consciousness, C1: 84
non-sinning, C4: 54
of a continuum, C4: 53
of fear, P2: 7
of phenomena-complexes, C4: 107
of self-encapsulation, C2: 60-61
of spinning energy, EG: 33
of turbulence, C1: 84
see C2: 93
selected, C2: 101
self-precipitated, C2: 66
sentient power, C2: 101
twilight, P2: 45, 50
Zoroastrianism
Says: There is law in nature; there is conflict in nature, C2: 101

About Eugene Halliday

Eugene Halliday (1911–1987), artist, writer, teacher and psychotherapist, was the founder of two educational charities, the International Hermeneutic Society (IHS) and the Institute for the Study of Hierological Values (Ishval—now known as the Eugene Halliday Association).

Hermeneutics is the art or science of interpretation of texts, for example in the fields of religion, philosophy or psychology. It is the means by which these texts are examined to investigate their meaning. Hierology relates to comparative religion, being the study of sacred writings or scripture, and the principles which underlie them.

Deeply versed in hermeneutics, art, religion, philosophy and science, Halliday recommended the reading of the major scriptures of the world and the works of the great philosophers. He taught that the whole visible universe is but a tiny portion of an infinite continuum of power. All worlds, from the great galaxies to the subatomic particles, are subsidiary worlds, or whirls, or whorls, of that same power. That power is omnipresent, that is, it fills all places; it moves and feels its movements—it is sentient. 'God', he said, is a short name for that which he called 'Absolute Sentient Power', or the 'Infinite Continuum of Sentient Power'. We are its activity, its whorls, its rotations. We are not separate from God.

Halliday had a theatrical background, his parents were music hall artistes. What he learned from them would have aided his ability to understand, relate and interpret the wide range of subjects he chose to study. Originally intending to be a violinist like his father, a childhood illness partially paralysed his left hand leading to a change of direction. He attended the Manchester School of Art from 1928 and in the 1930s-40s worked for Allied Newspapers as an illustrator and journalist. He was a conscientious objector in the Second World War and helped others in their tribunals. His work was shown in the Manchester Academy of Fine Art and other galleries, and he began giving talks on philosophy. Soon he became the catalyst for a community of creative people, including refugees from Nazi Germany. This led to the founding of the IHS (1959) and Ishval (1964).

From the late 1950s Halliday devoted more and more of his time to writing, teaching and therapeutic work. He taught that the highest centre of each of us is unique, and how to centre ourselves inwardly so as not to be swept off balance by the pressures of worldly life. One way of achieving this is through a new awareness of language that asks us to make our vocabulary active rather than passive by clearly defining the terms we use, through the study of etymology. His work was to help us to find ourselves, to become independent beings—including being independent of him. His aim was for all those who could rise to it, to become reflexively self-conscious.

Halliday was kind and compassionate—he was a healer whose psychotherapeutic work enabled the recovery of many troubled minds and souls. Yet he almost never gave advice, but taught people how to advise themselves.

He could be a ruthless taskmaster when he saw his students could be inspired to further development. His teaching was esoteric and profound, but also practical. He taught that our true place is in the eternal world, yet he did not despise the time-process, which he explained was essential for our spiritual development. He was a charismatic teacher who embodied the principles he taught and inspired many to follow in his footsteps.

Halliday's work was founded in Love, which he defined as 'working for the development of the highest potentialities of being'. Love, he wrote, 'is a feeling or activity directed at the development of the highest possible functional relationship between beings, an activity which contains, indissolubly bound together, elements of thought, feeling, and will, so that this activity is conducted with clarity, sensitivity, and power.'

Halliday wore his wisdom lightly and had a profound effect on everyone with whom he came into contact. More than thirty years after his death he is still held in affectionate reverence. None of those who met Eugene Halliday could ever forget him, and those who were taught by him regard him as a great sage, a true, reflexively self-conscious being, and a man of great humour and compassion.

Hephzibah Yohannan (2019) after David Mahlowe & Donald Lord

Further Reading
For those new to the work of Eugene Halliday, the first five chapters of his Contributions from a Potential Corpse, Book I, are a good introduction to his work. For further information on the work of Eugene Halliday, visit Melchisedec Press, including the Links page. (melchisedecpress.net)

The Collected Works of Eugene Halliday

Defence of the Devil—978-1-872240-00-8
Reflexive Self-Consciousness
Hardback 1989—978-1-872240-01-5
Paperback 2018— 978-1-872240-39-8
eBook— 978-1-872240-40-4
The Tacit Conspiracy—978-1-872240-02-2
Contributions from a Potential Corpse
Book I—978-1-872240-03-9
Book II—978-1-872240-04-6
Book III—978-1-872240-06-0
Book IV—978-1-872240-07-7
The Conquest of Anxiety—978-1-872240-09-1
Essays on God—978-1-872240-08-4
Through the Bible
Book I—978-1-872240-10-7
Book II—978-1-872240-13-8
Book III—978-1-872240-14-5
Book IV—978-1-872240-15-2
Christian Philosophy
Book I—978-1-872240-16-9
Book II—978-1-872240-17-6

Further works by Eugene Halliday

The Paradoxical Ego,
Eugene Halliday and Zhu Kabere
Hardback—978-1-872240-32-9
Paperback—978-1-872240-33-6
Ebook—978-1-872240-34-3

Who am I? How do I relate to my environment? The ego can offer a stable reference to support our development or it can become a barrier inhibiting it. Drawing on insights from medical practice, philosophy and science, this book considers the role of egoic dynamics in the ongoing evolution of consciousness. We hope that it will contribute to the quest for insight into these profound questions which have been with us throughout our history.

Die Eroberung der Angst
(The Conquest of Anxiety) by Eugene Halliday, translated by Christian Handschug
Hardback—978-1-872240-35-0
Paperback—978-1-872240-36-7
Ebook—978-1-872240-38-1

Den meisten von uns sind die Empfindungen von Furcht und Angst in manchen Lebenssituationen, und deren hemmende Wirkung auf unsere Fähigkeit mit anderen Menschen umzugehen und unser Leben zu genießen, wohl bekannt. In diesem Buch bietet Eugene Halliday praktische Übungen an, mit deren Hilfe wir beginnen können, diesen schwierigen Gemütszustand zu überwinden und ein glücklicheres und erfüllteres Leben zu führen. Der Autor stellt dieses Problem in dem Kontext einer umfassend holistischen und spirituellen Lebensauffassung dar.
Jede Seite führt den Leser weiter auf dem Weg zu einem ausgeglichenen eisteszustand, um mentale, emotionale oder physische Konflikte zu lösen, wann immer dies nötig ist.
Ich empfehle dieses Buch als perfekte Literatur, wenn Probleme zu lösen sind.
John Zaradin, Musiker/Autor.

Personal Journey:
John Zaradin in Conversation with Hephzibah Yohannan
Hardback—978-1-872240-29-9
Paperback—978-1-872240-30-5
Ebook—978-1-872240-31-2

This book is for readers who would reflect on, understand and come to terms with the contents of their own minds. It is for those who choose to value internal personal freedom and live within it.

This beautifully told unfolding of John's life—boy to man, intellectual to visceral seer—subtly, delicately reveals the genius of Eugene Halliday, a man for all men and women —literally, music for the senses!
Barbara Pidgeon, author of 'Shakti Manifest'

www.ingramcontent.com/pod-product-compliance
Lightning Source LLC
Chambersburg PA
CBHW080558030426
42336CB00019B/3237